AF251089

Jim Shaw

LUND HUMPHRIES | CONTEMPORARY PAINTERS

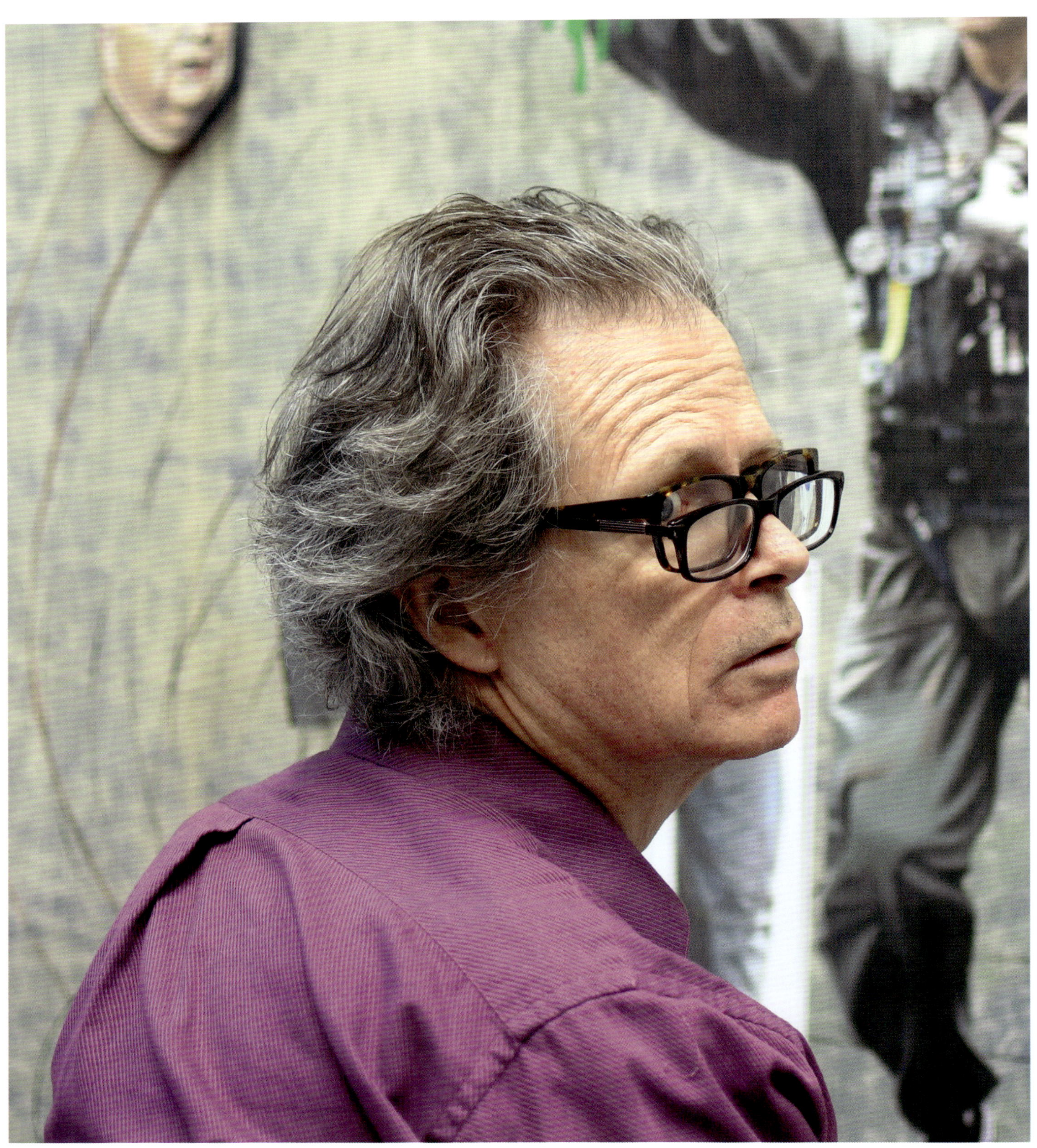

David Pagel

Jim Shaw

LUND HUMPHRIES | CONTEMPORARY PAINTERS

Contemporary Painters Series
Series Editor: Barry Schwabsky

The Contemporary Painters Series is a new, curated series of accessible, authoritative
and highly illustrated monographs on the world's leading living painters, which locates
painting as a vibrant and vital part of contemporary art.

The series is edited by American art critic Barry Schwabsky, supported by an
international advisory board with a specialist interest in contemporary painting.
It aims to redefine 'painting' in the contemporary context as work which is done within
the conventions and history of painting, but which may incorporate other materials
or techniques.

Advisory Board
Paco Barragán, independent curator and arts writer and Contributing Editor of ARTPULSE
Tony Godfrey, freelance writer and curator based in Singapore and the Philippines
David Pagel, Los Angeles-based art critic, curator and writer
Ida Panicelli, former Editor-in-Chief of *Artforum*
Simon Rees, Director of the Govett-Brewster Art Gallery/Len Lye Centre, New Zealand
Beatrix Ruf, former Director of the Stedelijk Museum, Amsterdam
Philip Tinari, Director of the Ullens Center for Contemporary Art, Beijing
Gilda Williams, art critic, writer, lecturer and London correspondent for *Artforum*
John Yau, poet, art critic and curator

Also available in the series:
Amy Sillman by Valerie Smith
Bernard Frize by David Rhodes
Etel Adnan by Kaelen Wilson-Goldie
Lois Dodd by Faye Hirsch
Mary Weatherford by Suzanne Hudson
Neo Rauch by Michael Glover
Philip Taaffe by John Yau
Tal R. by Martin Herbert
Thomas Nozkowski by John Yau
Verne Dawson by John Hutchinson

Contents

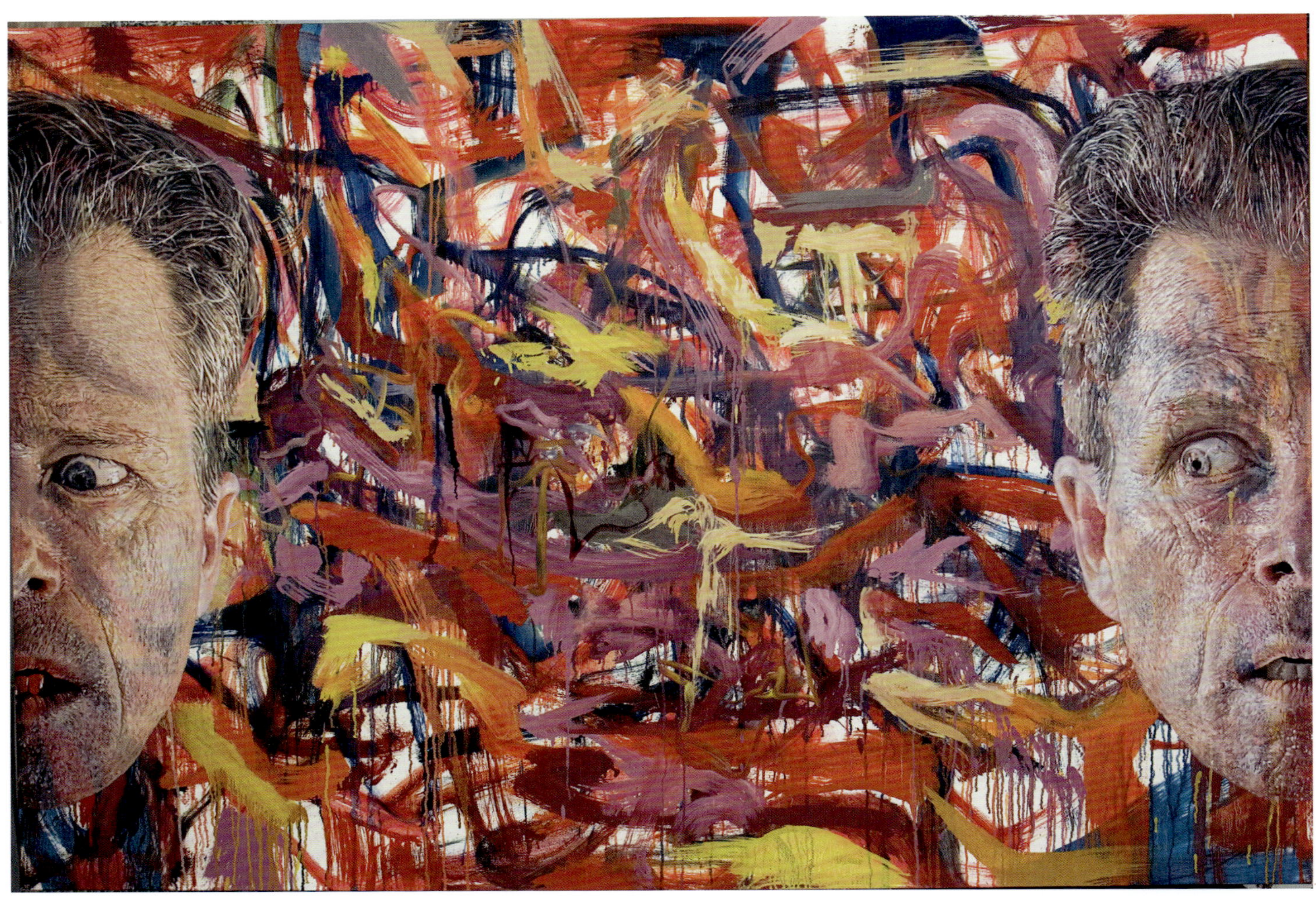

1. Split Head   2012

Oil on canvas
121.9 × 182.9 cm (48 × 72 in)
Private collection, Paris

Foreword

Although Jim Shaw has produced many paintings, some people might be surprised to be invited to think of him as above all a painter – as David Pagel does in this timely overview of the artist's career. It is not just that Shaw has also worked in other media (drawings, sculpture, installations, books, music) or that he is closely associated with a wave of Southern Californian artists (including Mike Kelley, Paul McCarthy and Jeffrey Vallance), whose aggressively abject oeuvres have not been much concerned with the art of painting. It is also that, even when painting, he seems to stand apart from the tradition of painting. Shaw's art is founded on an exploration of the artist's own psyche (as a stand-in, Pagel reminds us, for the collective imagination of an always somewhat unhinged America) by way of his immersion in many of the weirder meanders of modern American trash culture, from DIY religion and UFO-ology to conspiracy theories and manuals of dream interpretation. It accordingly reflects the influence of underground comics, the most grotesque sort of political cartoons and Sunday painters – some of whose works he famously gathered together in a legendary collection of *Thrift Store Paintings* – more than any high-art tradition, whether classical or modernist. This is not pop art, but something much more raw and disturbing, and it is unlike any other brand of painting out there. As the critic David Riesman put it in responding to Shaw's 2015 retrospective at the New Museum in New York, 'Shaw pushes representational art as far as he can before the temptation to subvert it with one form of weirdness or another becomes too strong for him to resist.'

In this book, Pagel examines six major bodies of work Shaw has pursued since 1985: the cycle of 170 works titled *My Mirage* (1985–91); the *Dream Drawings* of the 1990s and the *Dream Objects* he has been making since the middle of that decade; the vast body of work representing Shaw's imaginary religion of 'Oism', which has occupied him since the early 2000s; the 2004–12 *Left Behind* series inspired by a trove of huge painted movie backdrops that Shaw found; and the untitled paintings on stretched muslin he has been making since 2012. As Pagel concludes, Shaw's art demonstrates that reality is 'far more fascinating, improbable and mind-blowing' than we ever expected – and the same is true, I would add, of an art meant to contend with this bizarre condition of ours.

Barry Schwabsky

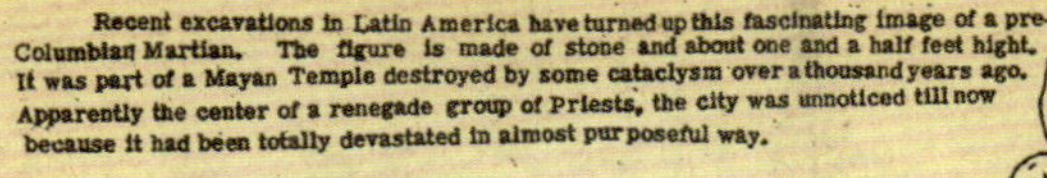

The DEVIL is a MARTIAN!

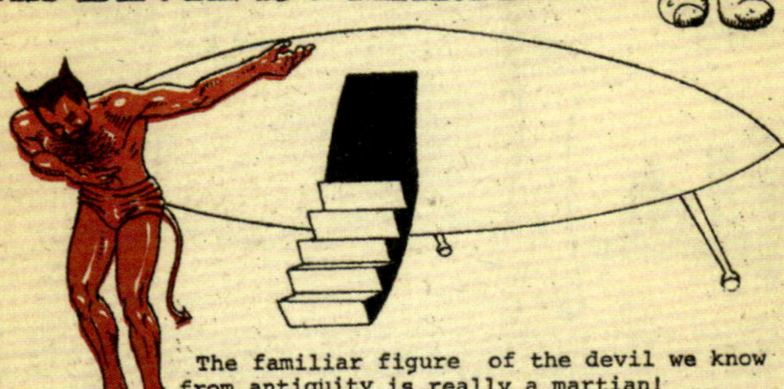

The familiar figure of the devil we know from antiquity is really a martian!

The image of god, a kindly old man with a long white beard and robe is an actual venusian! The martians have tried to fool us out of our pagan pantheistic beliefs into the notian of one god, one devil. In reality there were always many "gods" and many "devils", and numerous "angels" and "demons" That is, until the martians wiped out the venusians and the "gods" and "angels" with them.

There are still venusians left (we are their interbred descendants!), however when they have tried to tell the truth, they are ridiculed or ignored. In Mexico, when virgins were offered to the sun god they did not die as martian archeoligists have claimed, but bred with the aliens producing the fabled blond natives as offspring. Our own beloved queen Yma is a direct descendent of the venusian rulers of Peru, a true daughter of the gods

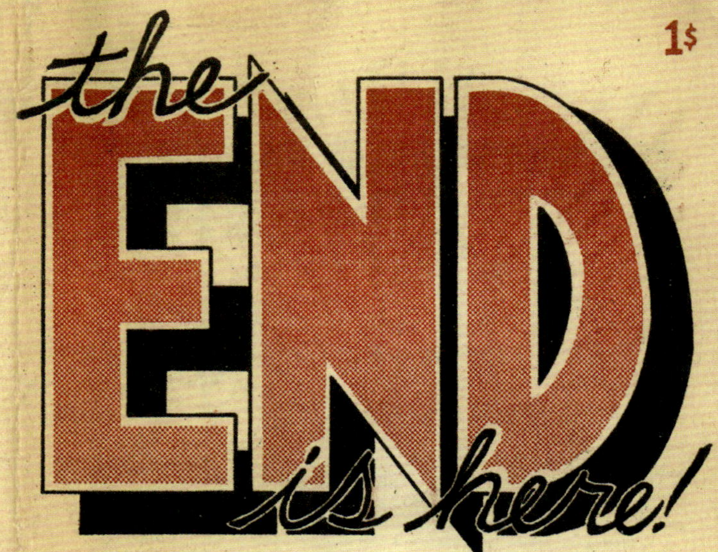

in this issue

2. The End is Here!   1978

Mimeographed booklet, 16 pages
21.6 × 18.5 cm (8½ × 7⅓ in)
Collection of the artist

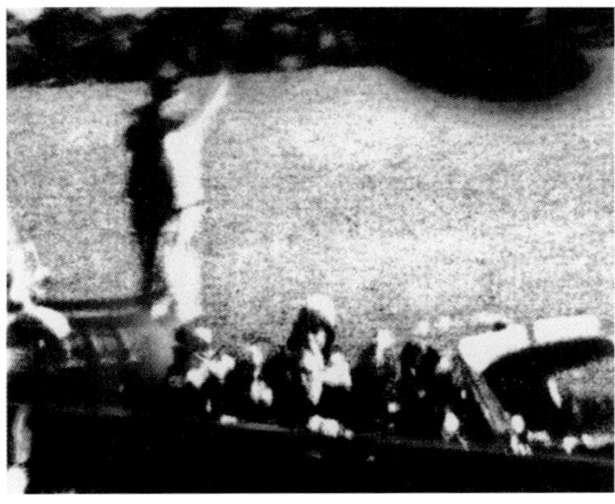
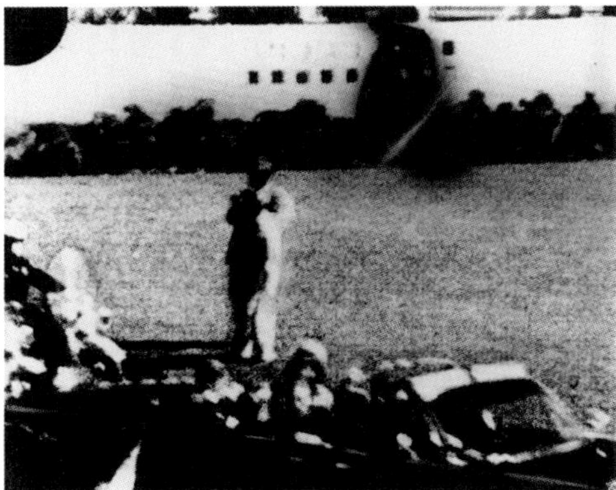

3. UFO Photos: Zapruder Film   1978–92

Black and white photographs, three parts
20.3 × 25.4 cm (8 × 10 in)
Courtesy Praz-Delavallade and Blum & Poe

In 1978, when Jim Shaw was wrapping up his graduate studies in the Master of Fine Arts program at the California Institute of the Arts (CalArts), he published a mimeographed pamphlet titled *The End is Here!* (fig.2). The 16-page volume sold for $1. Its two-color cover did double-duty as a table of contents, announcing, on page 3, an article based on new evidence in the slaying of John F. Kennedy; on page 5, a do-it-yourself personality quiz; and, on page 14, easy-to-use guidelines for identifying UFOs. Shaw's homemade chapbook accompanied his MFA exhibition, a rite of passage and academic requirement that all graduate students had to complete to receive their degrees.

So it was reasonable to assume that Shaw's publication was a catalog of his exhibition, *The Age of Lead*, which included two series of manipulated black-and-white photographs (fig.3); a hand-built table that Shaw had splattered with paint, Pollock-style; a series of transparent, vacuum-formed plastic abstractions he had spray-painted the backs of, leaving their surfaces shimmering with glossiness; a pseudo documentary video in the style of *Chariot of the Gods*; and a series of deformed Martian heads. All were installed around a faux-gold altarpiece: a triptych with a pair of hinged wings on which Shaw had airbrushed portraits of John F. Kennedy, Marilyn Monroe, Sharon Tate, Charles Manson, Lee Harvey Oswald and Martha Mitchell. On the night of the opening, Shaw kept the gallery doors locked for 30 minutes past show time, building the drama by playing selections from the soundtracks of Alfred Hitchcock's *Psycho* and Sergei Einstein's *Alexander Nevsky*. Guests were served what today might be called 'curated' refreshments: platters of Hostess Twinkies and Sno Balls, whose spongy surfaces Shaw had airbrushed orange, purple or green using food dyes, so that their palette matched the colors of the flag flown by the Martians who figured prominently in both *The End is Here!* and *The Age of Lead*. Venusians, who flew red, blue and yellow flags, played a secondary role and had no matching snacks.

But *The End is Here!* was not an exhibition catalog. It neither documented nor explained the works on display. Nor did Shaw present it as a work of art in its own right – a multi-page piece of image-and-text conceptualism that was autonomous and authoritative and aesthetically innovative. Instead, *The End is Here!* seemed to come out of the blue.

It riffed off of 'The End is Near' sermons preached by religious fanatics whose message was clear: everyone must repent because there is not much time left. Shaw took that idea one step further, proclaiming 'It's Over.' While his message was blunt, it was also absurd, especially since it was accompanied by an introduction Shaw made up and attributed to Queen Yma Sumac, a Peruvian-American coloratura soprano who

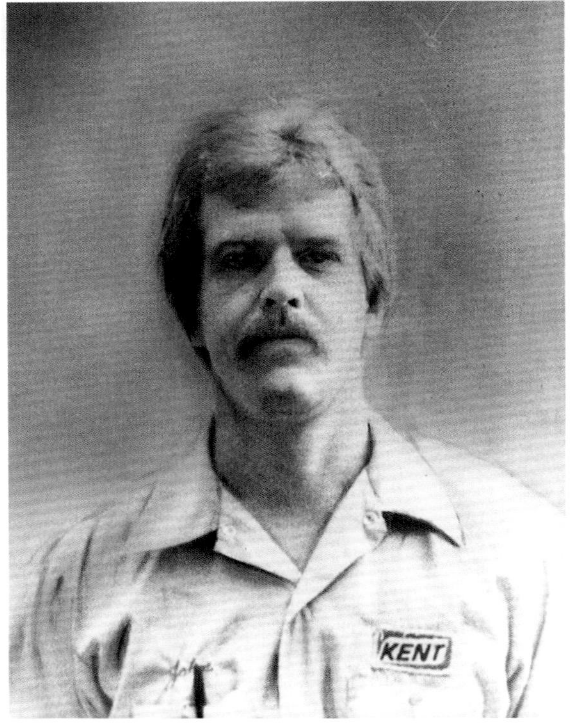
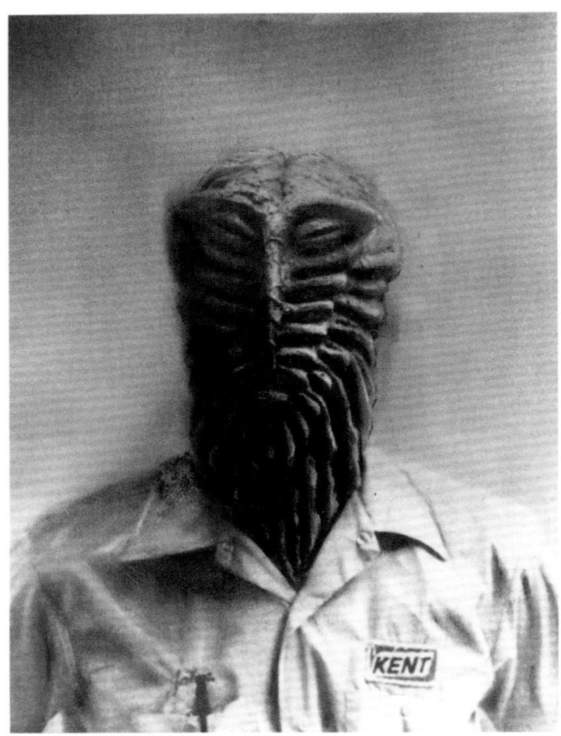
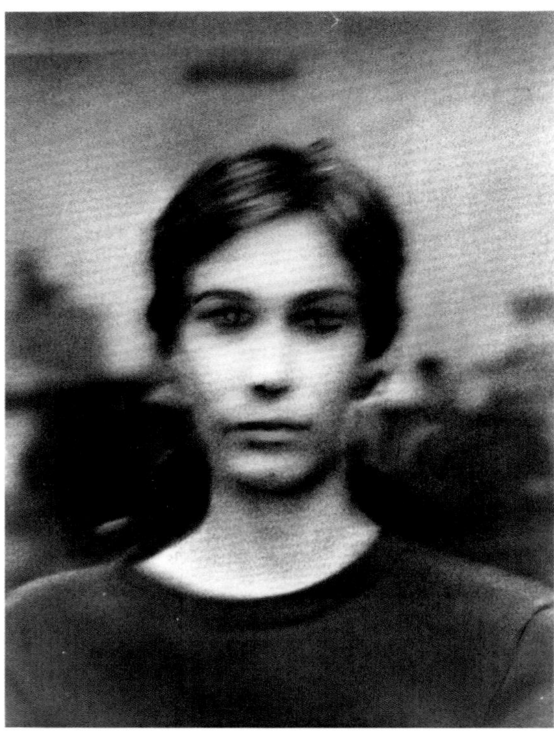
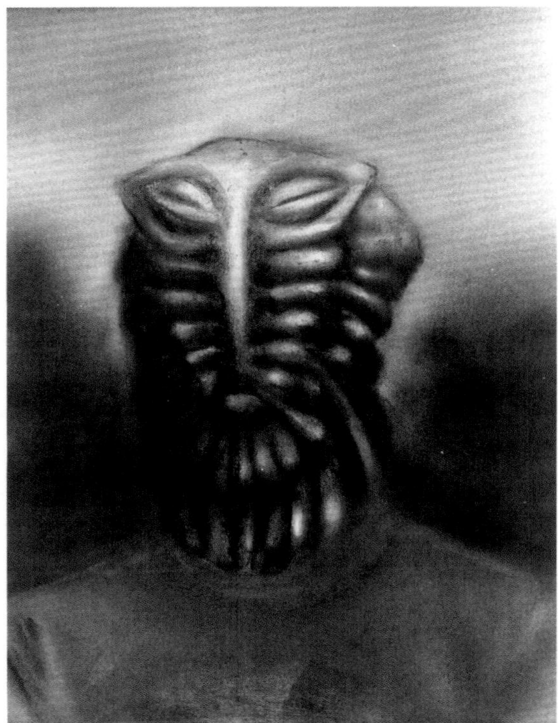

4. Martian Portraits   1978

Black and white photographs, four parts
35.8 × 28.2 cm ($14\frac{1}{10}$ × $11\frac{1}{10}$ in) (each)
Courtesy Praz-Delavallade and Blum & Poe

claimed to be an Incan princess and who predicted that a great religious revival was about to sweep the United States. Mimicking the format of tabloids, Shaw's pamphlet was also filled with the stuff of conspiracy buffs. The first article's headline read: 'Proof that JFK was Killed by Aliens'. The story that followed was fake news, pure and simple. It reported that Kennedy was a partially transubstantiated Martian who was preparing to reveal that he was a pawn in an intergalactic gambit for control of planet Earth. To keep that plot secret, the aliens assassinated him. The 'magic bullet', which reversed direction and struck both President Kennedy and Texas Governor John Connally, was actually a miniature guided missile. And Kennedy was killed when an explosive device embedded in his brain was triggered by a beam from a hovering saucer. When Jacqueline threw herself over his body, she was not protecting him but preventing spectators from seeing that her husband was turning back into an alien. As her reward, she got to marry a powerful Martian, Aristotle Socrates Onassis. Others involved in Shaw's stew of kookiness were Georges de Mohrenschildt (a Russian professor and friend of Lee Harvey Oswald), E. Howard Hunt (a CIA officer who would be convicted of perjury in the Watergate scandal), Dorothy Kilgallen (a gossip columnist found dead in her New York apartment after claiming she knew who assassinated Kennedy) and Mary Jo Kopechne (who died when Ted Kennedy crashed the car he was driving home from a party in Chappaquiddick, Massachusetts, in 1968).

In Shaw's typo-riddled 'news report', what began as an impossible-to-believe assertion quickly led in dozens of directions, each storyline a digression to be followed, sometimes like Alice down the rabbit hole, until the starting point, news about Kennedy's assassination, faded into the background and readers became immersed in a world that shared many similarities with the real one (in terms of people, places and things), but was profoundly out of step with it (in terms of the ways those elements are connected). Shaw had strung together the characters and plot points neither logically nor randomly but in a curious combination of the two: almost the way scenes and stories follow one other or run together in dreams.

Even though readers were not meant to believe everything – or anything – that was written in *The End is Here!*, Shaw's tall tales culminated in the conviction that something very strange was going on; that appearances did not tell the whole story; that conventional means for reporting and understanding reality were no match for its deep and abiding weirdness; and that art just might provide an effective way to capture and convey the truth of all that, in ways that made sense of the visible world as well as whatever might lie beyond it: Martians or mysteries, infinity or nothingness, the truth or more lies.

In doing that, *The End is Here!* set a precedent that Shaw would follow for the next 40 years: making works that introduced themselves as the nuttiest of non sequiturs only to become propositions that made a certain amount of difficult-to-articulate sense: certainly not the logical conclusiveness of sustained argumentation nor the lyrical resonance of poetic suggestiveness, but something far loopier and more

5. Untitled (Distorted Faces series)   1979

Graphite, airbrush and Prismacolor on paper
35.6 × 27.9 cm (14 × 11 in)
Courtesy Marc Blondeau

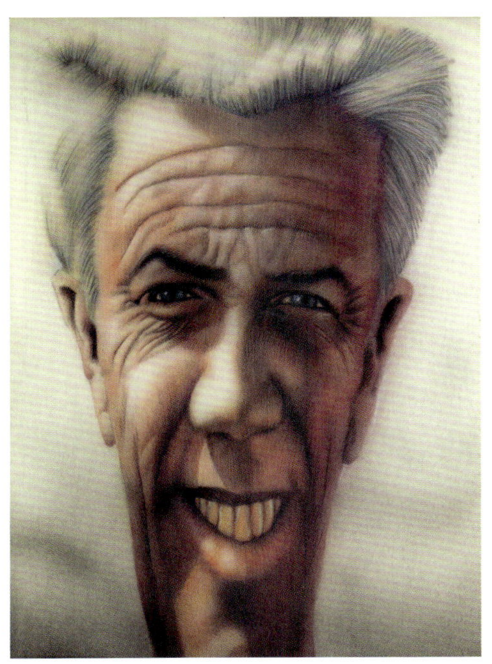

unsettling, particularly if you allowed their cock-eyed perspective on public life in the United States to align with the increasingly off-kilter reality of the public psyche, otherwise known as the popular imagination.

That is the way that painting functioned in *The Age of Lead*, entering Shaw's graduate exhibition not through the front door – as paint applied to rectangular panels or canvases – but through the side door: splattered, à la Pollock, over a handmade table; spray-painted, quasi-industrially, on the backs of translucent plastic forms; air-brushed, as if commercially, on a surrogate altarpiece; and dyed, like holiday deserts, into Twinkies and Sno Balls. Rather than embracing painting as an autonomous art form, with its own protocols and procedures, Shaw treated it as just another medium among many in his polyglot mélange of media, no better – or worse – than any other, and all the more potent for mixing it up with the mongrel mishmash of materials, formats and references that made up his exhibition.

In nascent, often bare-naked form, *The Age of Lead* and *The End is Here!* featured many of the artistic maneuvers and conceptual strategies that Shaw would develop into the driving concerns of his lifelong work as an artist: searching for truth on the fringes of respectability and traveling far beyond the limits of believability. By doing so he often discovered that the weirdness lurking in these spaces was not all that different from the weirdness that formed the heart and soul of mainstream society, especially when its veneer of middle-of-the-road normalcy was peeled back and middle-class culture was revealed to be what it is: a conflicted mixture of fantasies and fears that knows no limits and leaves everyone guessing about what might come next.

Over the last 40 years, Shaw has elaborated on the ideas and techniques in his graduate exhibition and its accompanying pamphlet in each of his six major bodies of work: *My Mirage* (1985–91); *Dream Drawings* (1992–9); *Dream Objects* (1995–present); 'Oist' works (2002–present); *Left Behind* (2004–12); and an untitled group of stretched muslin paintings (2012–present). Within all can be seen his relentless pursuit of confusion as a means for generating insights – for moving viewers (and readers) a little closer to the truth without downplaying the myriad twists and turns along the often mind-boggling journey. Over the last 15 years, Shaw has turned to painting more than ever before, treating it less as one medium among many, as he did for the first 25 years of his career, and more as the most effective vehicle for capturing the madness of reality and transforming it into something equally unbelievable while also being truthful. In the medium of painting, Shaw's loaded vision of the world and his understanding of art's place in society have found room to strut their stuff.

In the past, critics and commentators have treated each of Shaw's major bodies of work as a world unto itself: a universe jam-packed with so many vivid peculiarities and internal cross-references that making sense of it was a task unto itself. That approach went hand-in-hand with the tendency to see Shaw's obsessive art-making as an offshoot of, firstly, his obsessive collecting – of thrift-store paintings, religious manuals and the discarded backdrops of Hollywood movie sets – and, secondly, his freeform musical performances, which began in Detroit, when he and fellow artists Mike Kelley, Cary Loren and Niagra formed a band, Destroy All Monsters, which played at various art events. Shaw's association with Kelley has also tended to steer critical commentary away from his oeuvre as a group of interrelated series, and toward an understanding of it in relation to Kelley's work, as well as the work of other Los Angeles artists, including Paul McCarthy, Tony Oursler and Jeffrey Vallance.

What follows is an attempt to see the connections between and among Shaw's six major bodies of work. His musical performances, vernacular collections and relationships to his contemporaries will not be the focus. The goal is to identify the ways in which Shaw's vision of the world and his understanding of art's place in it have developed throughout his life as an artist, particularly in terms of their capacity to add up to a whole that is a lot more complex than the sum of its parts. Approaching Shaw's major bodies of work in relation to one another reveals that his art is much more engaged with painting and politics than has previously been acknowledged.

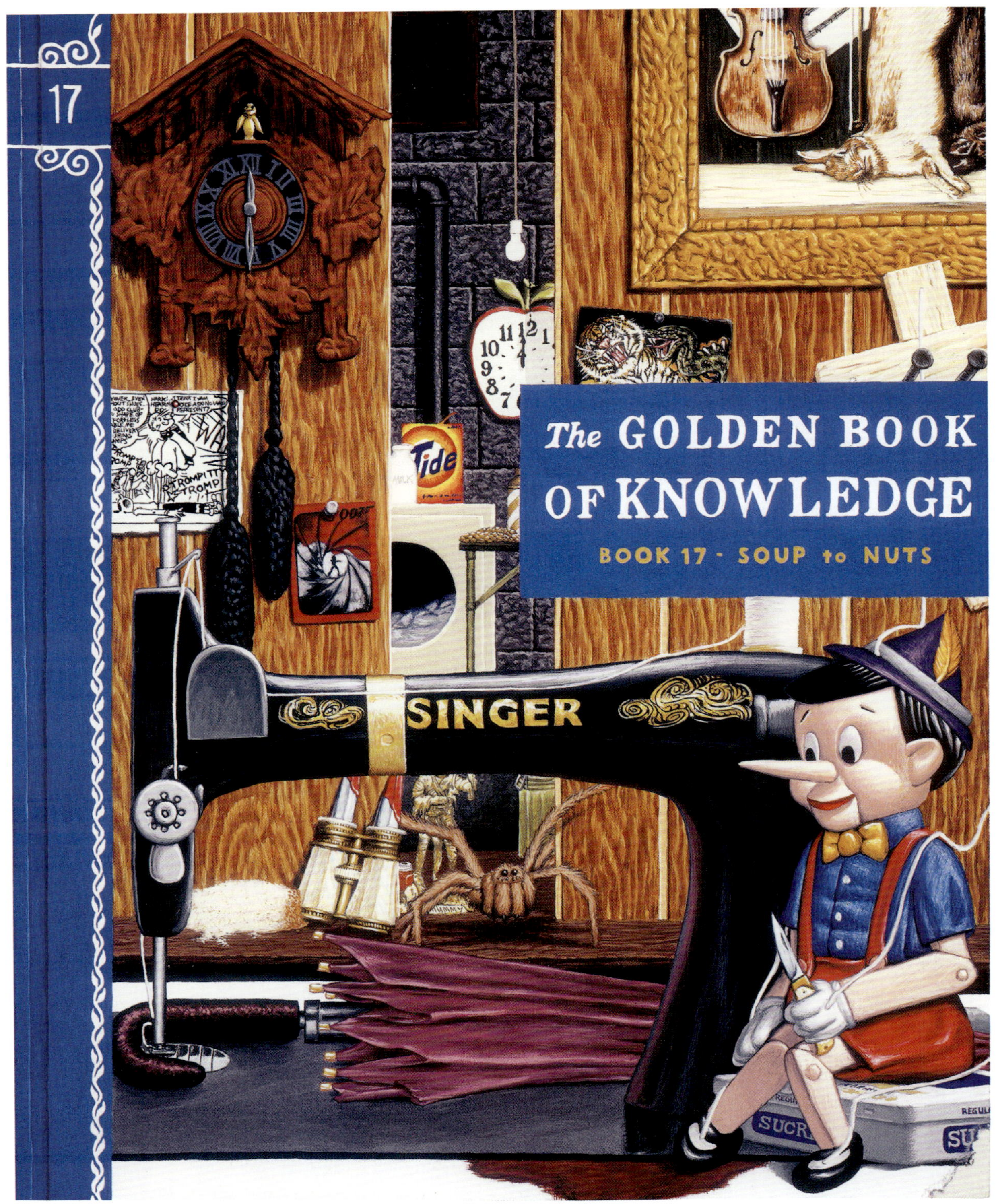

6. The Golden Book of Knowledge   1989

Gouache on rag board mounted on plywood
43.2 × 35.6 cm (17 × 14 in)
Collection of Eileen Harris Norton

2   My Mirage (1985–91)

The End is Here! also describes what it feels like for a student to graduate – to be cast out of the relative shelter of school and into the workaday world. In Shaw's case, that meant getting a job and making art on the side. In 1978, he moved to a small house in Echo Park, an Eastside neighborhood of Los Angeles, and began working on the fringes of the special effects world that had begun blooming in the wake of the success of *Star Wars*. He continued to make art: mostly small, black-and-white drawings on which he painted distorted faces but also airbrushed abstractions and expressionist cartoons. This set-up went on for four or five years, as Shaw moved from apartment to apartment in Hollywood and Silver Lake, hopscotching among a group of former classmates and friends that included Tony Oursler, Mike Kelley, Jett Jackson, Don Krieger, Benjamin Weissmann, Amy Gerstler, Tim Martin and Jim Isermann. To pay the rent, Shaw made backlit animation and storyboards for Mid-Ocean Motion Pictures and Robert Abel, the leading effects house in Hollywood. He worked on the films *A Nightmare on Elm Street* (1984) and *Earth Girls are Easy* (1988). He also undertook freelance projects: drawing storyboards for the earliest versions of Terrence Malick's *The Tree of Life* (2011); painting the psychedelic hippy bus that appeared in John Byrum's movie about Jack Kerouac, Carolyn and Neal Cassady's love triangle, *Heart Beat* (1980); and airbrushing the backdrops for *Tron* (1982). Without a studio of his own, Shaw painted wherever he could, in living rooms, basements and on patios. He was productive and relentless. But he felt that his art did not measure up to the expectations that went with a CalArts degree. He was plagued by the suspicion that his paintings were missing an essential ingredient, a conceptual component that would undergird them with the intellectual credentials deemed necessary for art at the time.

So he decided to make a masterpiece – in the 16th-century meaning of the term. Back then, an aspiring artisan was required to make a masterpiece to prove his competence to the guild authorities so that he might move up in rank, becoming a master of his craft. Shaw did not feel that that is what happened at CalArts so he took it upon himself to prove his own competence. He decided to make a series of 100 pieces, all measuring 17 x 14 in (43 x 36 cm). The painted, drawn, silkscreened, collaged, sculpted and photo-transferred images would together add up to an encyclopedic overview of Shaw's talents and tastes. This format would set the stage for a multi-layered narrative that would allow Shaw to demonstrate his facility as a draftsman, as a colorist and as a creator of eye-grabbing compositions. It would also allow him to pay homage to the artists he admired.

Shaw would call this body of work *My Mirage*, after a song on *In-A-Gadda-Da-Vida*, the American rock group Iron Butterfly's second album, released in 1968. By the early 1980s, the band's incantatory anthem to the transcendent power of sexual abandon was no longer a hit, but its reputation was legendary. That out-of-time, part-of-the-past quality suited Shaw. It meshed with his sense that time was ripe for a '60s revival, a rebellious backlash against the avariciousness of the 1980s, when the embrace of economic self-interest went hand-in-glove with the rise of multinational corporations and the commercialization of every aspect of everyday life. As Shaw approached his mid-thirties, he dove into *My Mirage* – and never looked back.

The project occupied the next six years of his life. In the end, it included more than 170 pieces. Once Shaw got started, he found it very difficult to stop. Most of the works were two-dimensional, but some were low-relief assemblages. A smattering of sculptures, a couple of boxed objects and four videos rounded things out. Aside from the videos, each image or object was formatted in the manner of a single frame of a comic book. But unlike conventional cartoons, Shaw's uber-comic could not be read sequentially. There was no beginning and no end, just a sprawling compendium of vivid fragments, some connected stylistically, others thematically, and still others by format, genre or topic. That is also how Shaw exhibited it, selecting highlights from the ongoing series while still working on it. A trio of exhibitions took place in 1989 and 1990: in Los Angeles at Dennis Anderson Gallery; in Santa Monica at Linda Cathcart Gallery; and in New York at Feature Inc. Each exhibition consisted of at least 30 pieces. The nearly complete suite was presented in 1990 in an exhibition organized by MATRIX at the Berkeley Art Museum at the University of California. It then traveled to the Saint Louis Museum of Art and the Whitney Museum of American Art, in New York, where it was part of *The 1991 Biennale Exhibition*. Twenty years later, in 2011, Shaw's masterpiece became a book, a 216-page volume with 148 images, published by JPR/Ringer in Zurich, Switzerland. That format suited the story perfectly, allowing readers to flip back and forth through the narrative as various strands of various storylines came into focus and then faded, like a dream seen through the kaleidoscopic eye of a fly.

At the center of Shaw's de-centered story was Billy, a suburban kid from Middle America, loosely based on Shaw as an adolescent. Shaw was born on 8 August 1952 in Midland, Michigan, a company town where Dow Chemical and Dow Corning were headquartered and manufactured silicone breast implants, napalm and the herbicide, Agent Orange. Shaw's father was a packaging designer for Dow. His mother was a homemaker and medical secretary. His three older sisters overshadowed him academically. After high school, Shaw attended a local community college for two years and then transferred to the University of Michigan, Ann Arbor, where he met Mike Kelley, co-founded Destroy All Monsters and earned his Bachelor of Fine Arts in 1974.

My Mirage was an impressionistic coming-of-age story in which youthful innocence was not destroyed so much as it was refracted through the multifaceted lens of a culture that was itself fracturing, its bittersweet beauty residing in the collision

between the dashed dreams of one generation and the possibilities such traumas
opened up for the next – even if those possibilities were darker and more dreadful than
anticipated. Although redemption was pursued, often furiously, by the characters in
My Mirage, no one discovered what they were originally seeking, much less anything
that resembled transcendence. Dreams were not dashed so much as they mutated into
corrupted versions of themselves. Despite the accumulating disappointments, Billy
carried on stoically, never wallowing in self-pity or presuming that the daily distress of
being an unpopular kid in high school was anything other than ordinary – absurd, to
be sure, but also run of the mill.

Shaw's sprawling storyboard was also a self-portrait, a tour-de-force depiction
of the artist as a shape-shifting chameleon, a jack-of-all-trades laborer who was able
to move among styles and materials and media to tell stories whose meanings were
equally elusive, fleeting and fugitive – and all the more potent for inhabiting a reality
just beyond the grasp of consciousness. The works that comprise *My Mirage* fall into
three categories: (1) Repeated motifs, with up to five versions of each; (2) The covers
of books and magazines and the pages of newspapers; and (3) Misfits: one-off oddballs
that would stick out like sore thumbs if not for the overall idiosyncrasy of the whole.

The first group includes five versions of a *Frontispiece*, five versions of *Billy's Self-
Portrait*, five versions of *Girls in Billy's Class* and five versions of *Anima* (earth, water, fire,
combustion and air). It also includes five versions of *My Mirage Logo* (in illusionistic
bone, blood, chrome, jism and a sliced apple) and five versions of *Utopian Landscapes*
(depicting dinosaurs, mushroom clouds, tripping hippies, monsters in jars and Christ's
crucifixion). These 30 works form the narrative spine of *My Mirage*. The frontispieces
chart Billy's experimentation with mind-altering substances, from cough drops and
model airplane glue to pot, LSD and heroin, before settling on the body and blood of
Christ and the religion he rejected as a teen. Similarly, the *Girls in Billy's Class* works
record Billy's attempt to make sense of the mysteries of femininity. Depicted as they
would be on the page of a high school yearbook, the 16 young women in the first version
are identified not by name but by religion (Presbyterian, Methodist, Mormon, and so
on). In the second version, the girls' portraits are captioned with the names of the drugs
they appear to have taken (nicotine, mushrooms, smack, and so on). In the third (fig.7),
their names have been replaced with popular phrases ('Keep on Truckin', 'You Are What
You Eat', 'All Power to the People', and so on). Also in the third version, some of Billy's
classmates have had their places taken by famous women, including Jane Fonda, Raquel
Welch and Ursula Andress. Others have had their places taken by men: Sean Connery,
Tiny Tim and Wally Wood, along with an actual classmate of Shaw's, who looked like
Jesus, a political protester, and Nguyen Van Lem, the North Vietnamese soldier executed
in the street by the Chief of Police in Saigon, South Vietnam.

The fourth version is the only one that lists the girls' names (Ursula, Kelly, Stacey,
and so on), but their portraits have been replaced with graphite drawings of common
household items, including a coffee Thermos, an electric can opener, a Tupperware

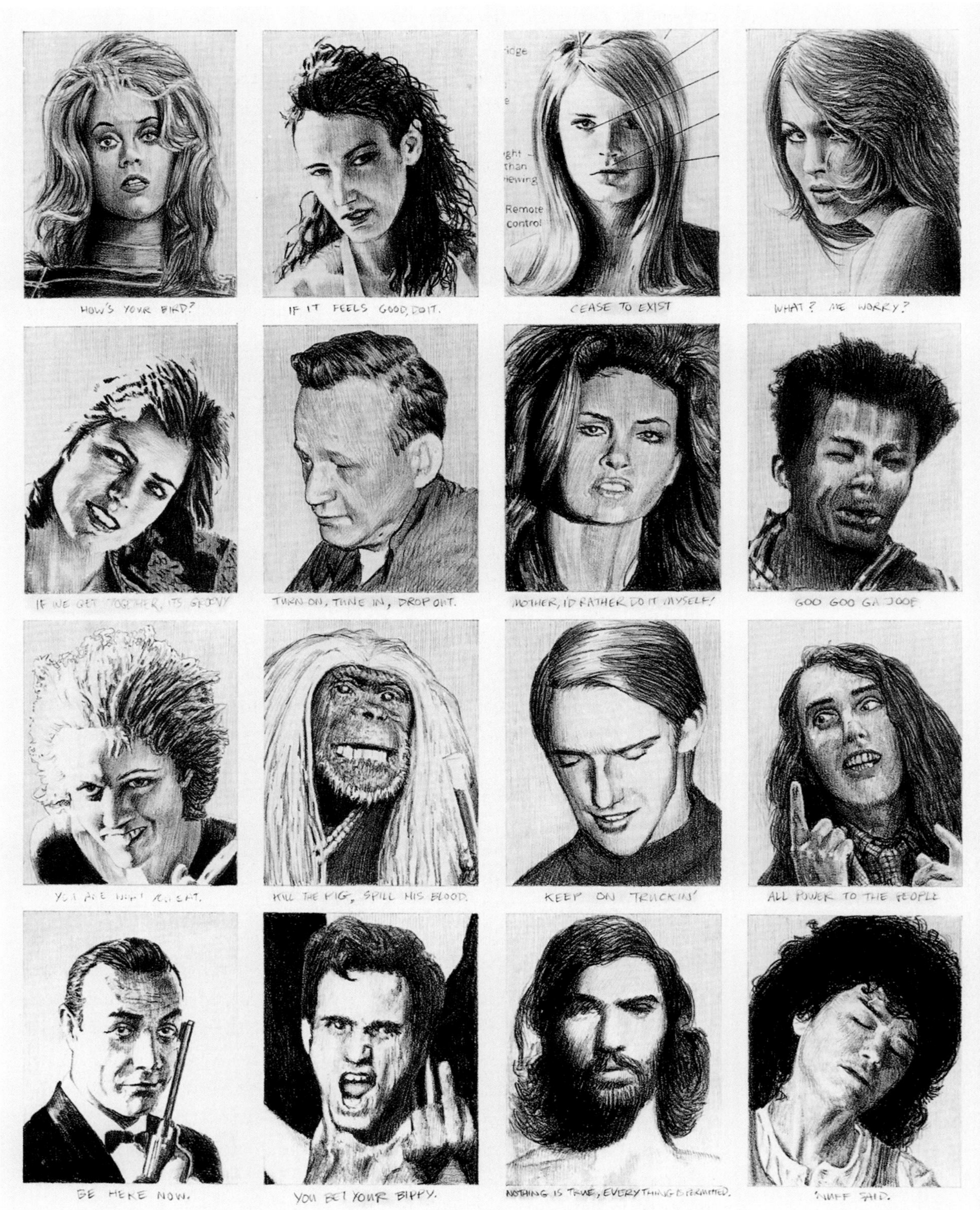

7. Girls in Billy's Class III   1986

Graphite on paper
43.2 × 35.6 cm (17 × 14 in)
Collection unknown

18

container, and so on. Its title, *Girls in Billy's Class IV (Self-Portrait IV)* reveals that this drawing does double-duty as Billy's fourth self-portrait. That doubling-up prevents the works in *My Mirage* from falling into mutually exclusive categories. It also embodies the anarchistic impulse at the heart of Shaw's project – his love of those moments when structures break down. Such dissonance takes disturbing form in the fifth version. *Girls in Billy's Class V* identifies each of the 16 women in one of two ways: as Lost or Saved. Shaw drew their portraits from the pictures of the eight student nurses who were kidnapped and tormented by Richard Speck in Chicago in 1966 and eight female members of the Manson Family. The eight listed as 'Saved' were murdered by Speck. The eight listed as 'Lost' were the Manson Family members, some of whom were involved in the Tate and LaBianca killings. In Shaw's drawing, the language of religious redemption gets recast as the tragic consequence of horrifying crimes.

The second group of works that make up *My Mirage* riffs off of popular publications, using their logos and graphics to send messages that conflict with the purposes and sentiments of the originals. In Shaw's hands, fake news and fake art rub up against each other, creating situations in which first impressions are not to be trusted, double-takes are a matter of course and there is always more to reality than meets the eye.

News Clippings (1988) (fig.9) masquerades as a page from a small-town newspaper. Its stories appear to be real. The same goes for an advice column by Ann Landers and several classified advertisements. But something is off. Landers' first name has been misspelled, as Anne. And the content of her column slips, gently but irreparably, from something the nationally syndicated advisor might have written to a parody of that. An article about a local art class is similarly ambivalent – or double-edged. To read between the lines is to glimpse Shaw's own ambivalence about the relationship between art and illustration, as well as the antagonism between artists and authorities, whether they are high-school teachers, graduate faculty or art world institutions.

In other works, Shaw reconfigured nationally recognized brands. His version of *Time* magazine has a Lichtenstein-style image of a raised middle finger on its cover. His unauthorized *Life* magazine links rebellion and selling out. His bootlegged rendition of *The Saturday Evening Post* shows that when life imitates art it is not always pretty. And his customized rendition of *The New Yorker* targets the troubled relationship between high art and low. *The Golden Book of Knowledge* (1989) (fig.6), based on a series of encyclopedia-style booklets by Golden Publications, is a pictorial essay on surrealism, trompe l'oeil painting, folk tales, action movies and newspaper comics. Similarly, in *Manlicker* (1991) (fig.10), Shaw added a fake volume to Ian Fleming's series of James Bond novels, its title a reference to the brand of rifle used to assassinate J.F.K. In Shaw's tromp l'oeil gouache, the torn cover of the fake paperback is collaged among pages apparently ripped from *Playboy* magazine and a book about the assassination. In fact, both texts were made up by Shaw, written in the manner of E. Howard Hunt, a prolific author whose talents were overshadowed by his role in the Watergate scandal and his subsequent convictions for burglary, conspiracy and wire-tapping.

8. Advent Calendar   1990

Vacuformed styrene, acrylic paint
43.2 × 35.6 cm (17 × 14 in)
Collection unknown

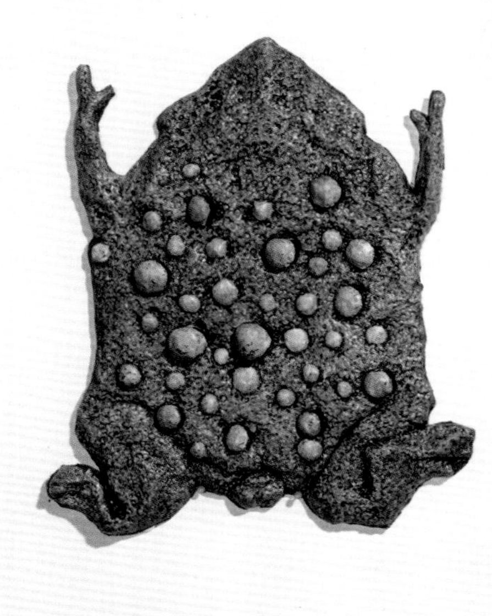

Dear Anne Landers: All the kids at school were hoping you would reprint a quiz we heard about from our older brothers and sisters. Some teens had sent it in and you could use it to rate yourself. Signed—Just a Good Kid.

Dear J.G.K.: You kids are just too darn curious, but here goes—I have updated it a bit from the original I received several years ago. I always get lots of response when I run this one.

(Rate yourself from 1 to 12 for each yes answer)

1. Have you ever dated a member of the opposite sex?　4
2. Have you ever lied to your parents?　2
3. Have you ever stolen worthless items from a dimestore just for fun?　5
4. Have you ever been kissed?　4
5. Do you smoke?　2
6. Have you ever lied to your pastor?　2
7. Have you ever played with yourself?　3
8. Have you ever peeled out in front of a fast food joint?　2
9. Have you ever told on your friends to authorities　3
10. Have you ever been French-kissed?　4
11. Do you drink?　2
12. Have you ever cheated on schoolwork?　2
13. Have you ever been kissed while in a reclining position?　5
14. Have you ever put water in your parents' liquor bottles to replace what you drank?　4
15. Have you ever gotten someone else to do your homework?　5
16. Have you ever been kissed in the nude?　7
17. Have you ever broken your vow at Lent?　2
18. Have you ever sniffed airplane glue?　5
19. Have you ever gone all the way?　10
20. Have you ever performed an animal sacrifice?　5
21. Have you ever sniffed spray-paint of Bactine in a bag?　6

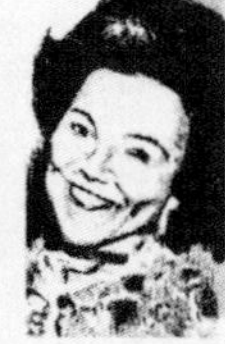

Ask Anne Landers

22. Have you ever had sex with a member of the same sex?　12
23. Have you ever smoked pot?　7
24. Have you ever struck your parents?　5
25. Have you ever participated in an orgy?　12
26. Have you ever dropped acid or STP?　10
27. Have you ever worshipped the devil?　8
28. Have you ever given anyone a social disease?　12
29. Have you ever had to go to the hospital for an overdose?　10
30. Have you ever attempted suicide?　12
31. Have you ever gotten anyone pregnant?　13

Scorecard

15 or less-Uncool
16 to 30-Triangle—a square with something missing
31 to 45-Alive and kicking
46 to 60-Average Joe or Jane
61 to 75-Too groovy for words
76 to 90-Unreal and in trouble
91 to 105-Don't let your [...] see if you marked the p[...] 106 and Over-Going to [...] hell for all eternity

Dear Anne Landers: My [...] is driving me crazy with [...] urges. He wants "it" all [...] Sometimes he surprises [...] middle of the day when [...] he's at the office and wa[...] drop my housework [...] satisfy himself. The m[...] animal! What should [...] Signed-Had it in Pittsbu[...]
Dear Had It: First tha[...] stars he isn't chasing secr[...] the office. Then ask him [...] a guidance counselor.

LOCAL NEWS

Bizarre Dog Abduction

Local police were baffled by the disappearance today of Osiris, pet dog of Dr. and Mrs. Joseph McCay. The dog, a German shepherd, was apparently given tranquilizers in his dog food. His dog dish showed traces of P.C.P. (an animal tranquilizer), and his rope had been severed with a knife or other sharp object. "He must have been drugged or he would have barked his head off" said Mrs. McCay. No ransom has been demanded and the police have no motive in this unusual case. "We miss him and just want him back alive and unharmed" said daughter Julie McCay.

Tomorrow Is Law Day

National Law Day occurs on Wednesday and Mayor Christensen will address the subject at a fathers and sons prayer breakfast at city hall tomorrow morning in a speech entitled "The Law and Our Country—Partners in Progress." Other festivities include a poster contest in the schools' art classes and an afternoon social given by the Moose women.

Police Put On Pressure

Local police have set up a special anti-drug task force to combat growing abuse by the town's youth. In an announcement from city hall, police chief Jablonski said "We are alarmed at the information we are getting as to the amount and type of drugs flowing into this community. It is largely due to outsiders who have moved into town. We intend to clean up the streets and make them safe again." Surveilance of individuals as well as Central High School is planned.

Mosquito Spra[...]

Experimental sprayi[...] new insecticide which d[...] mosquitos but will steri[...] begins in our area this [...] Scientists from Bell Che[...] the new compound wil[...] impossible for them [...] duce, thus eliminating [...] insects from spoiling ou[...] fun. Bell will begin spra[...] airplanes next month.

Break-In At L[...] Church

Authorities are invest[...] burglary at Saint [...] Reform Church Thursd[...] The pastor said he hea[...] giggling and saw the lig[...] the church's basement so[...] ed the doors and ca[...] police. When they arr[...] ficers surrounded the [...] and gave orders for the [...] ers to come out with th[...] up. However, the intru[...] already escaped through [...] basement window, taki[...] church items which were [...] monetary value", acco[...] pastor Moench. Police [...] the sickly-sweet odor [...] juana smoke inside and [...] couple of scurrilous dr[...] hymnals.

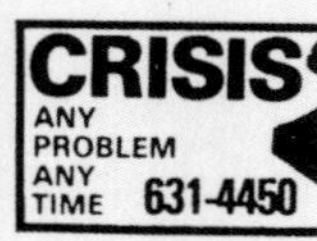

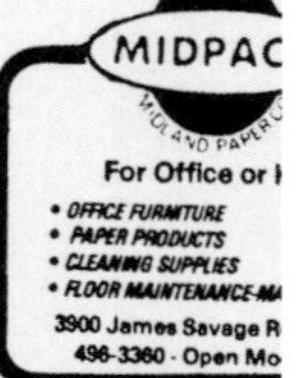

The photograph caption:

Showing off her students' handiwork under an experiment to tune in to a new kind of muse is art teacher Miss Foot (right). Seated next to her superior work is Central High's prize art student Mary Williams.

EXPERIMENT IN LOCAL ART CLASS

By JOSEPH R. SCHWINKENDORF
Daily News Staff Writer

The music of NOW echoed into the normally silent halls of Central High school today. It was all part of an attempt to involve our youngsters in their school work, in this case, Miss Foot's art class. "We are trying to get down to their level, to communicate in their language" she said.

While a long cut with a driving beat by the popular rhythm group "Iron Butterfly" played, the students were encouraged to make art that described what the music meant to them. "We were given a demonstration at the state teachers convention last month" said Miss Foot. "It really gives them encouragement to open up and free associate." The long, abstract instrumental section provides much room for exersizes on a mental jungle-gym, while the sparse lyrics are vague and idealistic.

One rather excited student was working out an abstract-expressionist form from modeling clay mixed with natural materials when I querried him. "I'm just grooving to the vibes, man" was his explanation. Another worked intently on a vision of Adam and Eve in paradise. Other takes ranged from racing cars to geometric abstractions to pretty fashion models to, simply, the words "Iron Butterfly" in a appropriately convoluted swirl.

The prize was awarded to star art student Mary Williams. Miss Williams, who had also won this year's Halloween window painting and Christmas card contests, came up with a brightly colored and incredibly detailed painting in the (relatively) short span of seventeen minutes the song takes to wind its way to an end. "We just worship the Butterfly" she said by way of explanation. Miss Foot says she has quite a career as an artist or art teacher ahead of her.

Others outside of the school system are not so approving. Dr. Daniel Rodgers said "It has been proved that frenzied beats have a deleterious effect on the youth of our country. I object strenuously to the forced exposure of innocents to this communist-inspired "underground" music in our public schools." Dr. Rodgers is a spokesman for the local John Birch Society.

Regardless of the controversy over rock 'n' roll music in our schools, Miss Foot said today's experiment was so sucessful she's having her students bring in records of their own choice to listen to and create to starting tomorrow.

9. News Clippings　1988

Photostat on paper
43.2 × 35.6 cm (17 × 14 in)
Collection unknown

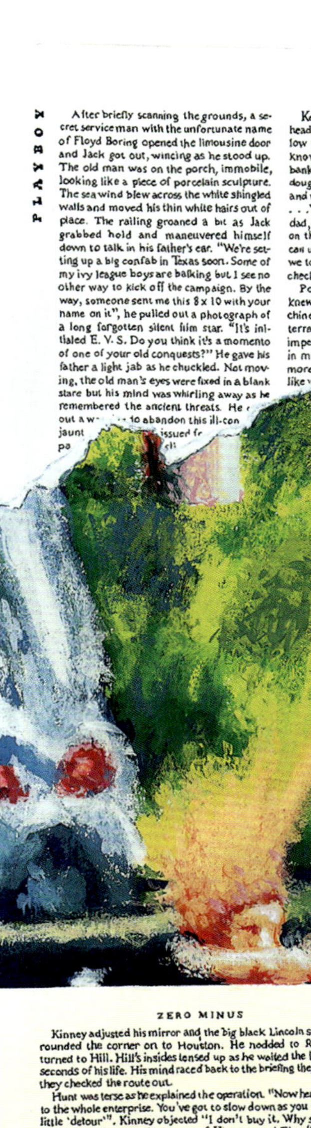

10. Manlicker   1991

Ink and gouache on paper
43.2 × 35.6 cm (17 × 14 in)
Collection of Linda Janger

Fake comic strips, fake board games and fake art also appear. In *Young Pillars* (1990) (fig.12), Shaw transforms Charles Schulz's beloved comic strip *Peanuts* into a Biblical parable about belief, betrayal and suffering. The gullibility, hope and cruelty that transpire among cartoon characters play out against a backdrop of Christian symbolism, suggesting that Charlie Brown and Jesus Christ have more in common than is usually seen by their fans and acolytes – and that religious ideals often play out in ways too mundane to be noticed. The catholic nature of faith is a touchstone for Shaw, as is the conviction that religious myths are most potent when they are down-to-earth and ordinary: no more transcendent than comic strips and just as easy to understand. That was also the point of *Game of the Stations of Life* (1990) (fig.11), a wall-mounted shadow box in which Shaw sabotaged a popular board game by turning its circuitous path into an ouroboros-style loop, trapping its players in a closed circuit of eternal recurrence, or *Ground Hog Day* repetition.

Modern art also gets turned inside-out. Made of Lincoln Logs (a popular American toy-set) and mass-produced knick-knacks, *Ecology Box* (1990) (fig.13) is a ham-fisted rendition of a Joseph Cornell shadow box. Shaw's knock-off dispenses with the preciousness of the original for the ordinariness of cheap souvenirs, because those items convey meaning just as meaningfully as fine art does. Shaw smuggled his punk populism into a miniature rendition of a text painting in the style of John Baldessari. Titled *Conceptual Art* (1987), it asserted that the supposed stylelessness of conceptual art was itself a style, and that that style could be put to diverse uses. Shaw treated the conceptual strictures of academic art-making in the same way he treated any other kind of authority: as something to be messed with.

When he turned to concert posters, album covers and underground graphics, his works were less barbed – more like works done in the style of an admired master by someone who wanted to learn the tricks of the trade and carry them on. *My Mirage* included a dozen such homages. Most focused on individuals, including Wes Wilson, Victor Moscoso, Rick Griffin, Peter Max, Robert Williams and Martin Sharp. Others were inspired by Dutch art, design and music collectives, including Kelley/Mouse Studios and The Fool. One riffed off of the *Chicago Seed*, an underground newspaper, and another sprung from an imagined collaboration between Wes Wilson, who designed psychedelic posters in California in the 1960s, and Käthe Kollwitz, whose political graphics and sculptures were banned by the Nazis.

All shaped the terrain of Shaw's imagination. They also reflected his acute awareness of power relationships, particularly as they played out in the art world, where fine art out-ranked commercial art, illustration and graphic design. *My Mirage* made room for such supposedly second-class forms, emphasizing their visual sophistication while taking a jab at the pretensions of art that presumed it had a better pedigree – as if it were a purebred dog show champion and not a multilayered mixture of various cultural strands and styles. Works in the style of Henri Matisse, Marc Chagall, Henry Moore, Pablo Picasso, Ferdinand Leger, Jean Miro and Joan Arp appear as runners up (i.e.,

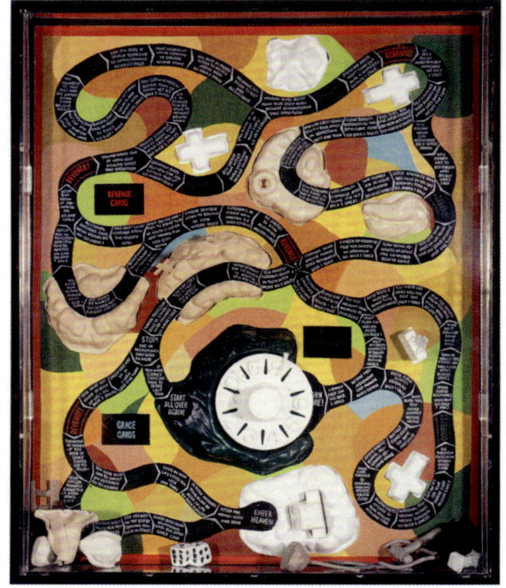

11. Game of the Stations of Life   1990

Gouache on board with game
43.2 × 35.6 cm (17 × 14 in)
Courtesy Marc Jancou

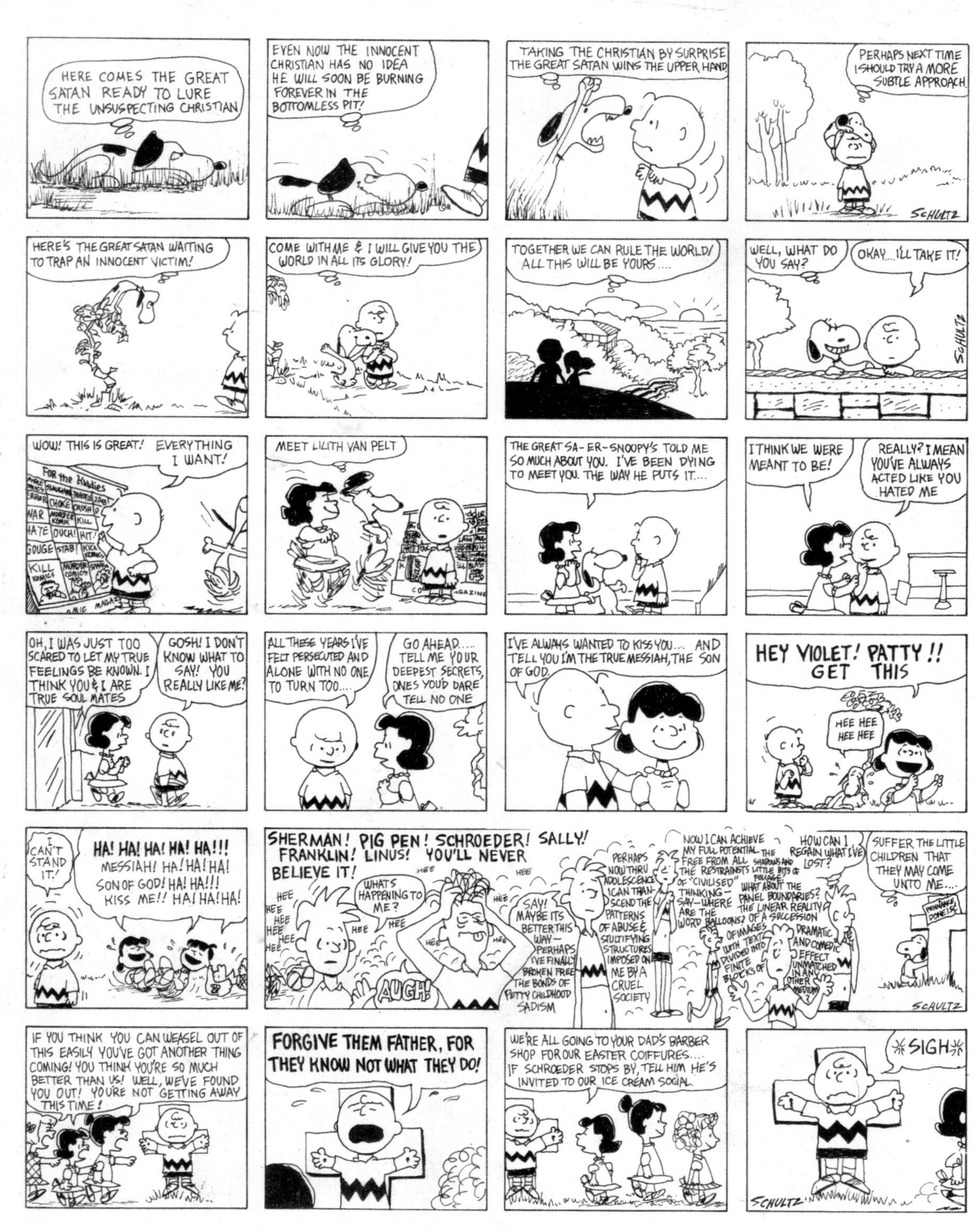

12. Young Pillars   1990

Ink on paper
43.2 × 35.6 cm (17 × 14 in)
Collection unknown

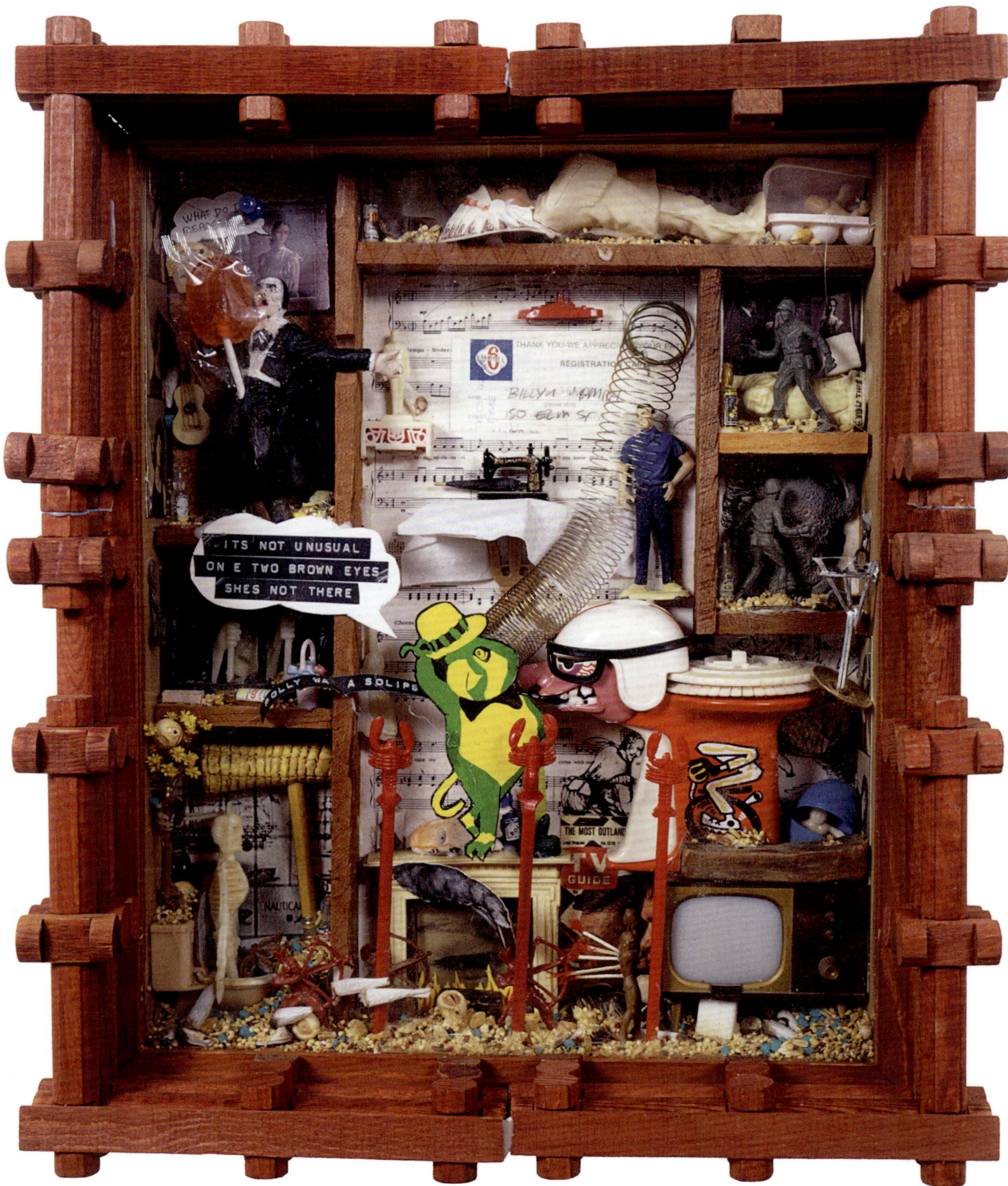

13. **Ecology Box**   1990

Mixed media, found objects, gouache, ink
43.2 × 35.6 cm (17 × 14 in)
Collection unknown

losers) in a high school Christmas card competition (*Christmas Card Contest Runner Up*, 1990). Salvador Dalí, René Magritte, Giorgio de Chirico and Hieronymus Bosch get better treatment, each inspiring a piece in Shaw's series. And *What Bitter Irony* (1989) used sarcasm to mock the critical shibboleth that caused more than one generation of art students to believe that the best art had to offer was ironic detachment, emotional distance and intellectual superiority. In Shaw's view, such thinking was myopic, even puritanical, especially when applied to works by Marc Rothko, Andy Warhol, Robert Indiana, Tom Wesselmann, Mel Ramos, Alan Jones, Robert Graham, Richard Linder and Douglas Huebler, many of whom, Shaw believed, made works that prioritized physical sensation, sexual and otherwise, and had nothing, whatsoever, to do with irony, detachment and cerebral superiority. Throughout *My Mirage*, high and low rubbed shoulders and more, making sparks fly in the mind's eye while stimulating the senses like nobody's business – often to the point of embarrassment.

The largest group of works in *My Mirage* was the leftovers, those that did not fit into any category but had the presence of misfits. Included in this eccentric compendium of stuff and symbols were lumps of Silly Putty, gobs of fake gum, an ant farm overrun by plastic bugs, a puddle of novelty vomit, a Rothko-red monochrome that seemed to be oozing goo from its bottom edge, and a roll of gold-leafed toilet paper tangled in the branches of a leafless tree. Still lifes, in various styles and media, depicted the Venus of Willendorf, Christ's face on a pepperoni pizza, and Richard Nixon as a chunk of deep-green kryptonite. Realistic images presented a tie-dyed mandala, various collections of bubblegum cards, an illegible ransom note, and a swathe of wallpaper overtaken by angry embryos and flip-flopped swastikas, their right-angled forms turned against one another so that their normal messaging was subtly disrupted, but still disturbing.

Misunderstanding and misinterpretation are integral to Shaw's sense of how meaning gets made and how art works in the world. That can be traced back to the origin story of *In-A-Gadda-Da-Vida*, a drunken mispronunciation of 'in the garden of Eden.' For Shaw, such misconstrued messages are often more meaningful than clearly conveyed ones. In a sense, *My Mirage* is a slippery slope on which there is no toehold for know-it-all superiority. Expertise meets its match in Shaw's ad-libbed extravaganza, where the textures and tones of images and words exist on a level playing field, no one more important than another. That radically democratic ethos carries over into Shaw's use of materials and conventions: whether drawing, in pencil or ink; painting, in gouache or oil; or sculpting, three-dimensionally or in shallow relief; he never presumes that any one material or technique, genre or style, is any more effective than any other. In fact, mashing them all together – along with abstraction and figuration, super-realism and surrealism, cartoons and photo-realistic illusions – seems to suit his picture of things: complex and fractured and in need of multiple perspectives if its reality is to be grasped or intuited, rationally or magically.

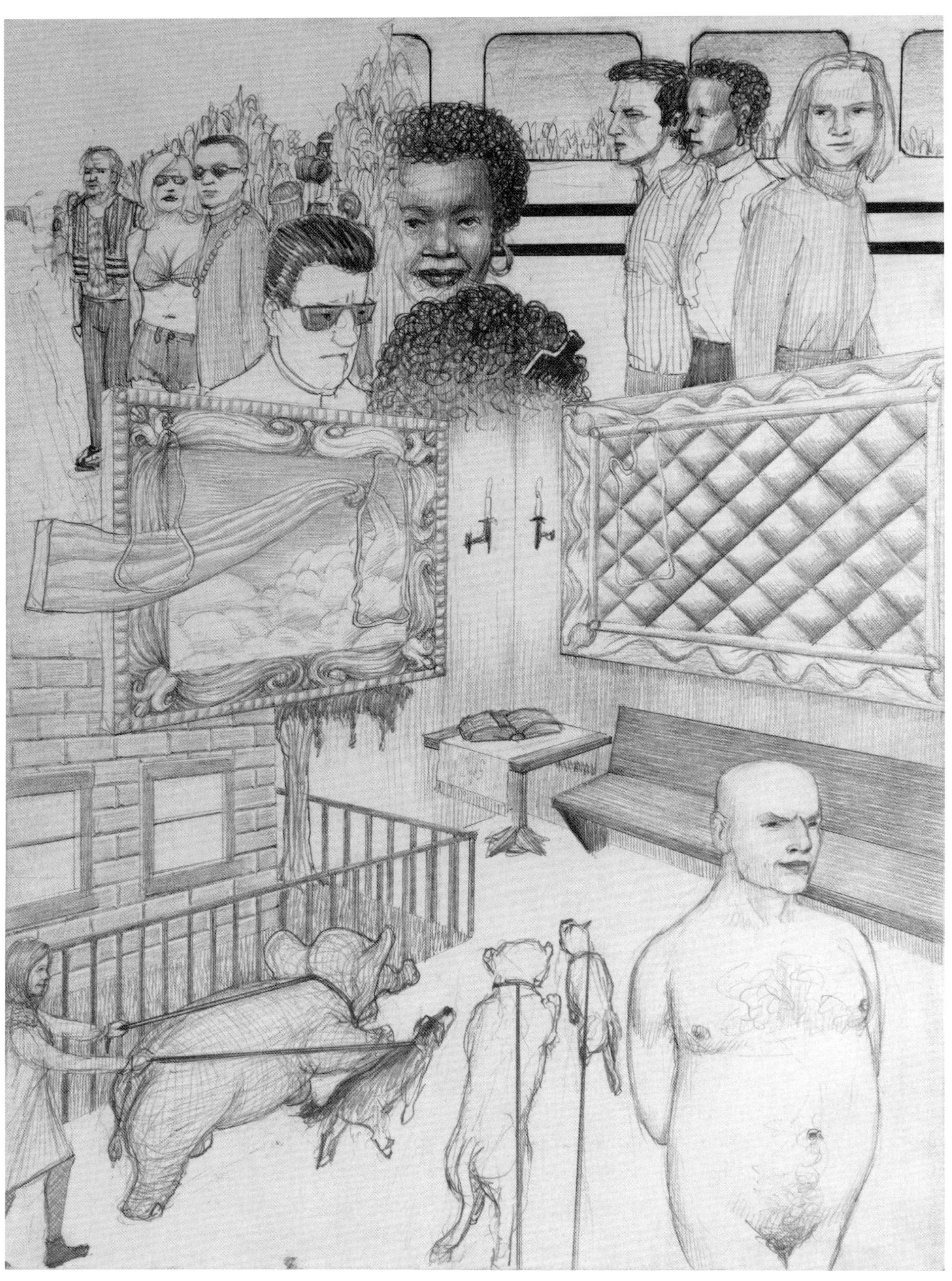

14. Dream Drawing
("On the TV movie bio of Frank
Sinatra...")   1996

Pencil on paper
30.5 × 22.9 cm (12 × 9 in)
Courtesy Praz-Delavallade
and Blum & Poe

3 Untitled (Giant Face Paintings) (1991–2);
Dream Drawings (1992–9);
Fake Dream Drawings (1992–4);
Other People's Dreams (1996);
and Dream Objects (1995–present)

In 1991, Shaw rented his first real studio, from Edward Ruscha, in a building in Los Angeles on Western Avenue just south of Santa Monica Boulevard. He hired, for the first time, an assistant. And he started painting a series of giant black-and-white portraits. The series included only two works, but each of his *Untitled (Giant Face Paintings)* measured 7 x 88 ft (around 2 x 27 m) and was comprised of 616 1-sq-ft (around 57-sq-m) canvas panels. Each was based on a pair of photographs of two friends or co-workers. Shaw wanted to see if any element of a sitter's identity remained after he had scrambled, more or less randomly, all of the panels that made up the four portraits. He also wanted to discover if the rearranged faces held together compositionally – if they worked as abstract paintings. While it was impossible to identify any of Shaw's sitters, their presences lurked, ghostlike, in the rearranged details of their facial features. Their identities were camouflaged in a mismatched mélange of information, lost, as it were, in transmission. What was gained was more elusive, inarticulate, alien.

While working on the series Shaw met artist Marnie Weber. He was 39 and within two years they would be married. Shaw moved into her house in Garvanza, northeast of downtown Los Angeles. He kept his apartment as a studio, office and library. Eventually the couple purchased a house in Eagle Rock and have lived there ever since. In 1999, their daughter Colette was born.

Upon completing his *Untitled (Giant Face Paintings)*, Shaw shipped the black and white group to Metro Pictures gallery in New York and the colour group to art dealer Massimo DeCarlo in Milan. In New York, he installed the whole group as a single mural that covered two walls. The installation resembled a discombobulated Chuck Close painting, as if a blast of static had interrupted the picture's ordinarily clear transmission. Shaw's ambivalence about artistic authority – particularly the sort that accompanies large-scale paintings – was embodied in his process: the ambition to work monumentally countered by the misaligned fragments, no two of which worked together to give viewers a glimpse of the big picture. It was as if Shaw was conflicted about his relationship to large-scale painting, fascinated by its potential but suspicious of its singularity, its size, its authority.

Just before Shaw sent off his paintings, Los Angeles erupted with violence. On 29 April 1992, following the acquittal of four police officers who were charged with assault and using excessive force in the arrest of motorist Rodney King on 3 March 1991, riots broke out. President George H.W. Bush declared a national emergency, and the California National Guard was called in, along with federal troops. For nearly a week, Los Angeles burned: 3,600 fires were set all over the city, 1,100 buildings were destroyed, 63 people were killed, 2,383 were injured and innumerable stores were looted. From his apartment, Shaw – like many people in Los Angeles – watched. During the day, smoke rose in thick black columns. At night, flames blazed, illuminating the sky with an ominous glow. When the riots began, Shaw dismissed his assistant. When they ended, he terminated his lease.

And just after that, he embarked on a project that would grow into two major bodies of work (*Dream Drawings* and *Dream Objects*) and two related series (*Fake Dream Drawings* and *Other People's Dreams*). Once again, Shaw decided to work small, making his *Dream Drawings* on 12 x 9 in (30.5 x 23 cm) sketchbook pages. Without a studio, he could work almost anywhere. He used only pencil, eliminating both color and the expansive inventory of media in *My Mirage*. And he eliminated the mimicry – or homage-paying – of that body of work, drawing in a way that did not borrow from other artists but came to him naturally: quickly and casually yet meticulously and judiciously, with just enough shading to suggest volume without suggesting that the finished work was anything more than an attentively observed study, which would serve as a preparatory sketch for future works.

Shaw's *Dream Drawings* occupied the lion's share of his artistic life for the next seven years. Each was structured like a single page from a comic book: with individual frames, gridded variously, always reading from upper left to lower right. Some were single-scene dreams. A handful had two scenes, like diptychs. The vast majority had more – many with six, eight or even more scenes. And some of those scenes depicted scenes within scenes, creating worlds-within-worlds. As the series progressed, the drawings grew in complexity, their narratives denser, more elaborate and packed with detail. On the back of each drawing Shaw wrote a basic description of the dream it depicted. His summaries were blunt; all steered clear of interpretation.

In *Dream Drawing ("Cookie (from* Beetle Bailey*) was hiding out in* Peanuts*...")* (1997) (fig.16), a central image is sandwiched between Shaw's sabotaged Charles Schulz comic strip and his own mongrel strip. The flipside description reads:

1. Cookie (from *Beetle Bailey*) was hiding out in *Peanuts*, sheltered by Charlie's kite, but his hair was shedding everywhere, which angered Charlie. Pig Pen said he smelled and Sally talked about the beauty of smells. 2. I was making a crayon banner for my basement, which I needed to go to the library to research.

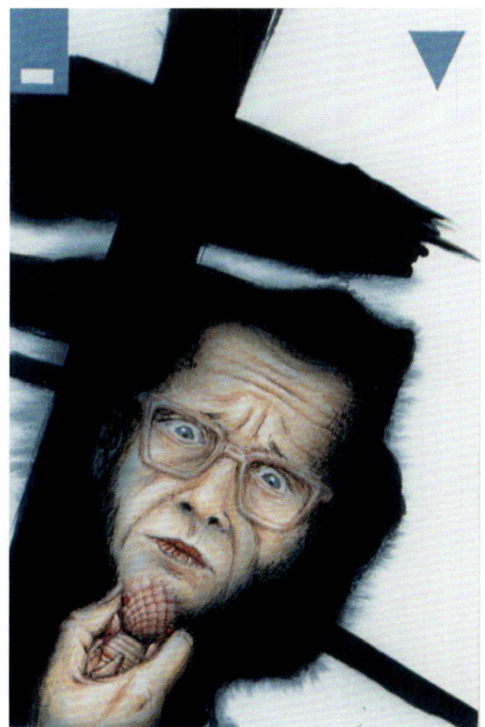

15. Dream Object ("On the Road to Rochester...") 1999

Gouache on rag board mounted on plywood
24 × 16 cm (9½ × 6⅓ in)
Private collection

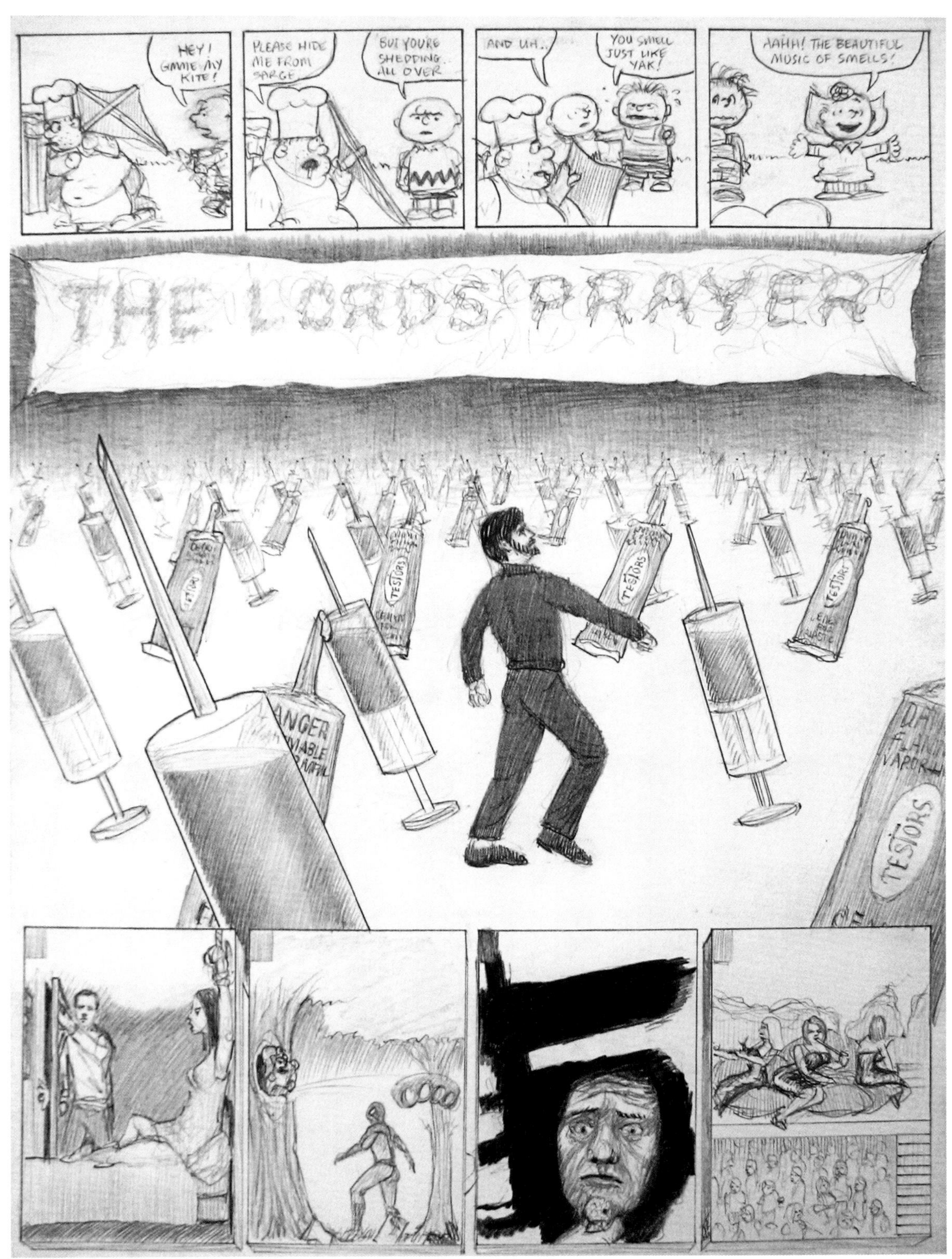

16. Dream Drawing ("Cookie (from Beetle Bailey) was hiding out in Peanuts…")   1997

Pencil on paper
30.5 × 22.9 cm (12 × 9 in)
Private collection

Then there was a scene from a never produced film about Sgt. Pepper's
with a guy dancing in a field of hypodermics & glue tubes. 3. On the road to
Rochester I had the idea to do a series of paperback paintings that would just
be the illustrations minus any texts (from a movie with Nick Cage & Katherine
Bigelow, she's been tied by her wrists to a bed & he suspects someone's behind
the closet door & it turned out to be a nerdy 18 year old she'd had an affair with
who was still obsessed with her & gave her a New Kids on the Block poster—
Spiderman was carrying a bunch of evidence in his skintight suit's pockets
so people called him Droopy Drawers so he placed it in a tree & the squirrel
occupant threw it all over the forest floor, pulling a scaly embryo out of my chin
during a party with hundreds of blond children—upstairs sexy women in red
dresses do drugs on cushions.)

Real comic strips (*Beetle Bailey* and *Peanuts*) run together and then fuse with Shaw's
made-up comic strip, in which pop music, popular movies and more comic strips
commingle and cross-pollinate, all making for a kind of multi-layered information-
overload both dizzying and fascinating – and way beyond Freud's wildest dreams.

The pedestrian regularity – and plodding daily labor – of Shaw's project contrast
dramatically with the eccentric singularity of his dreams. No two tell the same story,
or even repeat the same scenarios. Many pack a superabundance of improbable,
beyond-belief adventure – and even more nonsensical, impossible-to-make-up
juxtapositions – into a small format. The productivity of Shaw's dream life makes it
seem as if his unconscious took the Protestant work ethic both seriously and literally:
like his waking self, it never rests, matching, and surpassing, Shaw's daily labors. He
made hundreds of *Dream Drawings*, losing track of the number and never keeping
accurate records.

Shaw exhibited his *Dream Drawings* regularly, first in solo shows in 1993 at Linda
Cathcart Gallery in Santa Monica and at Metro Pictures in New York, and in 1994 at
Rena Bransten Gallery in San Francisco. Over the next five years, selections from the
series were displayed in solo shows in Las Vegas, London, Milan, Detroit, Paris, Tokyo,
Frankfurt and Salzburg, as well as in group shows in Houston, Vienna, Copenhagen,
Miami, Munich, Prague, New York, Victoria, Los Angeles, Rotterdam, Turin and San
Diego. In 1995, Smart Art Press published *Dreams: Jim Shaw*, a thick 8 x 6 in (20 x 15 cm)
picture book in which 148 *Dream Drawings* appeared. Most occupied a single page and
alternated with the description that had been written on their backs.

Sex enters the picture frequently and explicitly. Rendered in the same detached,
no-nonsense style that characterizes everything Shaw depicted, sexual activity is just
another fact to be reported. The dispassionate tone of Shaw's drawings strip sex of the
psychological significance that Freudian analysis brings to it. Shaw calls his sexually
explicit images *Erotic Dream Drawings* and thinks of them as a subset of his *Dream
Drawings*. Now that his daughter has gone off to college and he is no longer worried

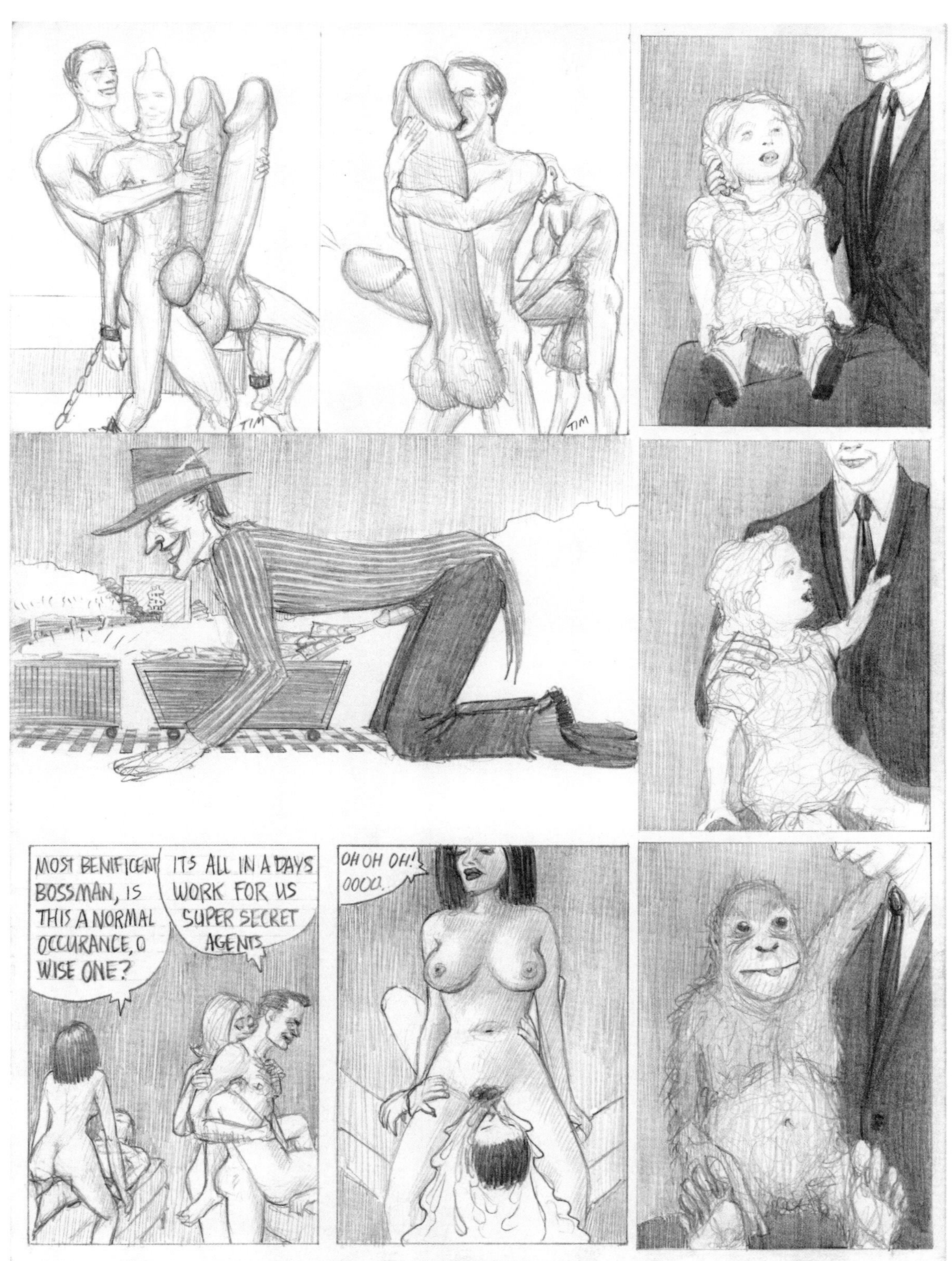

17. Dream Drawing ("An ad in a fake Tom of Finland catalog had guys with giant penises...")   1995

Pencil on paper
30.5 × 22.9 cm (12 × 9 in)
Courtesy Praz-Delavallade

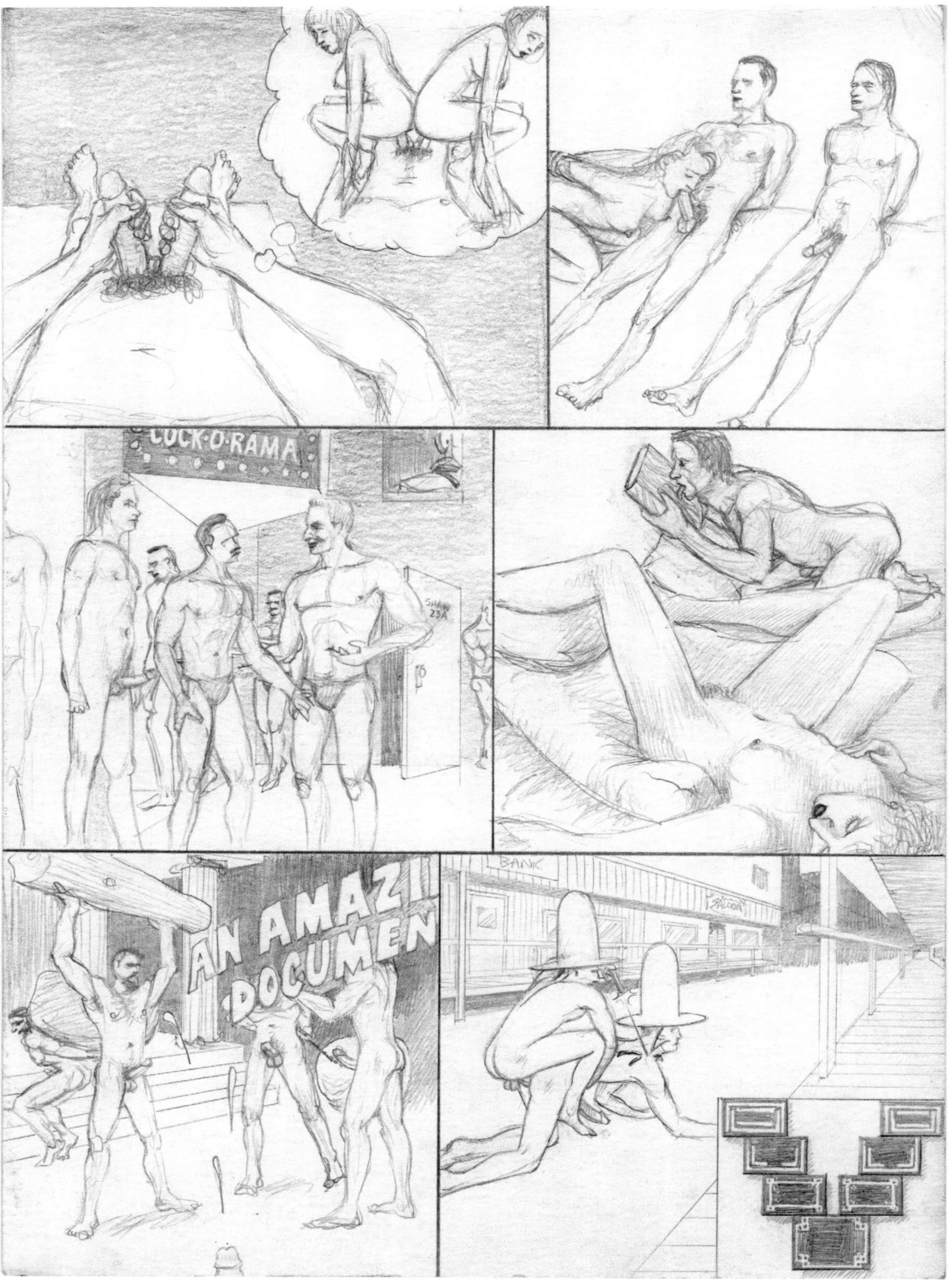

18. Dream Drawing ("I had 2 cocks and I was masturbating, wishing I had 2 women sitting on them...")

1993

Pencil on paper
30.5 × 22.9 cm (12 × 9 in)
Courtesy Praz-Delavallade

about embarrassing her, he allows them to be exhibited and reproduced in catalogs. But while he was making them, and well after that, Shaw refrained from exhibiting them, except for a solo show in Paris, where he felt that they would not be seen as salacious.

Throughout all of Shaw's wild adventures, the detached, just-the-facts tone remains the same: unflappable and matter-of-fact. The images and texts are recorded with a nothing-to-get-excited-about flatness, an almost monotone drone that makes their craziness seem ordinary, just like any other everyday occurrence. As a series, Shaw's *Dream Drawings* account for the most straightforward reportage he has done as an artist. In them, his waking self chronicles the adventures on which his sleeping self had embarked, recording, like an exceptionally restrained travel writer, the basic features of the places he had visited and the basic contours of the events that had unfolded there. The pencil, pastel and oil-stick drawings commonly made by court reporters are far more extravagant and expressive that Shaw's unadorned drawings. Neutrality is their overriding feature. No fake news, whatsoever.

The only caveat is that Shaw is the only witness to his dreams. Suspicious viewers might not believe that he is telling the truth. But he comes off as a convincing witness – not a braggart or egomaniac but as if he were just as puzzled as any one of us, amazed by the places his unconscious had taken him in the night, and now, in the light of day, almost dumbstruck by what he has witnessed. Unlike Dante, who has Virgil to guide him through *The Divine Comedy*, Shaw has no one to guide him through his dreams. He is on his own, a kind of innocent in a land in which anything might happen.

Shaw was drawn to dreams because they are not authored by their dreamers. His congenital antipathy to authority – whether that power resides in others or in himself – takes shape in the relationship he established to viewers of his *Dream Drawings*: as fellow travelers through a world of otherwise unimaginable occurrences, where what is learned in one situation is inapplicable to the next; where the most rational response is to acknowledge the limits of rationality; and where there is no end or goal, other than to be as attentive as possible. For Shaw, attentiveness is its own reward, partly because there is no guarantee the future will unfold in a way that may be predicted, and partly because the present is a wildly fascinating place to be – especially when seen through his eyes.

Over the first three years that Shaw was making *Dream Drawings*, he was also making *Fake Dream Drawings*. That series of approximately 25 works consists of larger-than-life-size images of larvae, pupae and cocoons, as well as tics, vines and parasites, each centered on a plain sheet of white paper that measured 19¾ x 16½ in (around 50 x 42 cm). At the bottom of each sheet appears a handwritten caption that matter-of-factly describes a program or advertisement that Shaw had seen on TV. The plots are preposterous. In one, a scrawny white guy is visited by tiny people, before he turns into a matador who uses a big can of bug spray to kill a bull and seduce a woman who turns into a bearded fortune-teller who advises a beautiful

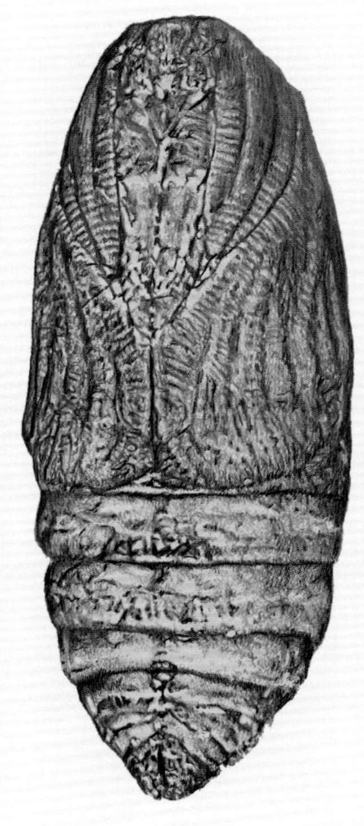

19. Fake Dream Drawing ("Vaginal Cocoon: As he sleeps, a wimpy wasp…") 1992

Pencil on paper
50.3 × 41.9 cm (19⅘ × 16½ in)
Private collection

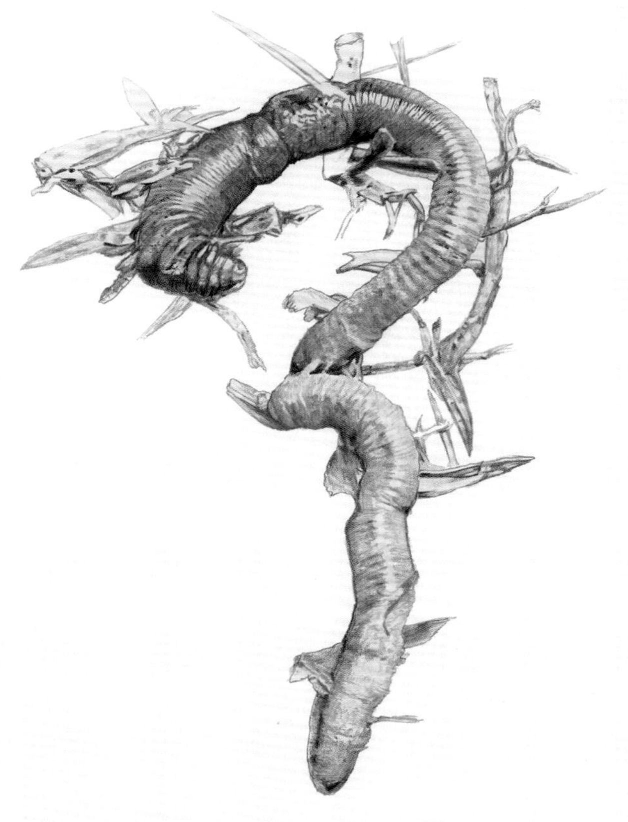

20. Fake Dream Drawing ("Worm: A bottle floats forward…")   1993

Pencil on paper
50.3 × 41.9 cm (19⅘ × 16½ in)
Private collection

woman wearing a boot-shaped hat. In another, a tennis player swats a tennis ball into the air, where it turns into a bottled soft drink that flies further into the sky, where it attracts beautiful women and then multiplies, forming a flotilla of bottles from which more women drink through long straws, causing a whirlpool of logos to spiral into outer space.

The flat-footed descriptions in Shaw's *Fake Dream Drawings* echo what takes place in his *Dream Drawings*. Scenes shift with no regard for continuity. Logic falls by the wayside. Narrative consistency is nonexistent. Non sequiturs abound. But there is a fundamental difference between the two series: while Shaw's *Dream Drawings* originate in actual dreams, his *Fake Dream Drawings* originate in deliberately conceived, carefully staged, meticulously scripted, beautifully lit and expensively produced programming. TV narratives may share many of the features of real dreams, but they are not real dreams. They are fake: manufactured fantasies conceived and designed and engineered to make people think that they have to have certain products. The strategy and format the ads deploy may have been invented by the surrealists, but the purposes they serve would have made the original surrealists cringe – or roll over in their graves. Rather than startling people into seeing reality more clearly and vividly and truly – awakening them, in other words, to the strangeness of the real world – the illogical juxtapositions that unfolded in the televised snippets are used by companies to seduce consumers into thinking that our needs and desires might be satisfied by a soft drink, or a big can of bug spray.

Shaw's *Fake Dream Drawings* harbor no such illusions. Like his *Dream Drawings*, they preserve the true weirdness of surrealism while getting rid of its bells-and-whistles, its slick surfaces, its mind-bending illusions, its splashy theatrics and its focus on momentous, life-changing events – whether the sexual trauma at the heart of surrealism or the sexual gratification promised by television. Even so, his *Fake Dream Drawings* lack the far-reaching freedom of his dream life, which was richer and more radically freewheeling than anything seen on TV.

While Shaw was drawing his dreams, he began to wonder about what other people might be dreaming. So he set up shop at Rosamund Felsen Gallery in Santa Monica, where, for one month in 1996, he made himself available, for the very reasonable fee of $200, to anyone who wanted him to draw their dreams. All Shaw required was a narrative. Some customers were very clear about what they wanted. Others were uncomfortable with the idea of seeing their desires realized so literally. One collector requested a picture of herself looking at a work by Shaw that she had recently purchased. Another wanted a portrait of jazz saxophonist Steve Lacy. And another hired Shaw to make a drawing that included the RMS *Titanic* and postage stamps. My wife, Alisa Tager, was working on a movie in Argentina (fig.21), so I asked Shaw to draw her at her dream job. He did that, depicting the stars, the director and three yaks, parachuting to the set while Che Guevara made a cameo, singing an ad-libbed rendition of *Don't Cry for Me Argentina*.

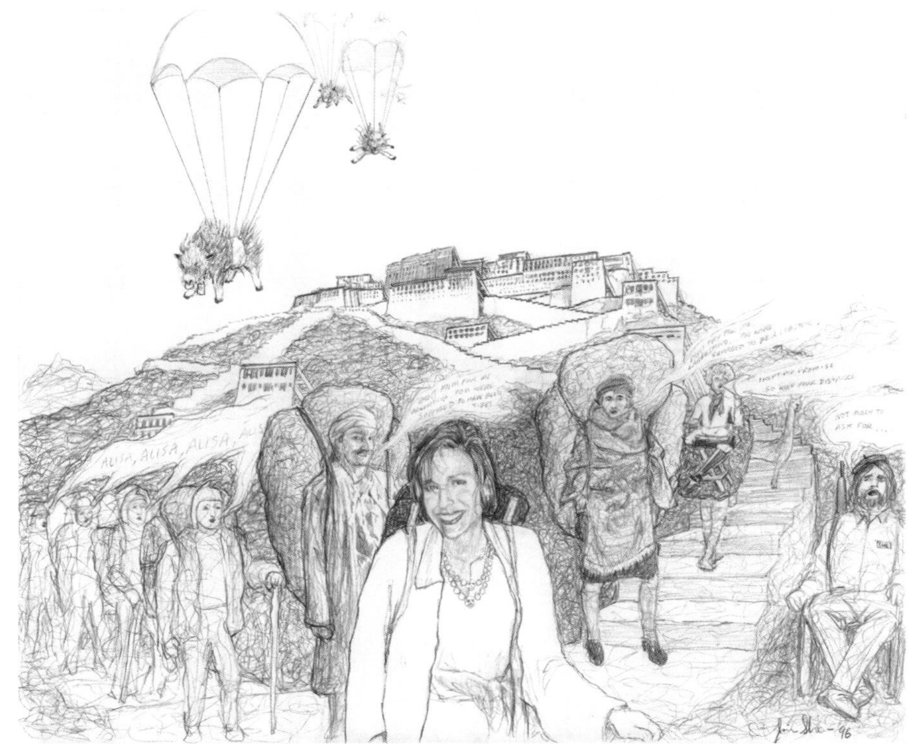

21. Other People's Dreams (Alisa Tager filming *Enemy at the Gates* in Argentina with Brad Pitt, David Thewlis and Jean-Jacques Annaud) 1996

Pencil on paper
35.6 × 43.2 cm (14 × 17 in)
Collection of David Pagel and Alisa Tager

22. Dream Object (Bone piece was missing top & bottom & odd vacuum parts were being added to it) 2010

Ink, wood, foam, aqua resin, fiberglass and gesso paint
46 × 115 × 88 cm (18 × 45½ × 34½)
Courtesy Blum & Poe

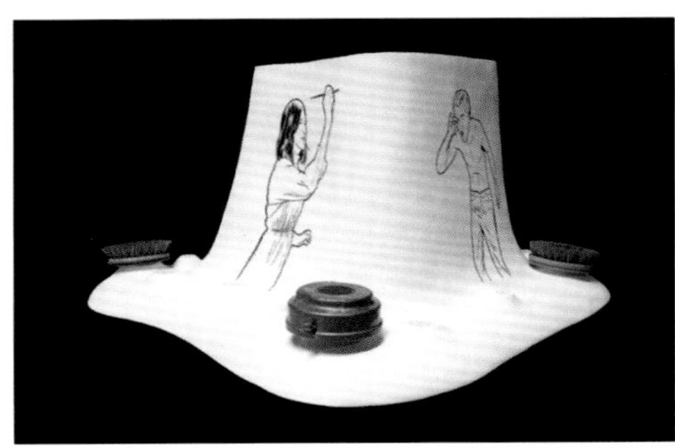

Other People's Dreams was a short-lived project. Part of the reason Shaw undertook it was to bring the two halves of his life together – the making-art part and the paying-the-bills part. That did not work out, so he went back to his day jobs: working part-time at special effects houses in Hollywood and the San Fernando Valley; designing a 3D thrill-ride for a Hello Kitty-themed amusement park in Japan; designing elements of a computerized stage show for singer-songwriter Graham Nash; and teaching for a semester as a visiting artist at the University of Nevada, Las Vegas. Shaw stopped making *Dream Drawings* in 1999, when he realized that he had already made far too many to ever translate even a fraction of them into *Dream Objects*, which he had begun making in 1995, three years after he had started drawing his dreams. By 1999, he decided to dedicate less time to drawing so he would have more time to realize his dreams – literally and figuratively – in paintings, sculptures and installations.

Shaw's *Dream Objects* are an ongoing project. They echo what he did in *My Mirage*, working in different styles and genres, with different materials and formats, to make works unconstrained by the expectation that they look similar and behave similarly. His *Dream Objects* gave him even greater range: without the narrative structure of *My Mirage*, Shaw could leap more freely from subject to subject, piece to piece, without worrying about how any of it fitted into a storyline, a format or dimensions. True to the image-glut of modern life, and to the multilayered nature of reality, Shaw's *Dream*

Objects included two-dimensional works (on paper, panel and canvas) alongside three-dimensional ones (some miniature, some life-size, others larger-than-life). Whether flat or volumetric, all were *Dream Objects* because they came out of his *Dream Drawings*. Each transformed the quickly sketched-in authenticity of those documentary works into the space our bodies occupy, presenting viewers with the opportunity to engage them the same way Shaw did: in full color, with the palpability and realness of real dreams, and, most important, with the untranslatable strangeness of dreams. It was as if the conceptual underpinnings of *My Mirage* were no longer necessary and Shaw could do what he most loved: make works as idiosyncratic and unpredictable as his dreams, free of logic and outside the bounds of rationality.

The most straightforward *Dream Objects* are enlarged, more meticulously rendered versions of *Dream Drawings*. To make them, Shaw selected a single frame from one of his drawings and recreated it, sometimes using pen-and-ink, on paper or rag board; sometimes using gouache, on panel or canvas; and sometimes sticking with pencil on paper, making works whose materials matched those of his *Dream Drawings* but whose resolution and finish distinguished them from that series. For example, *Dream Drawing* (*"Cookie (from* Beetle Bailey*) was hiding out in* Peanuts...*")* (1997) (fig.16) gave birth to *Dream Object* (*"Cookie (from* Beetle Bailey*) was hiding out in* Peanuts...*")* (1998) (fig.15), the latter a blown-up, full-color version of the third frame of the four-frame comic-strip at the bottom of the original. Shaw altered the composition of the drawn portrait, tilting it slightly to make it stronger. Painted with gouache on rag board, which Shaw then glued to a wood panel, his fake paperback's dimensions matched those of actual paperbacks, about 9 x 6 in (23 x 15 cm).

His *Dream Objects* include a library of fake paperbacks. No titles appear on any of their covers. Nor do the names of their authors. Each has the presence of an apparition; the story implied by the picture a mystery. Shaw's dreamed-up books tend toward pulp fiction, sci-fi and fantasy, along with low-brow who-dunnits, real-life adventures, surreal dramas, autobiographical intrigues, werewolf narratives and page-turning horror stories. Jesus Christ and the Whore of Babylon appear in different settings and situations, as do James Bond knock-offs and authentic Errol Flynns.

Comic books form another group. Some are based on actual superheroes, such as Superman, Green Lantern and Hawkman. But the scenes depicted and the stories promised within would never have been published by DC Comics. Other comic book covers have no match in reality. Each seems to have sprung from a world a lot like the real one yet significantly more cockeyed, its borderline distastefulness and cheeky irreverence a slap in the face to business as usual. The references to underground publications that percolated throughout *My Mirage* live on in Shaw's *Dream Objects* as the prevailing atmosphere of the whole project: a queasy stew of intertwined storylines, with plots impossible to disentangle from subplots, characters behaving uncharacteristically, and scenes providing more points of entry and exit than can be kept up with, much less explored, exhaustively or otherwise.

23. Dream Object: Paperback Cover (On the Road to Rochester ... I'm pulling a fetus out of my chin)   2008

Gouache on rag board mounted on plywood
24 × 16 cm (9½ × 6⅓ in)
Collection of Massimo De Carlo

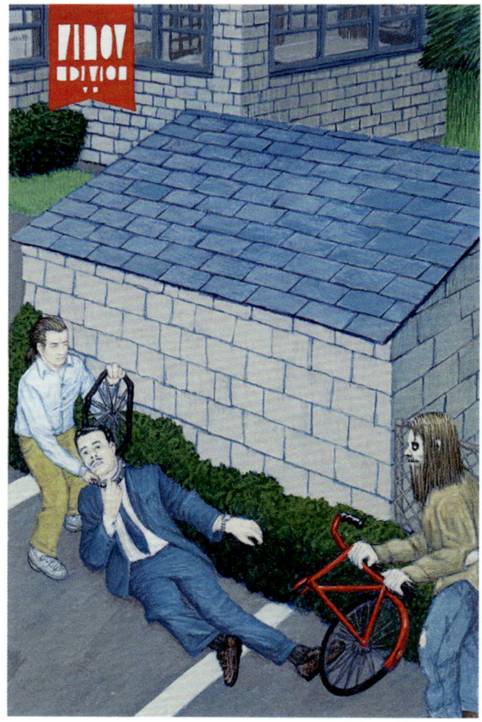

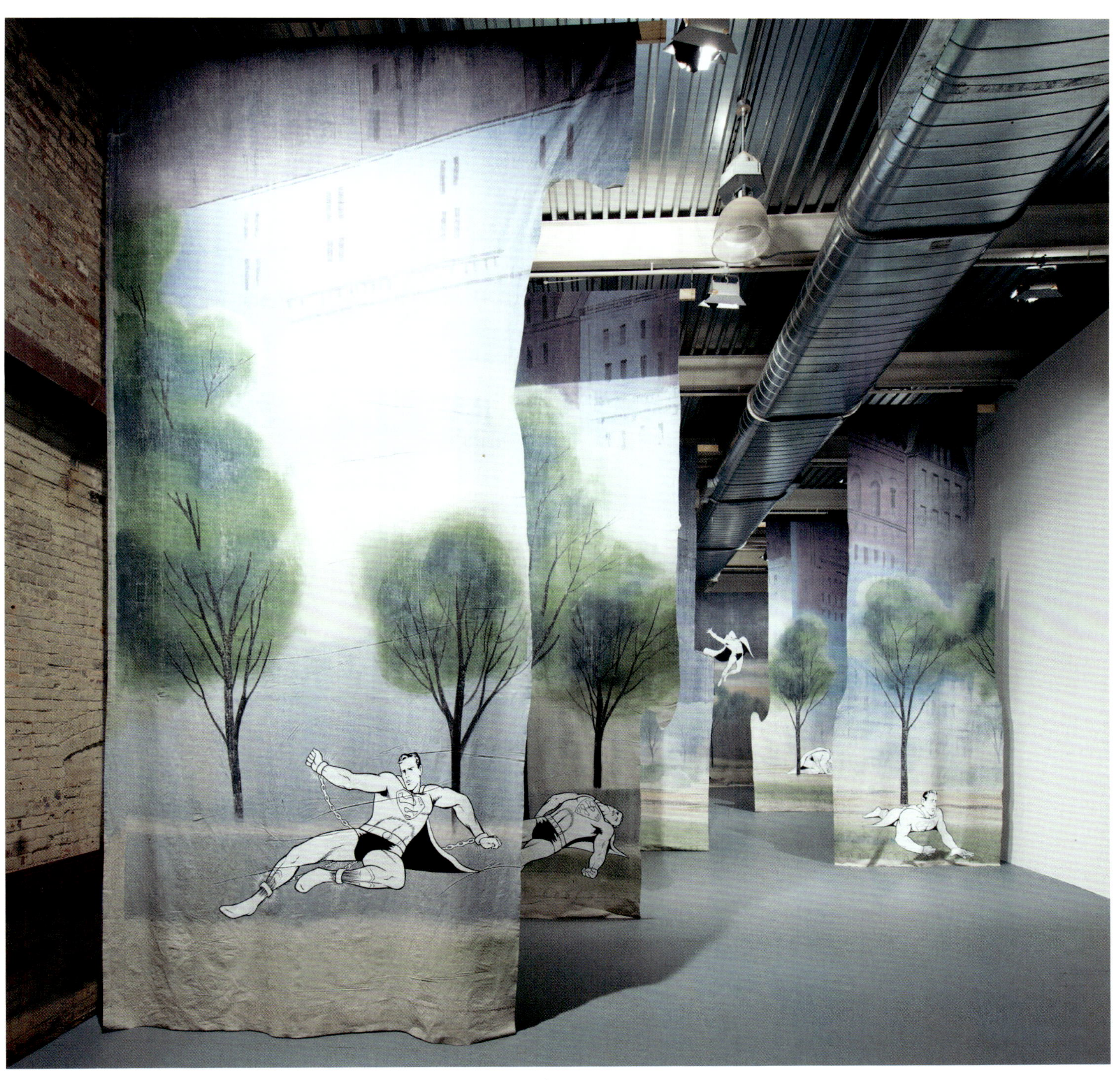

24. Not Since Superman Died
(installation view, Massachusetts
Museum of Contemporary Art,
North Adams, MA)   2014

Acrylic on muslin
8 parts, 685.8 × 1524 cm
(270 × 600 in) overall
Courtesy Blum & Poe

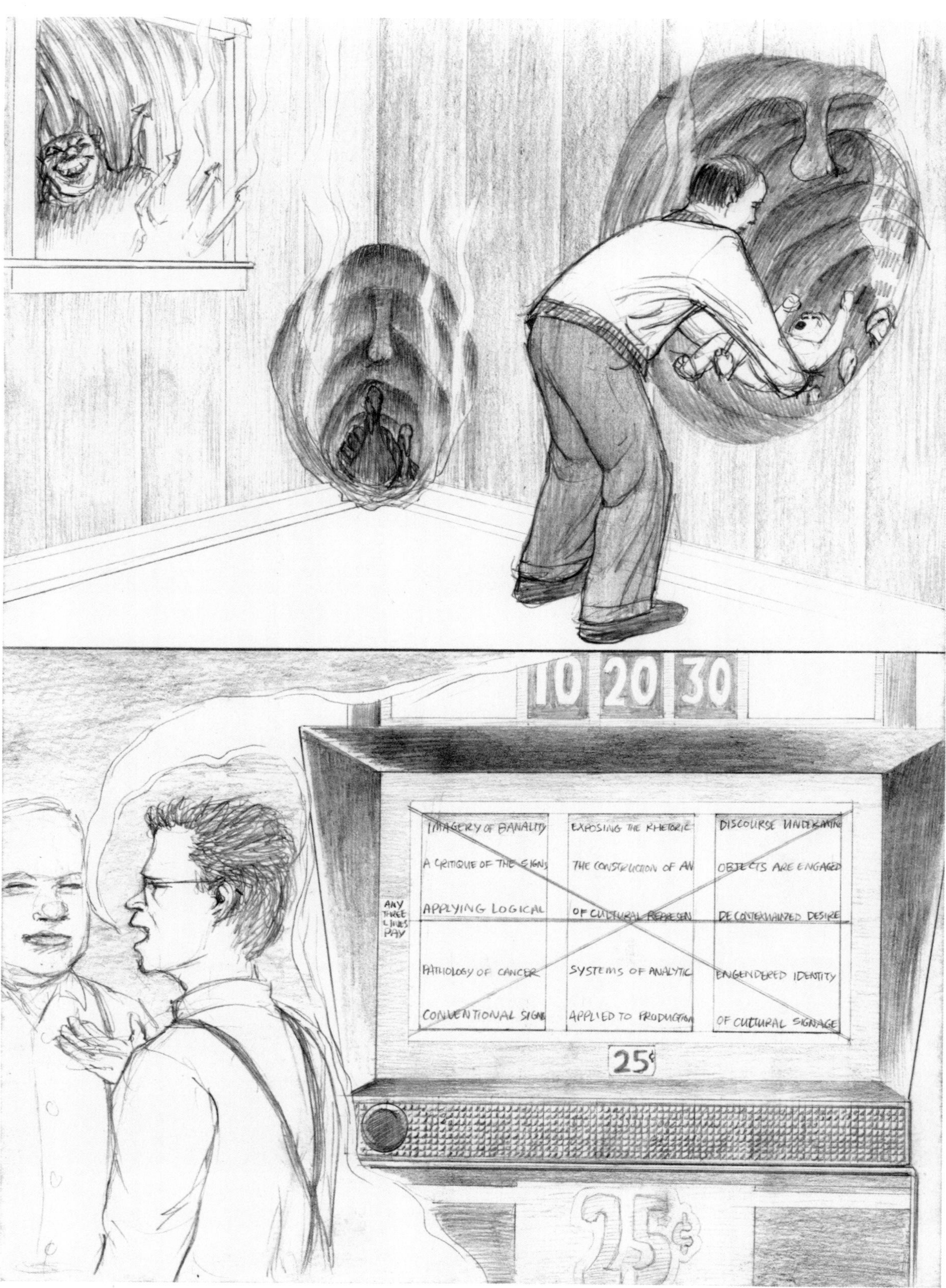

25. Dream Drawing ("A steaming fun house where adults pretend to feed babies into giant throats…")

1994

Pencil on paper
30.5 × 23 cm (12 × 9 in)
Beth Rudin DeWoody collection

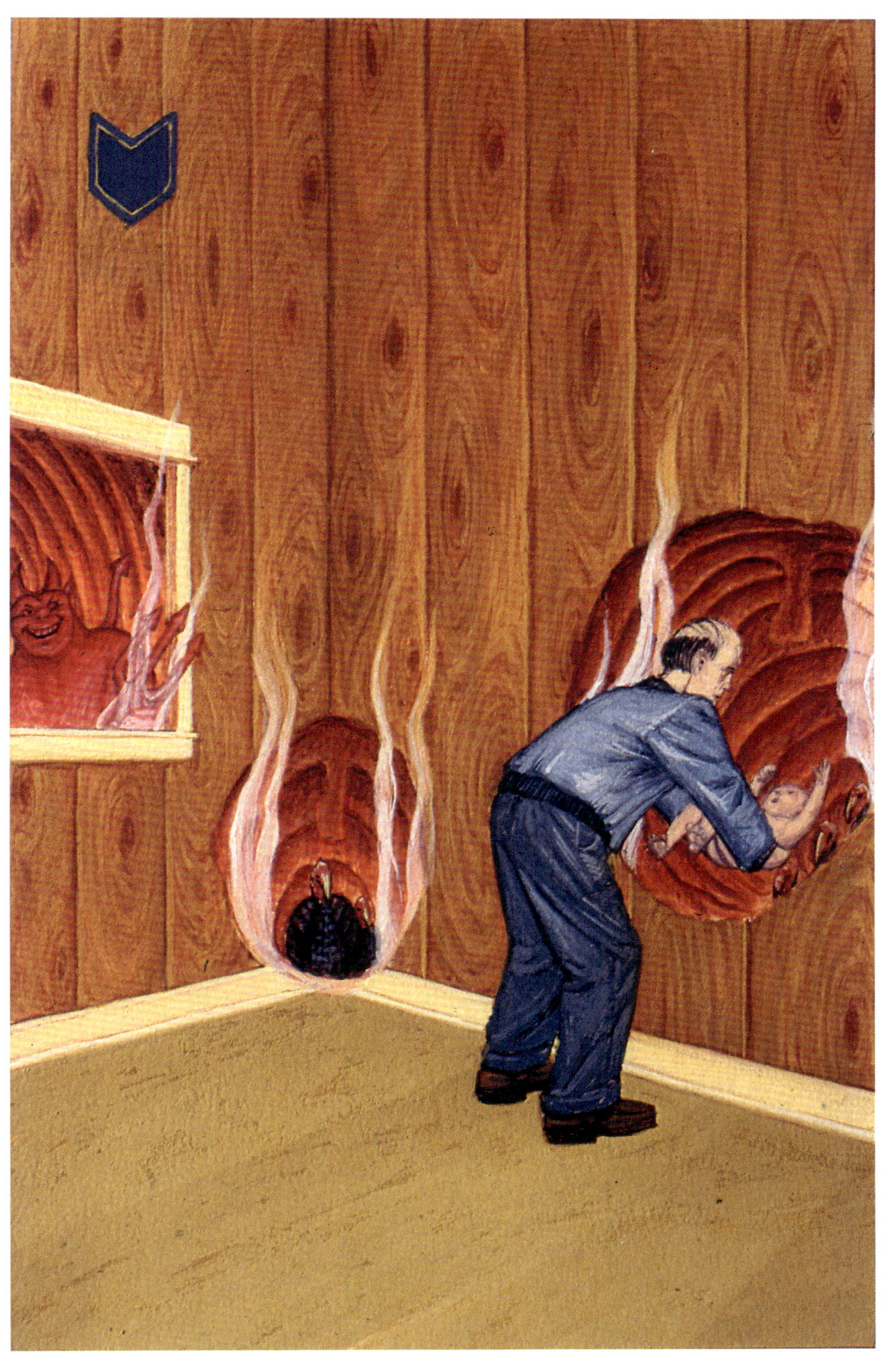

26. Dream Object ("A Steaming Funhouse...")   1998

Acrylic on rag board mounted on plywood
17 × 26.7 cm (6⅜ × 10½ in)
Private collection

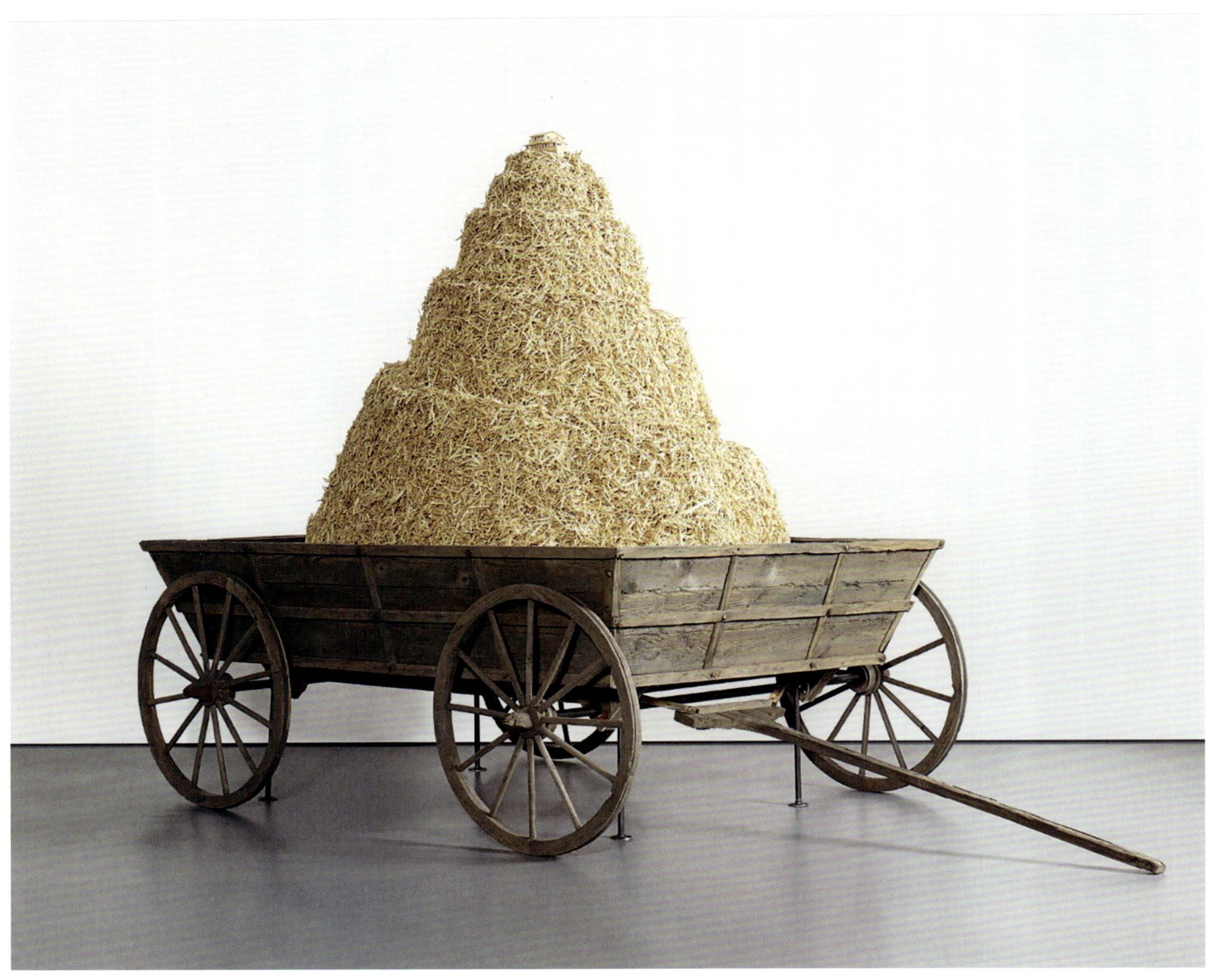

27. Dream Object (Haywain)   2007

Straw, wood, resin, metal
7.6 cm × 17.8 × 35.6 cm (9 × 7 × 14 in)
Private collection

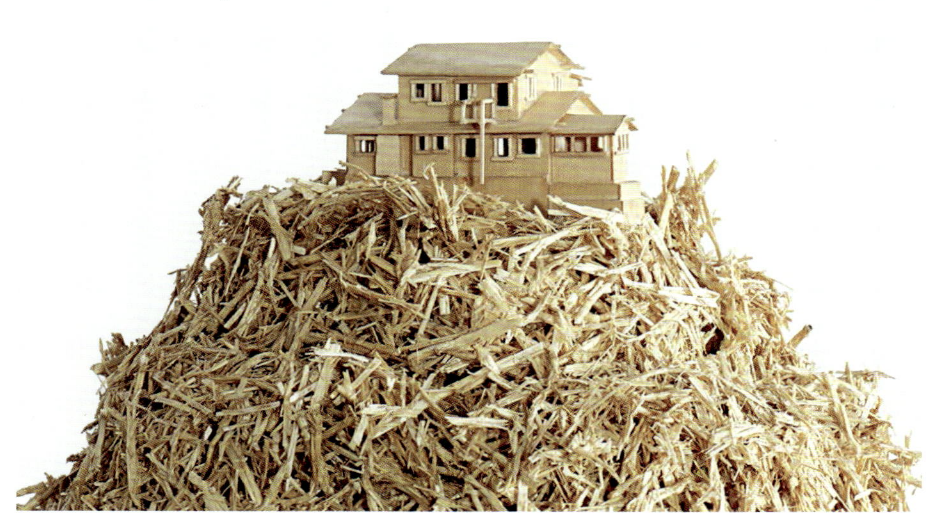

28. Dream Object (Haywain) (detail)   2007

A larger group is made up of the sculptures that sprung from the drawings, seemingly fully formed, like Minerva from Zeus's head. Included among these is an overwhelming inventory of disparate things: objects and organs, creatures and characters, costumes and models. If Shaw's sculptural *Dream Objects* were an iceberg, a glimpse of its tip would include: a hay wagon from the Middle Ages on which is perched a miniature model of Shaw and Weber's house (figs 27 and 28); a spiraling string of taxidermied turtles with chocolate appendages (fig.29); a dozen giant noses that function as sconces; a set of meat waves, crashing in the corner of a regal dining room; a hamburger tornado; a cave-monster piano; a mid-size Santa in a tire swing/ planter; the head of Jesus, with tiny saints sprouting from his flesh; rubbery intestines, eyeballs, brains and testicles; and more paintings, drawings and collages than it is possible to wrap one's head around.

One of the most surprising, and paradoxical, aspects of Shaw's sculptural *Dream Objects* is how comical they are. As three-dimensional entities that viewers must walk around to see fully, they are loopier and goofier than the book- and comic-book covers, which would seem, because of their subject matter and format, to grant faster access to a world of gags, wisecracks and jokes. But that is not the case. The images that make up Shaw's *Dream Objects* have an edge and bite that are not to be found in his sculpted dreams, which are far more cartoon. Part of that has to do with the fact that his three-dimensional pieces come with fewer narratives cues, scene-setting contexts and background information than his two-dimensional pieces. Rather than being part of a picture, they stand alone, much like the pupae and larvae in his *Fake Dream Drawings*, but even weirder because of the contrast between their hand-crafted materiality and the galleries they inhabit. Visiting an exhibition of them feels like

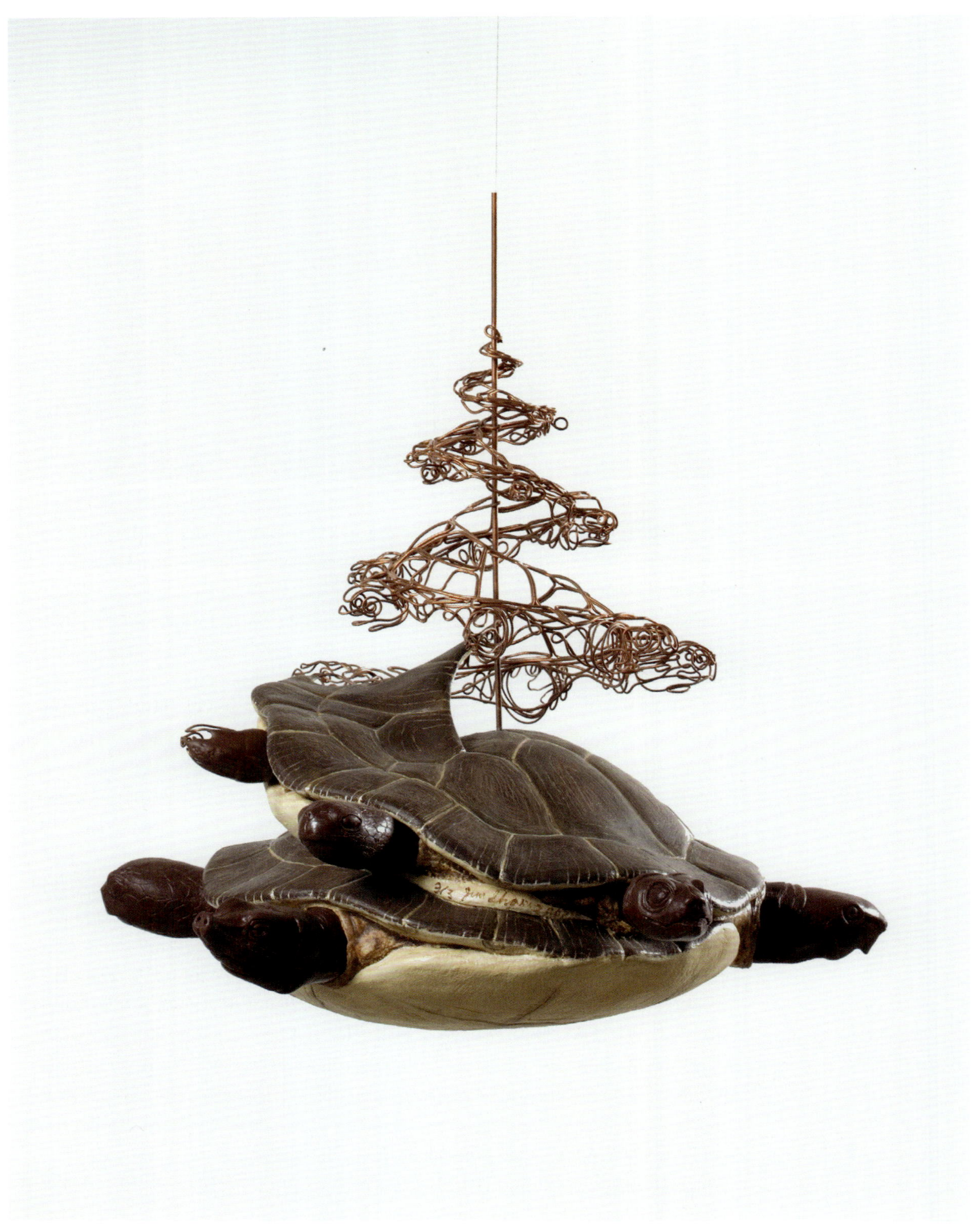

29. Dream Object ("I was looking for a red blouse that was by one of my students & found a complex spiraling wire frame structure which became a sort of infinite turtle whose appendages were all chocolate heads of various types of turtles.")   2007

Copper wire, polyurathane rubber, polyurathane foam and paint
53.3 × 58.4 × 53.3 cm (21 × 23 × 23 in)
Private collection

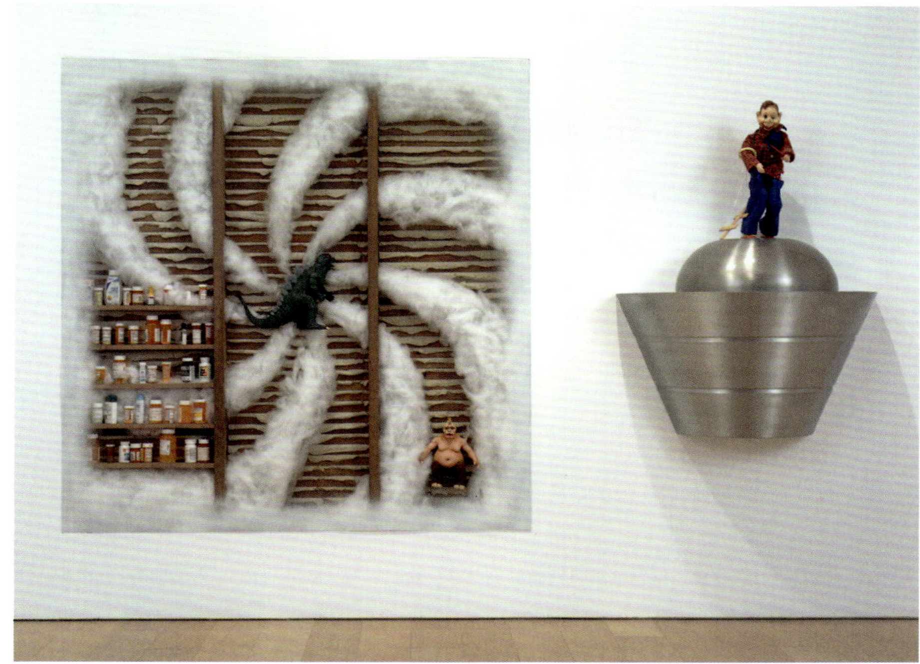

30. Dream Object ("I was washing some silverware in abrasive powder when I heard Linda outside with a client...")   2007

Mixed media installation
182.9 × 182.9 × 63.5 cm (72 × 72 × 25 in)
Private collection

stepping into a warehouse full of props for movies or plays that were never produced because something went wrong before that could happen. As if derailed from their original purposes, Shaw's three-dimensional *Dream Objects* inhabit a world of absurd, tragicomic possibility.

The third group of *Dream Objects* combines the drawn and painted imagery of Shaw's two-dimensional *Dream Objects* with the sculptural presence of his three-dimensional *Dream Objects*. These pieces take the form of tableaux, shaped canvases, geometric sculptures (on which Shaw has painted, drawn and written) and full-blown installations – dreams that you can stand back and look at, walk around or enter (or all three, sequentially and simultaneously).

Dream Object ("I was washing some silverware in abrasive powder when I heard Linda outside with a client...") (2007) (fig.30) translates the top half of *Dream Drawing ("I was washing some silverware in abrasive powder when I heard Linda outside with a client...")* (1993) into three dimensions, where its components appear in full color, blown-up to life-size. Transforming a 6-x-9-in (15-x-23-cm) image into an arrangement of actual objects transforms readers into viewers and, if all goes well, into authors of our own stories about Shaw's odd constellation of props, which are arranged in a cutout section of the wall or affixed to it, like a dysfunctional sconce or misbegotten minimalist sculpture.

A similarly complex relationship between pictures and things unfolds in a group of works that riff off of a dream about a perverted collector and *Presence*, the seventh studio album released in 1976 by Led Zeppelin. The album cover, designed by Hipgnosis and George Hardie, features a small black obelisk around which a family of four has gathered. Shaw saw the obelisk in a dream, both silhouetted and three-dimensionally, so he made shaped paintings and freestanding sculptures of it, transforming the 1-ft (30-cm) tall obelisk into 4-, 5- and 6-ft-tall works.

On a group of 17 oddly angled canvases Shaw superimposed images and media and styles. In *Dream Object (Irregularly Shaped Canvas: Hoover Vacuum Cleaner)* (2010) (fig.32), he used pencil to render a realistic standing figure, pen-and-ink to depict cartoon streams of water and acrylic to paint a vacuum cleaner. In *Dream Object (Irregularly Shaped Canvas: Pink Vacuum)* (2010) (fig.33), he sandwiched a super-realistic image of a pink vacuum cleaner between a pen-and-ink image of cartoon explosions and an airbrushed abstraction in which comic strip figures are embedded. Shaw compressed what had been spread out across many pieces in *My Mirage* into single works whose compositions could be seen all at once but whose meanings seeped out more slowly, the layered images never settling into a singular message but proving more elusive.

He began to customize some *Dream Objects*. His ten *Dream Object (Presence sculptures)* include images from different dreams, all brought together on a single object, where they either pile on top of one another or wrap around its angled planes (figs.34 and 35). In these pieces, Shaw loosened the relationship between his faithfully recorded dreams and the objects that sprung from them. He filled in details he had missed when he was dreaming. His objects and the dreams in which they originated began to interact more dynamically. And that was exacerbated by the fact that what Shaw was working on in the studio often showed up in his dreams, sometimes exactly as it had appeared in reality and at other times in different forms.

References to art history proliferated, as did nods to popular culture and occultist esoterica. *Dream Object (Presence sculpture: UN Jesus; Led Zeppelin's "Houses of the Holy" cover; Max Ernst's "Men Shall Know Nothing of This")* (2010) (fig.31) depicts everything listed in its title and more: the eye of providence; a frieze of musclemen teaming up to do Atlas's work; the seven dwarves holding up the seven deadly sins; a portrait of Aleister Crowley looking troubled; a nude woman parachuting, in the style of graphic artist Tadanori Yokoo; a copy of William Blake's painting of God creating the universe; a diagram of two men from an Ad Reinhardt cartoon; a blazing fire with smoke that resembles a chicken; and a teacher and student engaged in some kind of mystical communion over the obelisk. All were drawn in pencil, with great care and detail, except for the dwarves, who were rendered in ink, a little more quickly. Sometimes overlapping, but mostly occupying their own space, the images covered a plain white, vaguely X-shaped plinth. Each of the 13 planes that defined its volume formed a nearly rectangular shape. And those shapes met their adjoining sections at odd angles – none of them right. To circumnavigate the sculpture is to feel as if you are seeing seven or eight movies at once, each calling to mind the narrative arc it belonged to while interacting with others but never coming to a conclusion or eliminating other options.

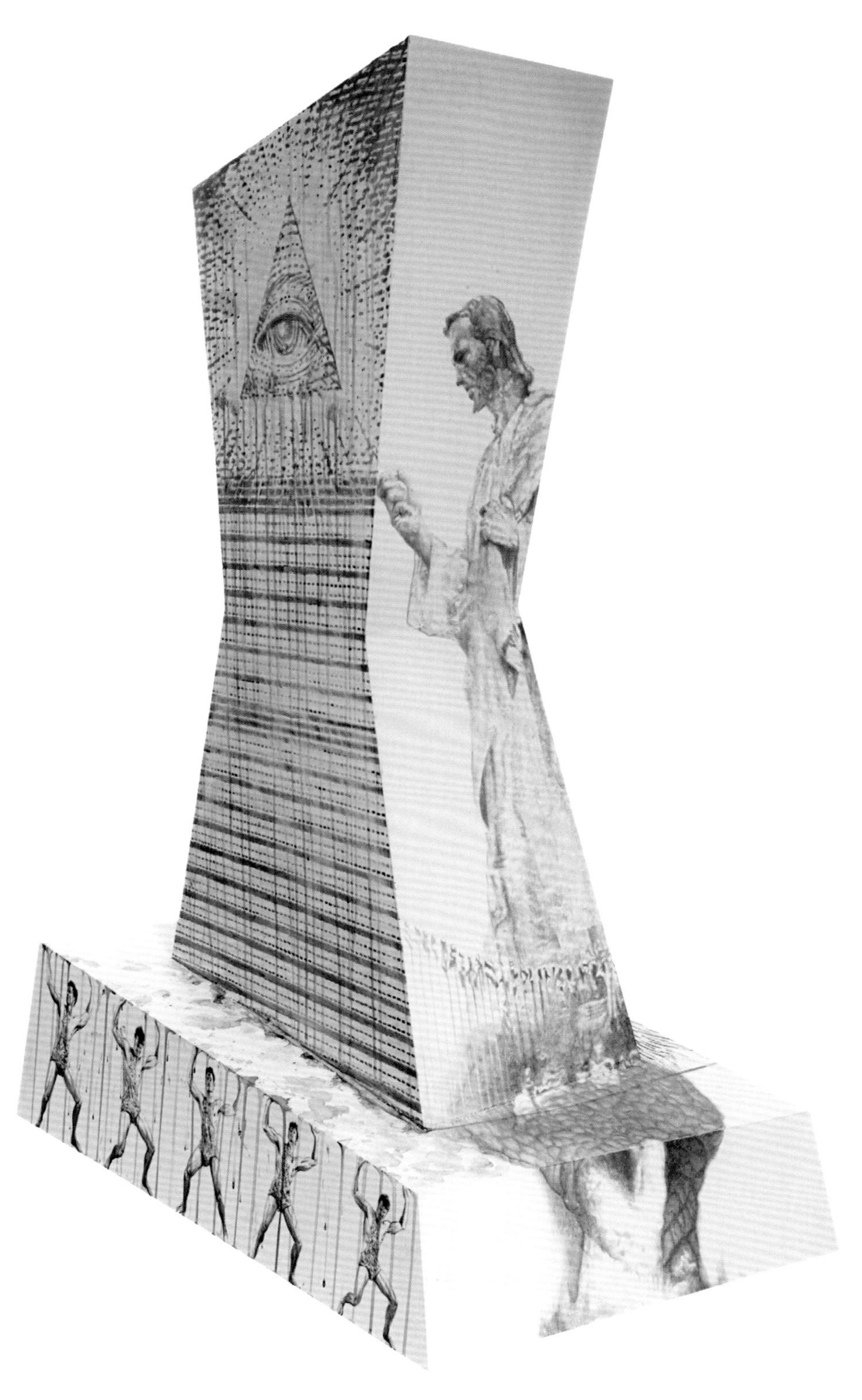

31. Dream Object (Presence sculpture: UN Jesus; Led Zeppelin's "Houses of the Holy" cover; Max Ernst's "Men Shall Know Nothing of This")   2010

Airbrush, acrylic, ink, pencil, MDF wood, aqua resin and fiberglass
120 × 57 × 83 cm (47⅓ × 22⅓ × 32⅘ in)
Courtesy Bernier/Eliades

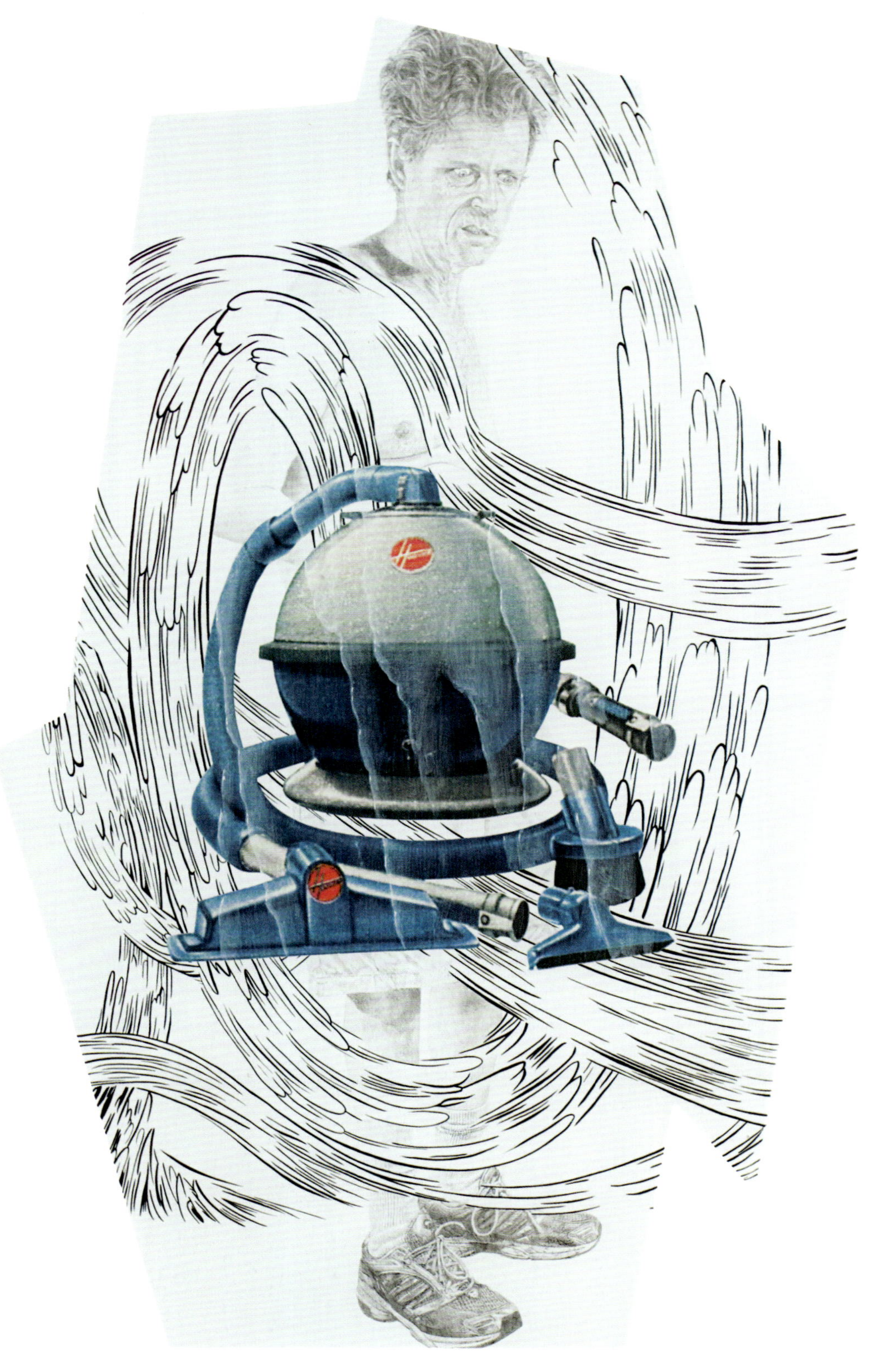

32. Dream Object (Irregularly
Shaped Canvas: Hoover Vacuum
Cleaner   2010

Acrylic, oil, ink, pencil and inkjet print
on canvas
138 × 92 × 7 cm (54½ × 36¼ × 2⅘ in)
Courtesy Blum & Poe

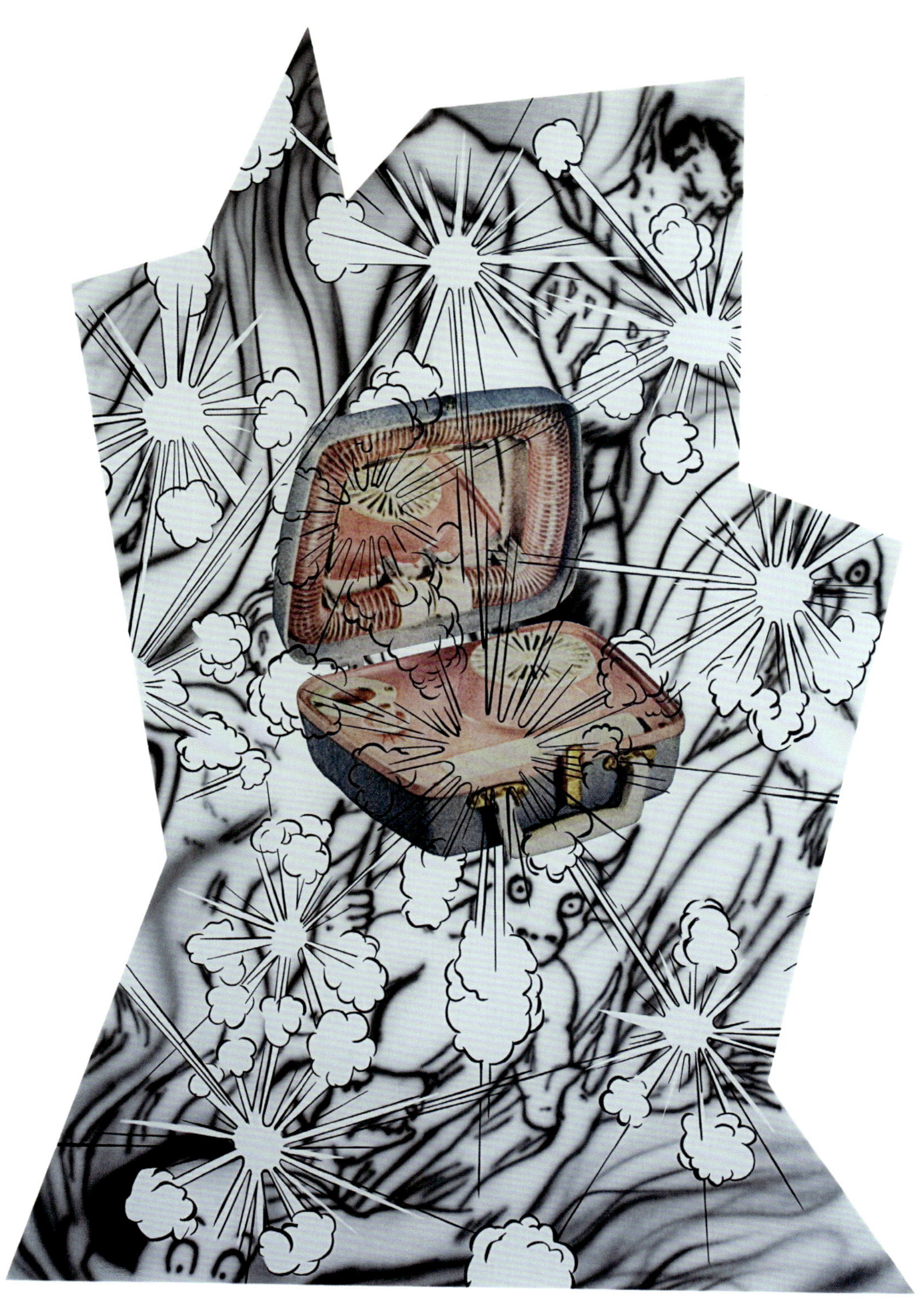

33. Dream Object (Irregularly
Shaped Canvas: Pink Vacuum)

2010

Ink and inkjet print on canvas
130 × 92 × 7 cm (51¼ × 36¼ × 2 ⅘ in)
Collection of Steven Hull

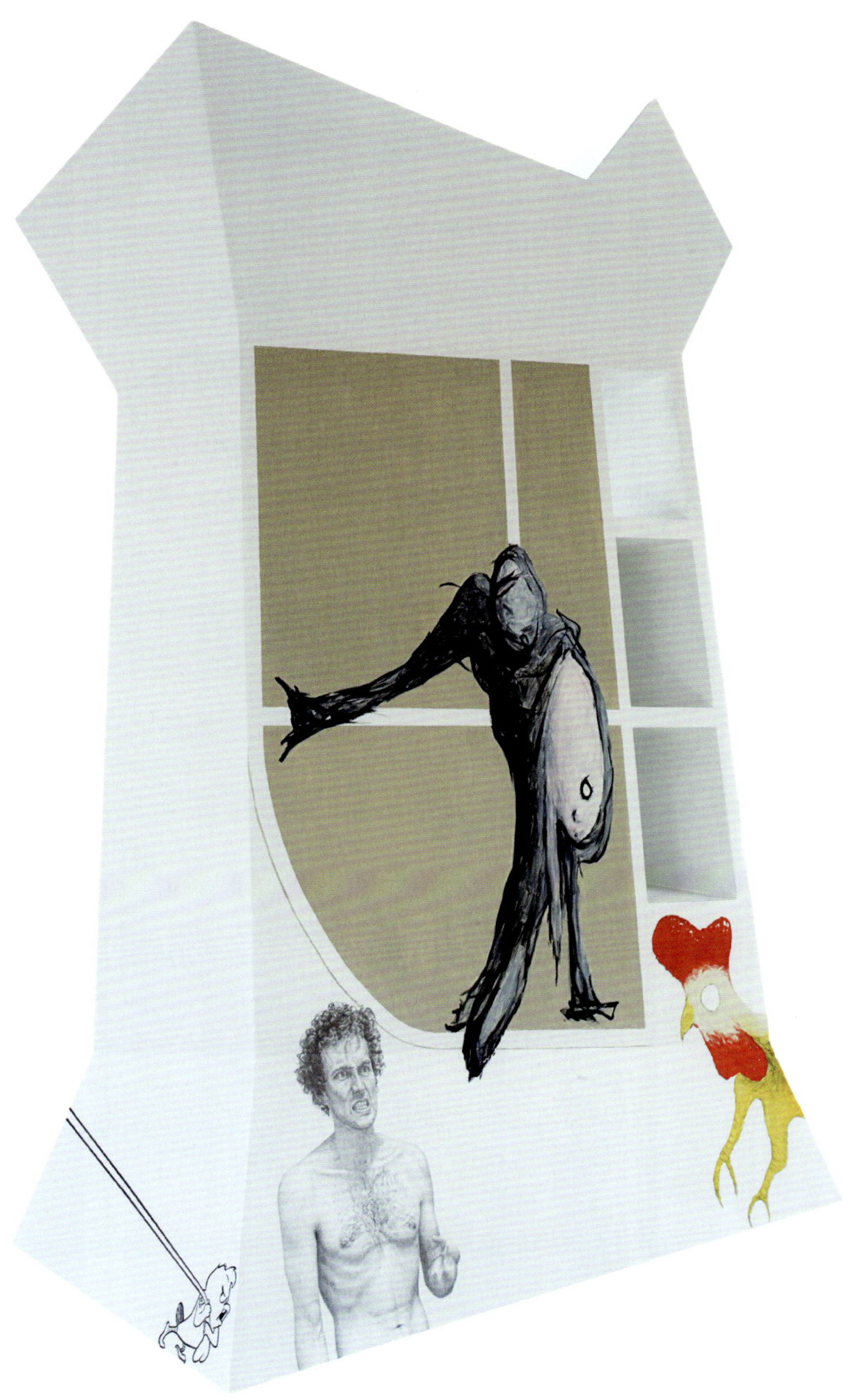

34. Dream Object (Presence sculpture: "I was working on these shaped canvases & sculpture that had printed blowups of appliances & added elements...")   2010

Acrylic, oil, ink, pencil, MDF wood, aqua resin and fiberglass
198 × 154 × 80 cm (78⅓ × 60½ × 31⅓)
Courtesy Blum & Poe

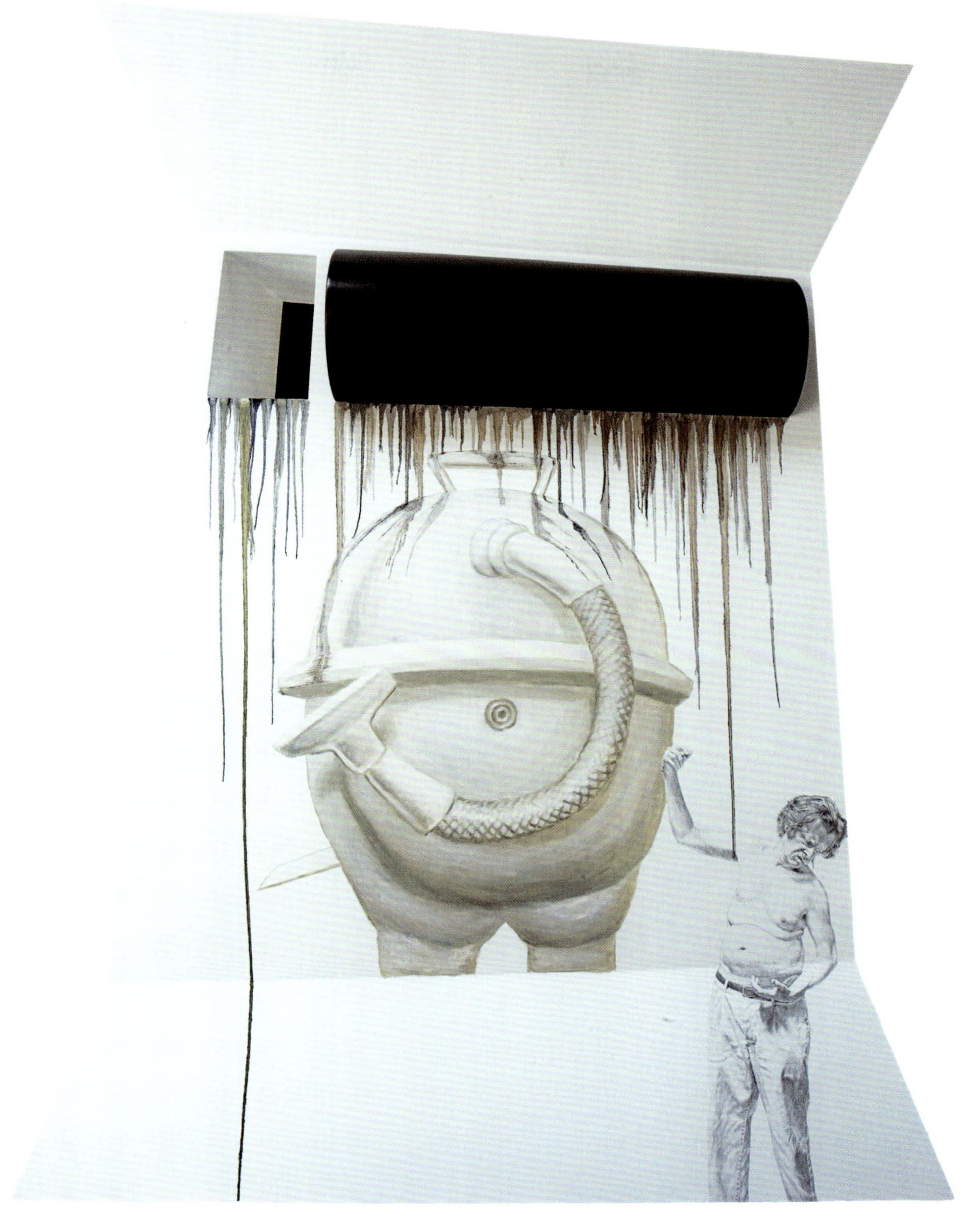

35. Dream Object (Presence sculpture: "I was working on these shaped canvases & sculpture that had printed blowups of appliances & added elements...") 2010

Acrylic, oil, ink, pencil, MDF wood, aqua resin and fiberglass
198 × 154 × 80 cm (78⅓ × 60½ × 31⅓)
Collection unknown

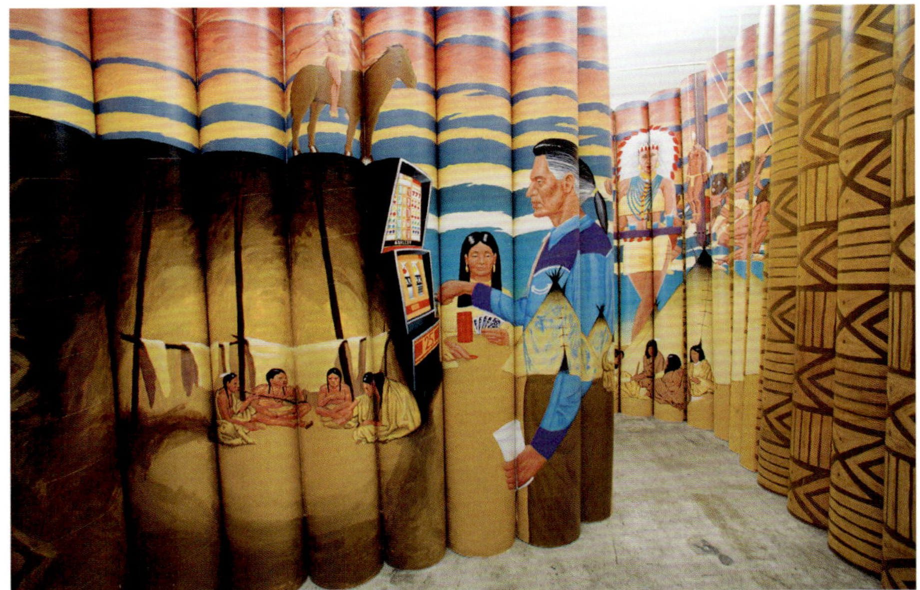

36. Dream Object ("I was in my gallery in Japan where the next show was of miniature landscapes…") 1999

Acrylic on cardboard half-tubes, approximately 51
Dimensions variable
Courtesy Blum & Poe

Shaw's dream-based installations turn his *Presence sculptures* inside out. Rather than rendering his dreams on the exterior surfaces of multi-sided plinths (or sci-fi bollards), he rendered them on the interior walls of a gallery. That transformation changes the relationship between his works and viewers: instead of moving around a sculpture to take it in, viewers move within it. Power shifts, slightly but significantly, transforming viewers into participants. It is no longer possible to stand back and regard Shaw's art from a distance. You are in it, often overwhelmed and made vulnerable, both by the size of the installation and the cascade of references that tumble through your mind's-eye.

For one of his first installations, *Dream Object ("I was in my gallery in Japan where the next show was of miniature landscapes…")* (1999) (fig.36), Shaw made his own walls, creating a tear-shaped room-within-a-room by standing 51 sturdy cardboard tubes, ordinarily used in construction, alongside one another. On them he painted clichéd images of Native Americans, dancing, hunting and operating modern casinos. For one of his most optically disorienting installations, *Dream Object ("A later room contains murals of Dan Quayle glad-handing rich white people at an art opening and now I'm Paul Drake (from 'Perry Mason')…")* (2007) (fig.37), he amplified the spatial disorientation by turning paintings into walls. In the booth shared by Praz-Delavallade and Patrick Painter galleries at Art Basel, Shaw painted three canvas murals and hung them so that they formed a rectangular space, the open fourth side functioning as the entrance. Each of the murals depicted the wall of an art gallery, on which hung paintings that had appeared in his dream: a Dr. Seuss-meets-Christopher-Wool word-painting; a psychotic rant in the style of Edward Ruscha; a gestural abstraction framed by illusionistic clouds; and the instructions for building a plastic model, which resembled

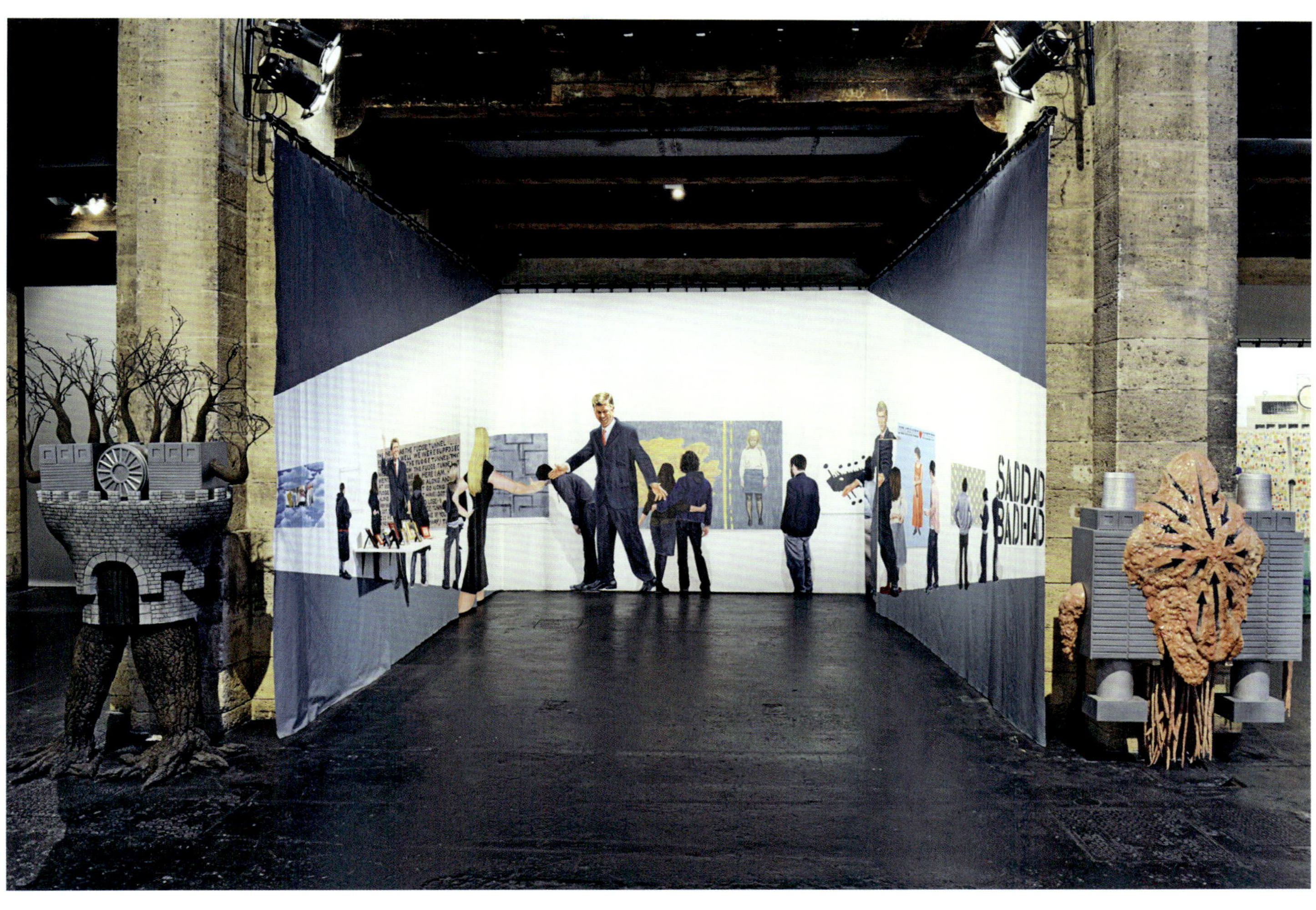

37. Dream Object ("A later room contains murals of Dan Quayle glad-handing rich white people at an art opening and now I'm Paul Drake (from 'Perry Mason')...) (installation view)   2007

Acrylic on muslin and mixed media
Dimensions variable
Courtesy Blum & Poe
Installation with two sculptures *Dream Object ("Mike had maxed out his warehouse space & wanted...")*

an abstract work by Kazimir Malevich. On his illusionistic walls, Shaw also painted 18 illusionistic people, all but three of whom were looking at the art. Those three were the same person, a giant Dan Quayle, the Vice President of the United States, who served under George H.W. Bush from 1989 to 1993.

The mural opposite the entrance was a frontal view of the wall it depicted. The two side murals were painted in forced perspective, the lines formed by the floor, wall and ceiling radically receding. That caused the entire space to feel warped and unstable. As you moved through it, the architecture seemed to buckle and tilt, as if the floor were the deck of a ship being tossed at sea. The wooziness continued until you found the single spot, just past the center of the room, where everything seemed to snap into place, the side walls appearing to form a single, continuous plane with the back wall. For a moment, the room, and everything in it, seemed to obey the laws of perspective. Order was restored. But that, too, was an illusion. Shaw did not hide the tricks he had played on your perceptions. True to his dream, his elaborate optical illusion recreated the experience for visitors, perhaps more vividly than any other of his *Dream Objects*.

As some of Shaw's *Dream Objects* grew in size and complexity, others got smaller but no less complex. *Dream Object ("I was working on a landscape sculpture that was actually a big garbage pile of all the dream objects I'd done and on top of it all was a sculpture of the Whore of Babylon riding the beast with 7 heads and 10 horns. It was in a Plexi box")* (2007) (fig.39) consisted of miniature renditions of every *Dream Object* Shaw had made, all packed in a Plexiglas box and topped by the Whore of Babylon astride the apocalyptic beast. But before Shaw glued his own version of Marcel Duchamp's *Boîte-en-valise* (1936) into his translucent cube, he asked his studio manager, Sachiyo Yoshimoto, to curate a miniature exhibition in a scale-model museum, which was built of foam core and printed wood floorboards by his studio assistant Brigitte Coleman. The show of Shaw's pint-size doppelgangers was installed and photographed. And those photographs were featured in *Dream Object Book*, a 168-page catalogue raisonné of the 334 miniature versions of the 334 full-size *Dream Objects* he had made from 1995 to 2007, each based on a *Dream Drawing* he had made from 1991 to 1999. No matter the form or media into which Shaw's dreams were translated, the objects, characters and creatures in them invited viewers into a world whose borders were porous and shifting, weirdly beautiful in their fusion of fact and fiction, truth and strangeness.

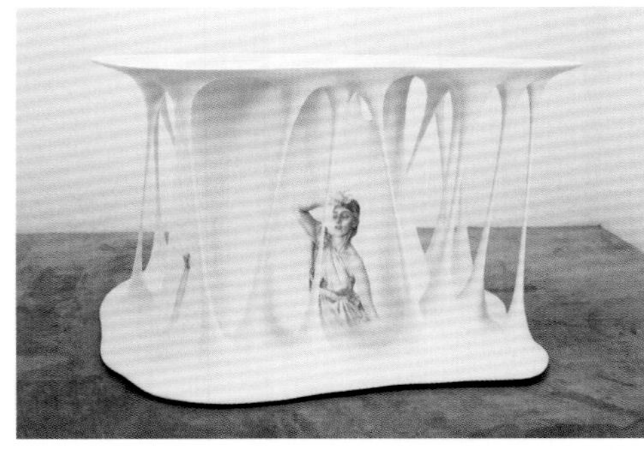

38. Bone Sculpture   2008

Graphite, wood, foam, aqua resin, fiberglass and gesso paint
132 × 261.6 × 177.8cm (52 × 103 × 70 in)
Private collection

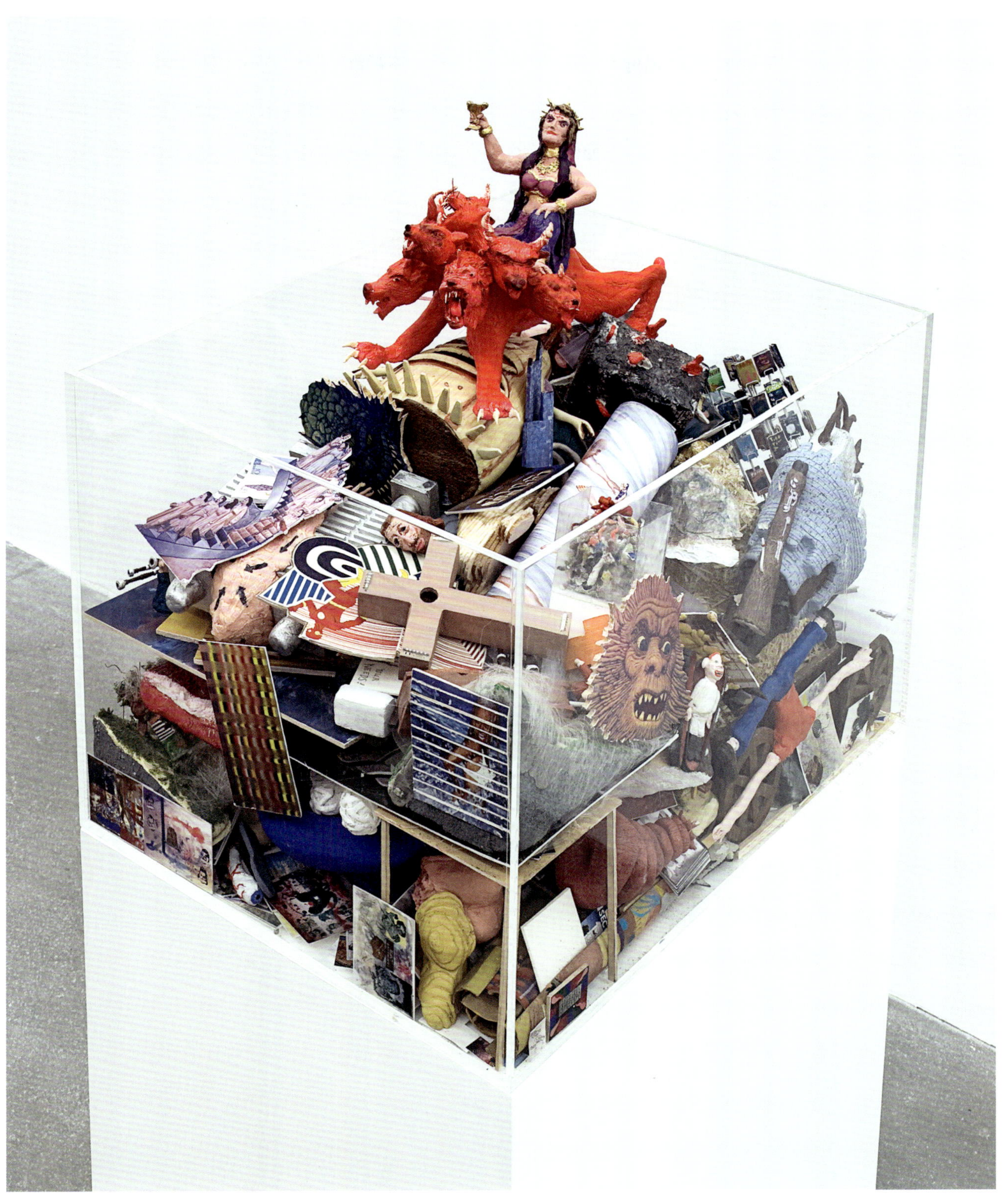

39. Dream Object ("I was working on a landscape sculpture that was actually a big garbage pile of all the dream objects I'd done and on top of it all was a sculpture of the Whore of Babylon riding the beast with 7 heads and 10 horns. It was in a Plexi box")   2007

Mixed media
31 × 21 × 37 cm (12⅓ × 18½ × 14½ in)
Private collection

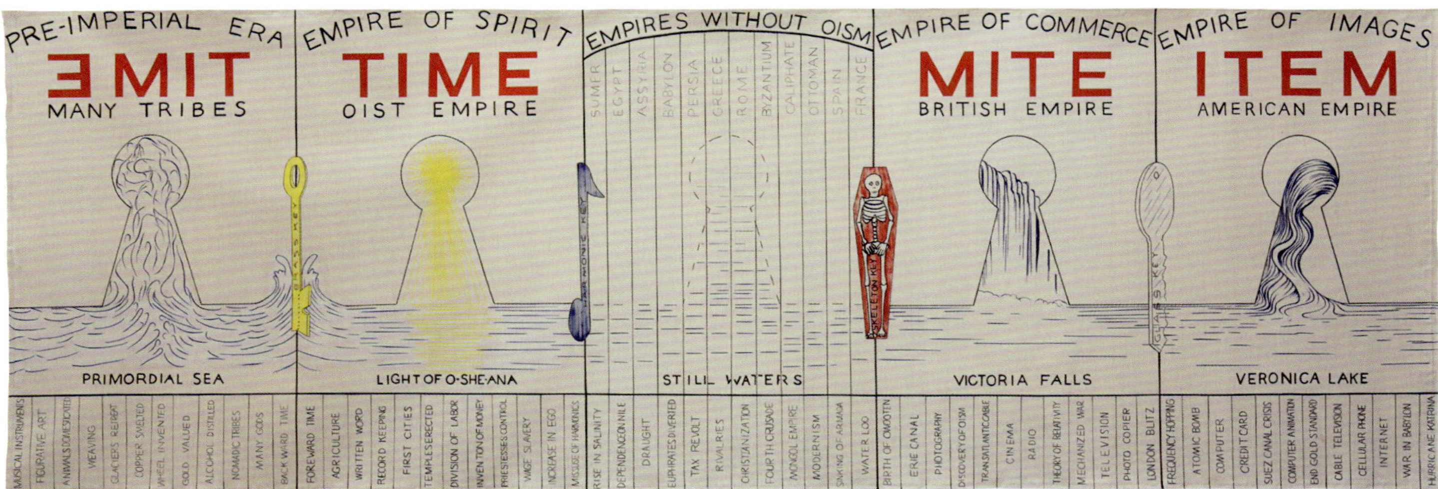

40. Timeline   2013

Acrylic on canvas
152.9 × 455.9 cm (60⅛ × 179½ in)
Courtesy Blum & Poe

4   Oist Works (2002–13 and continuing)

Belief is the middle ground between fact and fiction, and that is where Shaw turned his
attention in his 'fake religion project'. In a 1997 interview with Mike Kelley, that is how
he described his next body of work, saying that it was 'a fully conscious production'
and going on to explain, 'I may derive some element of it from subconscious sources,
but I'm doing a lot of research for it.'[1] That distinguished it from his *Dream Drawings*,
whose imagery came to him with no conscious effort. Eventually, Shaw's research
would lead him to the development of Oism, a religion he invented and presented in
an expansive body of work.

Shaw created his religion by collaging together various elements of other religions,
as well as episodes from the lives of comic-book superheroes and from his own life,
growing up Episcopalian in Michigan and then living in Southern California, where
congregations and cults of all sorts captured the popular imagination only to disappear
from the headlines. Like Mormonism, which was created by Joseph Smith in Upstate
New York in the 1820s, and Scientology, which was converted into a religion from the
discredited science of Dianetics by L. Ron Hubbard in New Jersey in 1953, Shaw's
Oism freely mixed fact and fiction, with an emphasis on the latter – belief lubricating
the slippage between the two. As he pursued his project, he accumulated an impressive
archive of pamphlets, brochures, books, flyers, posters, T-shirts, vinyl records and
other pedagogical materials, most commissioned from anonymous artists by various
religious denominations (including Scientology, Mormonism and Jehovah's Witnesses),
fraternities (such as the Freemasons) and assorted evangelical, fundamentalist and New
Age movements; but a good number of others were made by dyed-in-the-wool do-it-
yourselfers, including ultraconservatives and conspiracy theorists.

Shaw transformed what he had discovered about homegrown American belief
systems into his own religion by using many of the principles at work in dreams:
condensation, compression, wish fulfillment, symbolism, juxtaposition, free-association
and time-travel. On the one hand, Shaw's project departed from his *Dream Drawings*
and *Dream Objects* because he did not have to fall asleep in order to gather data: he
was wide-awake when doing his research. On the other hand, what he did with his
discoveries – collaging them into his own idiosyncratic, cut-and-paste religion –
mimicked the operations of his unconscious when he was dreaming: mixing disparate
elements in single scenes, creating unexpected narratives and freely jumping from one
time and place to another.

With Oism, Shaw's role as an artist got a lot more complicated than it had been
when he was making his dream works. It was as if, while still wide-awake and well

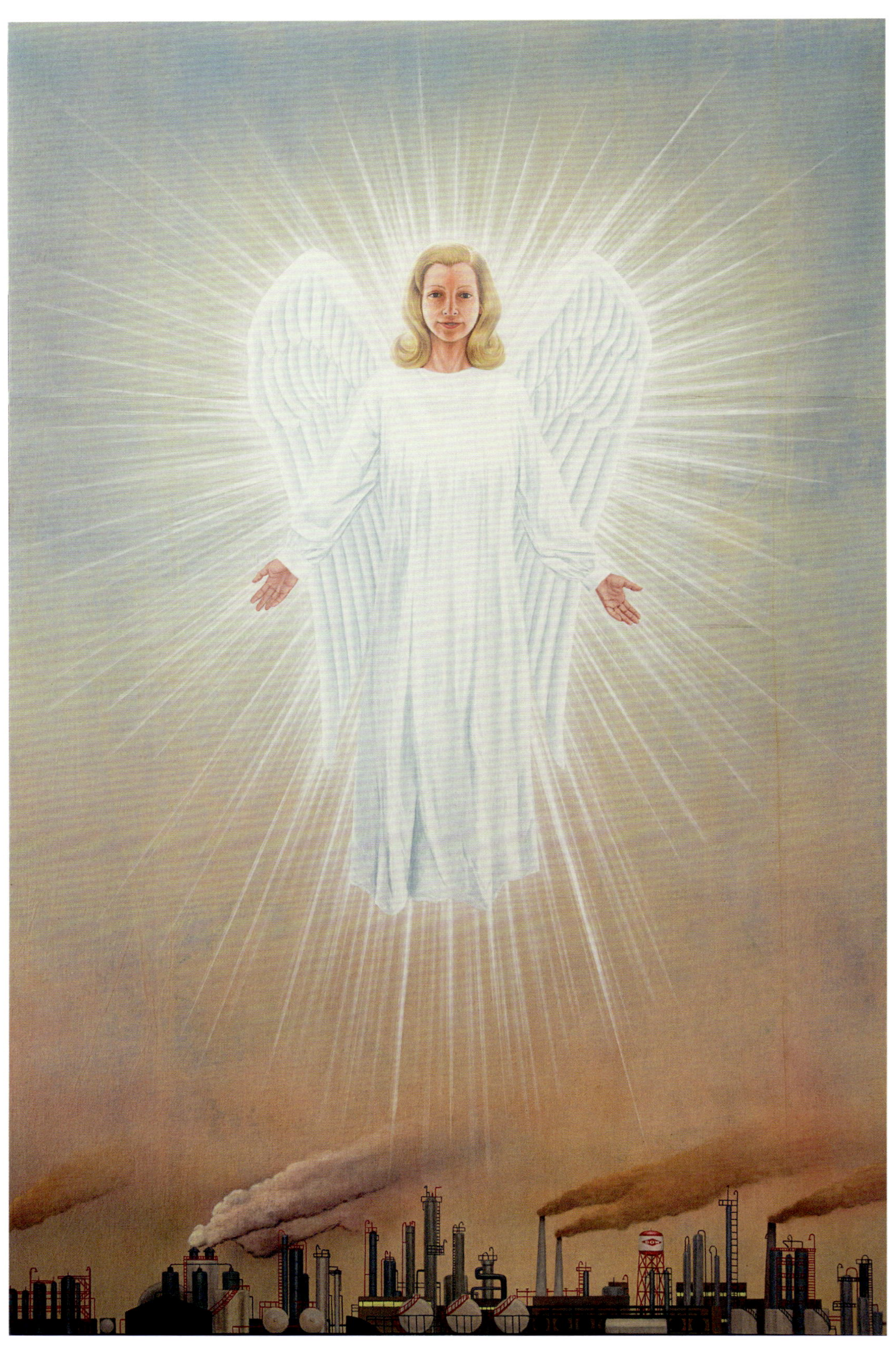

41. The Angel of the Chemical Plant   2015

Acrylic on muslin
188 × 127 cm (74 × 50 in)
Private collection

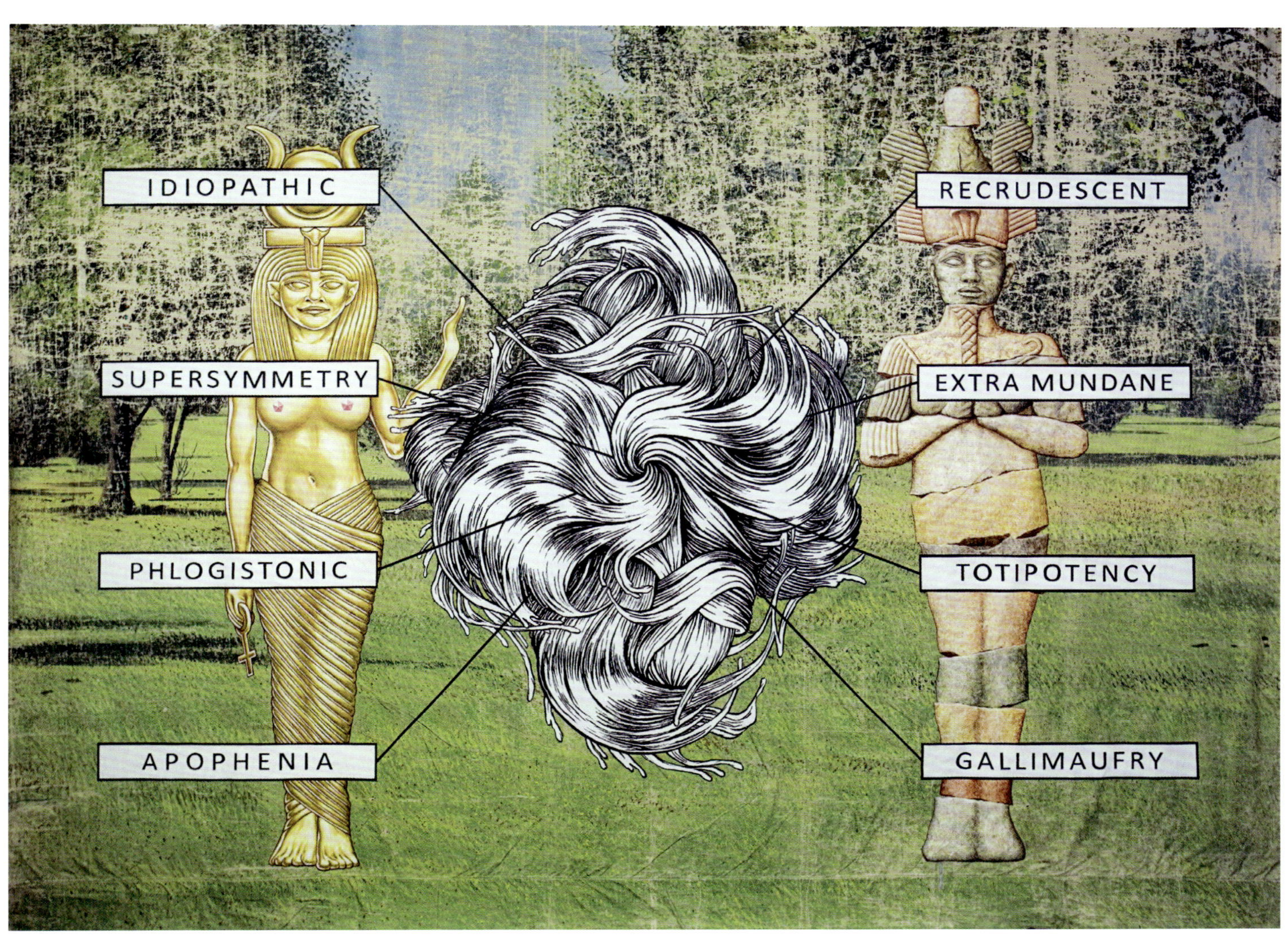

42. Anal/Isis   2012

Acrylic on muslin
243.8 × 304.8 cm (96 × 120 in)
Private collection, Paris

aware of what he was doing, he operated like his unconscious: processing the day's data by editing it and compressing it into a narrative filled with vivid details, illogical leaps, confounding collations and epiphanies that turned out to be as befuddling as everything else. As before, Shaw did all that in a pedestrian manner, describing otherwise unbelievable developments in plain language. In a sense, his religion was the result of conscious dreaming. And, ultimately, that is not all that different from real religions, which, like his, put forth stories with utopian components that explain how humanity has fallen from that condition, yet still might manage to get there if the proper path is followed.

Shaw created Oism not to be a work of art in its own right but to be the background (or backdrop) against which his art unfolded. The story of Oism is similar to the story that lies behind *My Mirage*: the coming-of-age tale of Billy, who leaves the religion of his childhood to experiment with just about anything that might expand his consciousness, only to become, as an adult, a born-again Christian. And, if the backdrop of Oism had a backdrop, that was the George W. Bush presidency of 2001 to 2009, which began after the former governor of Texas lost the popular vote to Democratic candidate Al Gore (by some 500,000 ballots) yet won in the electoral college – but only after the Supreme Court stripped the State of Florida of its right to recount the ballots in an election that was too close to call without a recount. Eight months into Bush's presidency, the World Trade Center was attacked and destroyed by al-Qaeda terrorists, killing nearly 3,000 people and injuring more than 6,000 others. That led to Bush's 'War on Terror'; war in Afghanistan in 2001; and the Iraq War in 2003; as well as to a resurgence, in the United States, of fundamentalist religion and nostalgia for a past that never existed. Opportunistic politicians exploited recycled religion and fake history in mythical stories that swayed the popular imagination and ultimately shaped reality – into their vision of it. Shaw could not bear to sit back and watch. He got in on the action.

The story of Oism goes like this: In Upstate New York in the 1840s, a young woman named Annie O'Wooton had a revelation. She recorded it in *The Book of Oism*, which begins with a virgin, named O, who, around 3000 BCE, gave birth to herself. She brought agriculture and writing to her people. Her appearance also reversed the direction of time. Thousands of years passed and a male entity, 'I', appeared, bringing the concept of Self to the Oists. Wars followed. Then an earthquake. And a tsunami. Survivors scattered to the far ends of Earth, where they remain to this day. After documenting her revelation, O'Wooton began evangelizing. She fled with her flock to Chicago, made bad investments and lost everything. Then, the Great Chicago Fire of 1871 destroyed nearly every trace of her work. A handful of survivors – all male elders – began manufacturing vacuum cleaners and vibrators, which turned into successful businesses.[2]

In 2002, three of Shaw's four solo exhibitions featured art based on Oism. The first, at Metro Pictures, was titled *Oist Thrift Store Paintings*. It presented 62 paintings

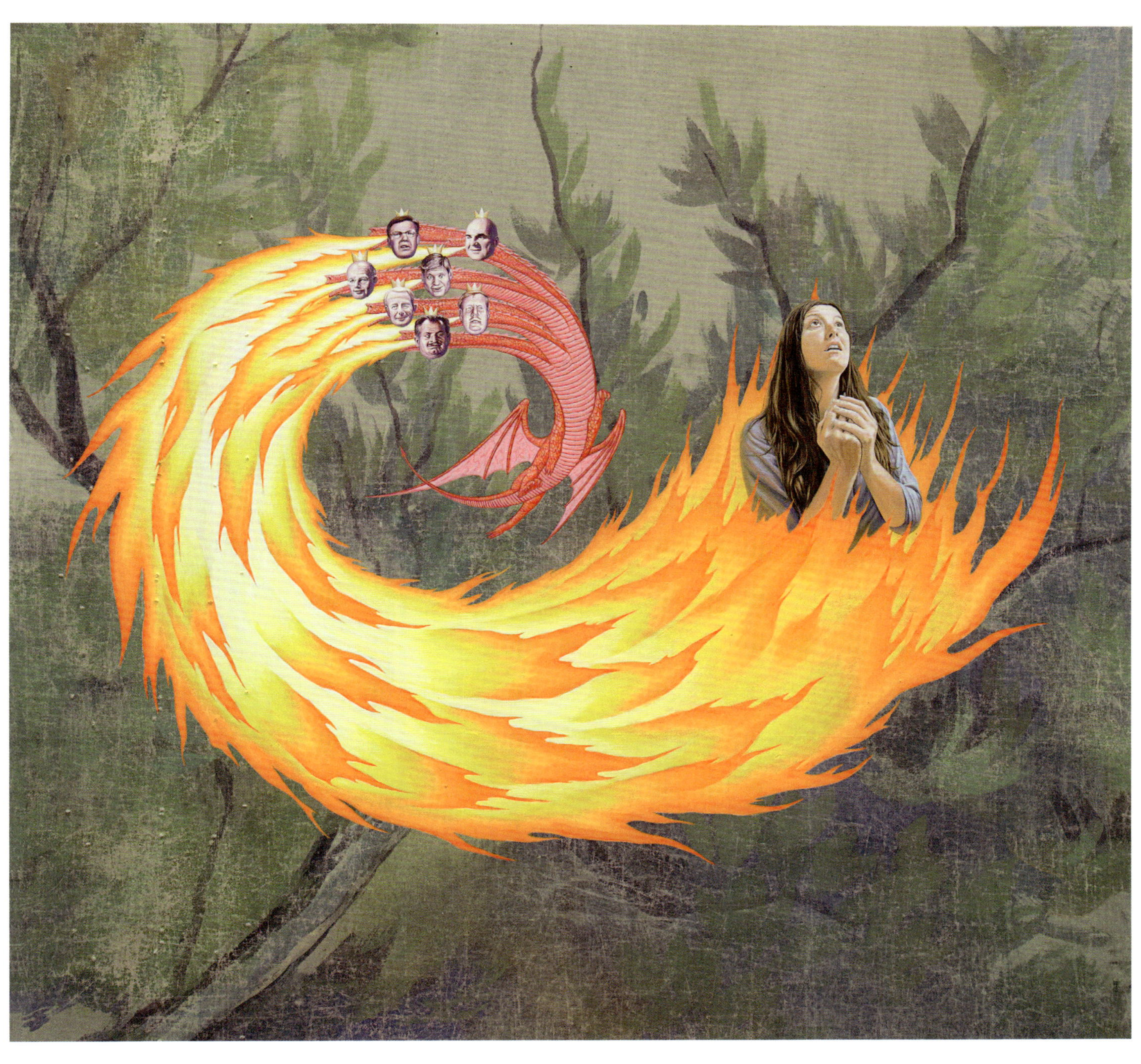

43. The Woman In the Wilderness   *2018*

Acrylic on muslin
121.9 × 134.6 cm (48 × 53 in)
Private collection

purportedly purchased by Shaw in thrift stores in small towns in Iowa and Nebraska, when he was researching homegrown religions. In actuality, Shaw and his assistants painted the pictures. Most illustrated scenes from *The Book of Oism*, which he had not yet gotten around to writing. But by placing his faux folk paintings in his growing archive of religious materials, Shaw made a place for Oism among other start-up religions, many of which had very short lives.

A precedent for Shaw's *Oist Thrift Store Paintings* was his own collection of paintings by anonymous amateurs he had purchased in second-hand shops, at weekend flea markets and via online auction sites. In the early 1990s, Shaw had arranged various selections of those cast-off paintings in salon-style installations and exhibited them, first at the bookstore at Los Angeles Contemporary Exhibitions, next at the Brand Library in Glendale, California, then at the Santa Barbara Contemporary Arts Forum and finally at Metro Pictures in New York. A book, *Thrift Store Paintings*, was published by Heavy Industries in 1992. The exhibitions and publication established Shaw's reputation as a connoisseur of a doubly marginalized art form: Sunday paintings made by enthusiasts who had lost their enthusiasm for them but still couldn't bear to dispose of their failures. Shaw was drawn to the earnestness of the paintings. He appreciated their unschooled, often crude idealism and the pragmatism that made them available at bargain-basement prices. He was fascinated by the equal and opposite currents of hope and desperation – as well as the eccentricity and ordinariness – that ran through them. Grouped together, Shaw's rescued rejects gave potent form to the weirdness pulsing through middle-American life.

Although Shaw never saw his *Thrift Store Paintings* as his own work, critics and viewers did, finding, in the blunt captions he wrote for each, a particular morphology, epistemology and ontology. His *Oist Thrift Store Paintings* – which were fake thrift store paintings – took advantage of that interpretation: fulfilling some viewers' desires to see Shaw's hand in his collection of paintings, they pushed the game of 'let's pretend' to the next level.

The second, at the Swiss Institute in New York, was titled *The Goodman Image File and Study*. It was exactly that: a group of file cabinets, arranged in a circular configuration, which contained an illustrator's morgue of image references, and seven circular paintings, all mandala-style abstractions that resembled Kenneth Noland-esque targets. The paintings were made by Shaw, but they were presented as if they were the work of an Oist painter named Adam O. Goodman, whose desire to work abstractly was thwarted by his need to make a living doing illustrative work.

The third one, at Praz-Delavallade in Paris, was titled *The Rite of the 360°*. It included an 11-minute video, *The Initiation Ritual of the 360°*; as well as the performers' costumes and the musical instruments they played. Shaped like body parts, all referred to the ancient Egyptian myth in which Osiris is murdered by his brother, Set. Many of the instruments in Shaw's reenactment had appeared in his dreams, making them both 'Oist Works' and *Dream Objects*. The video was as straightforward as Shaw's *Dream Drawings*, its clumsy costuming, dialogue and lighting colliding with the solemnity of the characters' performances. The mixture of portent and goofiness, absurdity and earnestness, was hard to cipher – and pure Shaw.

The next year, nearly all of the works from those three exhibitions were shipped to Grenoble, France, where they were joined by other Oist works Shaw had made in the meantime to form *Jim Shaw: O*. Co-organized by Le Magasin, Centre National d'Art Contemporain and the Kunsthaus Glarus in Glarus, Switzerland (where it was installed in 2004), *O* was – and still is – the fullest articulation of Oism. It included *Oist Movie Posters Paintings*, which were paintings meant to be the designs for posters that would advertise four Oist movies: *Killing Your Darlings*, *The Land of the Octopus*, *Birth of a Notion*, and *The Woman With No Name*. Each painting featured the faces of the film's stars, usually three or four. Nearly all wore headdresses – sometimes plain white scarves, but more often elaborately sculpted structures, including candelabra-style tiaras, crescent moon-style helmets, vase-like arrangements, tentacle-festooned pillows, geological anomalies, spaceship-shaped bonnets and wiggish configurations. All of the heads hovered in multi-hued fields of Expressionist brushwork, the bold gestures of that mid-20th-century style dissolving in a soft-focus dreaminess that left plenty of room for titles and captions to be superimposed later. Archie Gunn's signature appeared on all of the paintings. That was the pseudonym Adam O. Goodman used when he worked as a commercial illustrator (and another name Arshile Gorky considered using). Attuned to the rules that ranked fine art above commercial design – and troubled by that hierarchy – Shaw turned abstract painting into a step in the design process while acknowledging the travails of purists like Goodman, even if they were fictitious.

Shaw also presented a series of *Oist Movie Stills*. These glossy photographs, in black-and-white and color, depicted the stars and supporting actors. They bore a superficial resemblance to movie advertisements from the 1940s and '50s, as seen through the eyes of an outsider. Like the fake book covers that made up a good number of Shaw's *Dream Objects*, his *Oist Movie Stills* drew on the imaginations of viewers. A series of small works on canvas, *Oist Student Paintings* similarly emphasized potential. Made by Shaw and his assistants, these inchoate stews of abstraction and representation were muddled mélanges of gesture, text and figuration – a kind of primordial soup or painterly stew out of which possibility burbled, not forming fully articulated utterances but suggesting that no matter how hard it is to know the present, it is always reassuring to think that the future will be different.

The largest and most ambitious element of Shaw's traveling exhibition was *The Donner Party* (2003) (fig.44), an installation that riffed off of Judy Chicago's *The Dinner Party* (1979) by overlaying that icon of feminist idealism with a dystopian tale

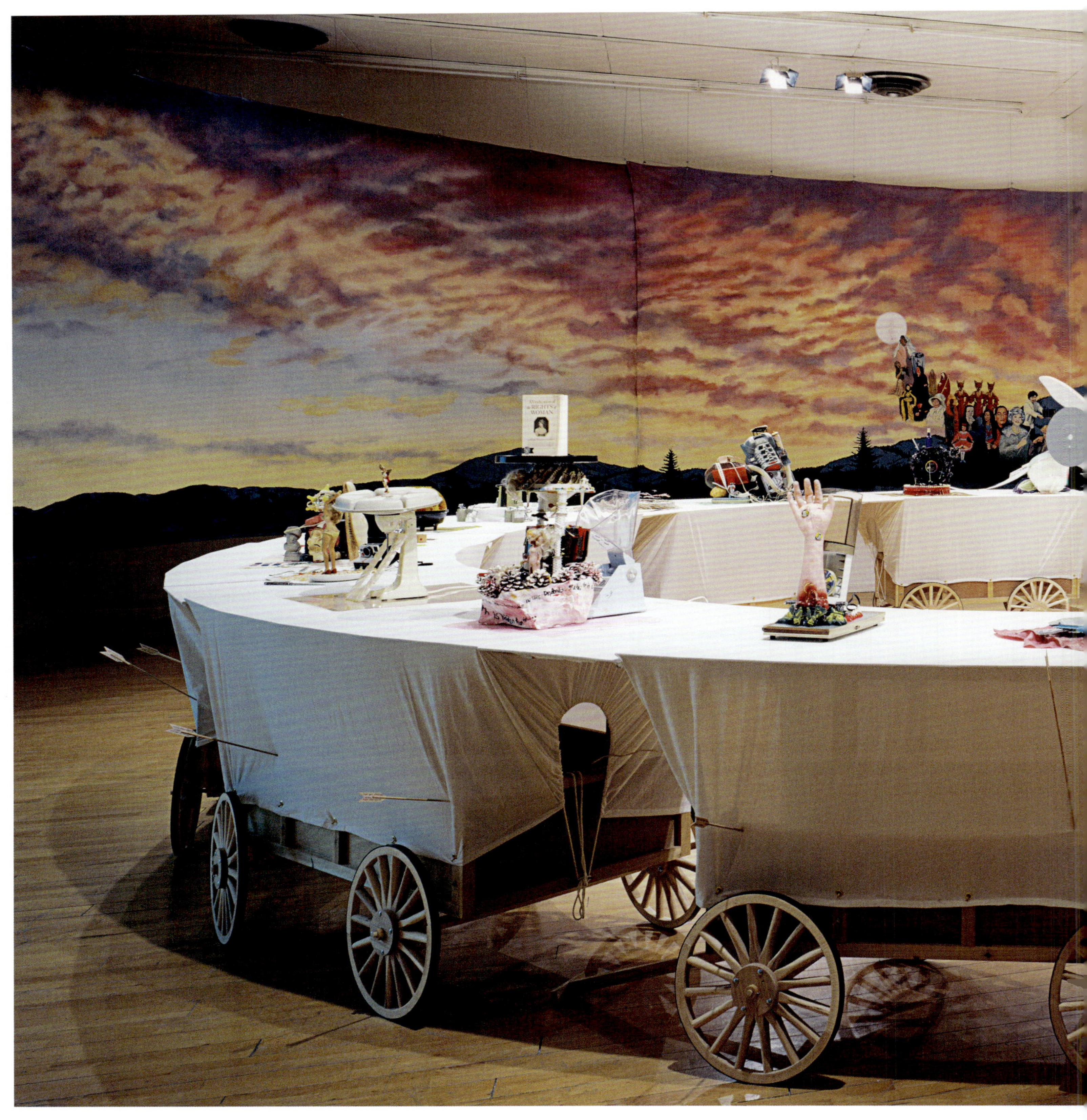

44. The Donner Party (installation view)   2003

Mixed media
Dimensions variable
Private collection

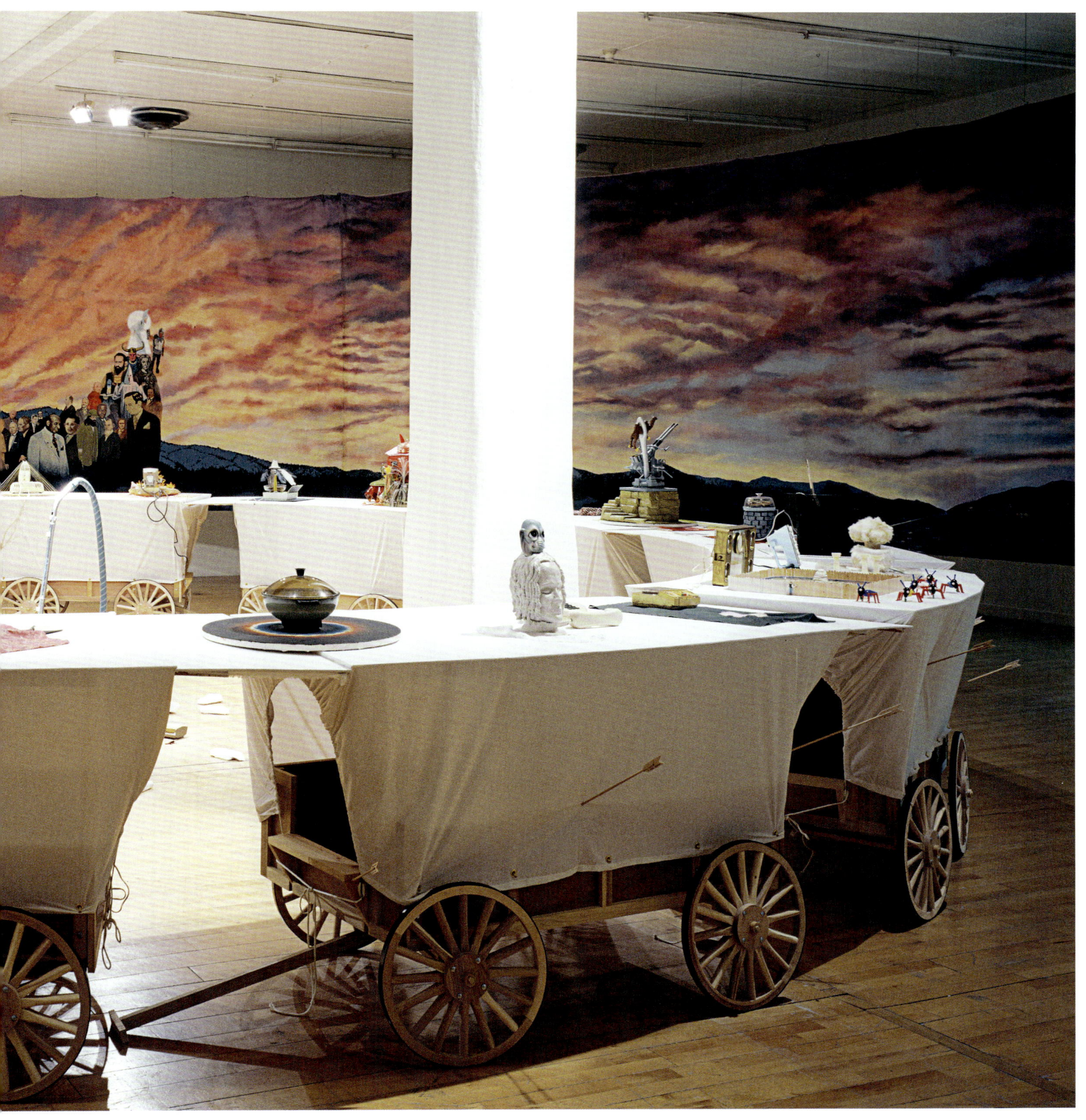

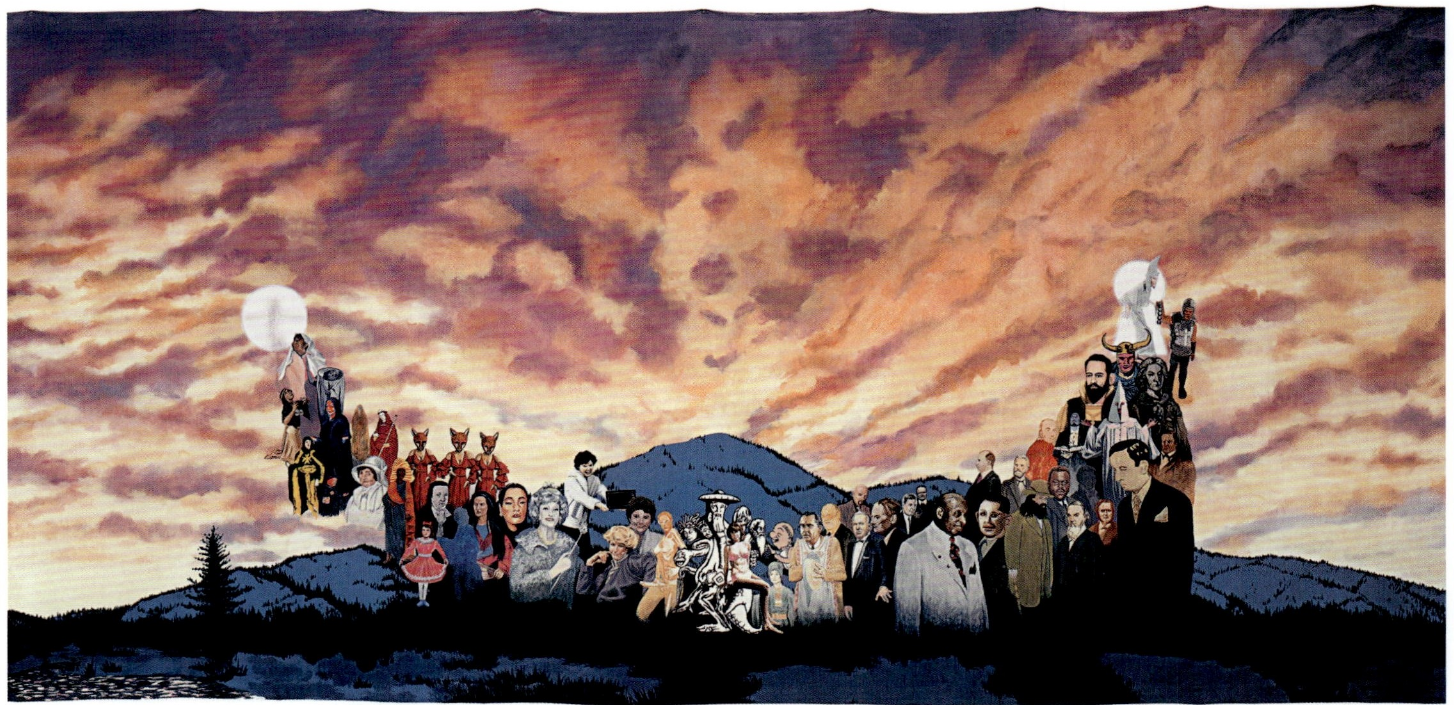

45. The Donner Party (detail)   2003

of pioneer life in the 1840s. By replacing the 'i' in 'dinner' with the 'o' from 'Oism', Shaw complicated Chicago's celebratory symbol of righteous feasting by aligning it with a dark moment in the history of westward expansion: the winter of 1846, when a wagon train got stuck in the snow on its way through Donner Pass in California's Sierra Nevada Mountain Range and 34 settlers died of disease, hypothermia and starvation. The 48 who survived did so by eating the flesh of their companions. Kind of like the Last Supper, but different.

Shaw's installation consisted of 12 child-size covered wagons arranged in the same manner as Goodman's file cabinet. And, like that piece, Shaw attributed *The Donner Party* to an Oist artist, Mandy Omaha. Atop the flattened covered wagons, Shaw-cum-Omaha, like Chicago, enlisted the help of collaborators – assistants and students who created 18 place settings, each a miniature installation that paid homage to historical women (and several men). *The Dinner Party* had 39 place settings (all but one featuring vulva-shaped forms) atop a triangular table; all paid homage to women who had been overlooked by history. *The Donner Party* focused on mythical figures that existed around the time 'O' brought farming and writing to her people (3000 BCE); historical figures who lived around the time when Annie O'Wooton had her revelatory vision (the 1840s); and figures from the present, including artists, musicians, dancers and TV personalities.

Behind the circled wagons hung a large theatrical backdrop that Shaw had painted (fig.45). It depicted a sunset over Donner Pass. Atop the glorious landscape appeared sharply rendered portraits of mythical, realistic and fictitious figures. All 50 had something to do with Oism, their place in its pantheon both clear and ambiguous because of the way time moves in Shaw's religion – in reverse for the faithful and the other way for everyone else. The people portrayed came from a wide range of faiths and represented disparate convictions and philosophies. Included were Loki, the Norse trickster god; Tituba, an enslaved Nigerian woman accused of being a witch in Salem, Massachusetts, in the 1690s; Elizabeth Clare Prophet, leader of the Church Universal and Triumphant; William Moulton Marston, the creator of Wonder Woman and the inventor of the lie detector; Lynda Benglis, artist; Teresa of Ávila, mystic nun; Uriel/Ruth Norman, leader of Unarius and prophet of 'Space Brothers' arrival; and Tina Louise, the actress who played Ginger in *Gilligan's Island*, a 1960s American sitcom. Also portrayed were many Oists, including Djed Okampu, the first priestess of Oism; Ba Alabar, the Keeper of Oist history after the destruction of Om; Um Thulum, leader of a splinter Oist reform sect; Joshua Carson, Annie O'Wooton's lover; anonymous members of the Oist knights; and 'I', the corruptor of Oism.

Suffice it to say that Shaw's interest in inventing a religion was not to establish any kind of clear doctrine. His purpose was to create a story with so many loose ends that there were plenty to grab onto – and take in just about any direction. Like most religions, Oism tested the limits of rationality. Yet unlike most religions, it made sense of reality by revealing the difficulty of doing just that – and relishing the absurdity of that.

Oism also provided Shaw with a back story for the videos and paintings he made. A pair of Oist videos, *The Hole* (2007) and *The Whole: A Study in Oist Integrated Movement* (2009), mirror each other. The first, a 6'30" black-and-white movie, starts with realism and ends with abstraction, moving from everyday reality to reverie-inducing blurriness by way of the herky-jerky movements of ten zombie businessmen. The second, an 8'50" color video, begins with gauzy swathes of billowing fabric and then follows the synchronized movement of eight dancing women until they arrange themselves around a fake banyan tree, which begins to spin, like a carousel.

If Oism allowed Shaw to make videos that indulged his love of low-budget, early 1960s horror movies, 1970s exercise videos, and the choreography of Busby Berkeley, it also allowed him to make paintings that were both abstract and representational, expressive and illustrative, carefully rendered and gesturally freewheeling. *Untitled (Ripped Up Zombie Face #1)* (2009) (fig.46) depicts a zombie businessman from *The Hole* in the manner of Shaw's *Untitled (Gigantic Face Paintings)* from 1992, as well as the various *Distorted Face Paintings* he made in the late 1970s and early 1980s. This time around, Shaw superimposes a carefully ripped-apart portrait of a zombie atop a gestural abstraction. The brushy web of overlapping and intersecting gestures bears a family resemblance to Pollock's drip paintings but never pretends to be anything more than a generic evocation of the abstract expressionist's famous paintings, whose original rebelliousness had filtered into popular culture as a widely recognized sign of general artistic freedom. 'That is enough,' Shaw's painting seems to say, 'artists need not reinvent the wheel every time they need some freedom.'

Similar experiences unfold before *Split Head*, *Gretchen and Fetal Wig* and *Eight-and-a-Half Dancers* (figs 1, 47 and 48), all from 2012. In the first, ab-ex gestures are bookended by Shaw's portrait, which has been split down the middle and flipped, so that the right half of his face meets the left edge of the canvas and the left half of his face meets the right edge. Shaw's wild-eyed expression makes it seem as if he is shocked – comically – not because his head has been split in two, but because drippy purple, pink, orange, gold and blue brushstrokes have come between the two halves of his head. Being of two minds about something never looked better, nor more absurd. The second painting portrays a dignified woman with impressively coiffed hair standing impassively and looking at a perfect square that seems to have been removed from the 8-ft (2.5-m) long painting only to reappear on the wall to the right, where it has become a black-and-white abstraction with small faces hidden amidst its gestural swirls. The third, a large oil on canvas, similarly hides realistically rendered figures in washy brushstrokes. The atmosphere is smoky and gauzy, like the last half of *The Hole* and the first half of *The Whole*. In all three paintings, multiple modes of mark-making cohabitate. The same goes for styles and formats, media and approaches. Such multiplicity suggests that Shaw's suspicion of single, all-encompassing explanations, which first emerged in *The End is Here!*, is as alive and well in 2012 as it was in 1978.

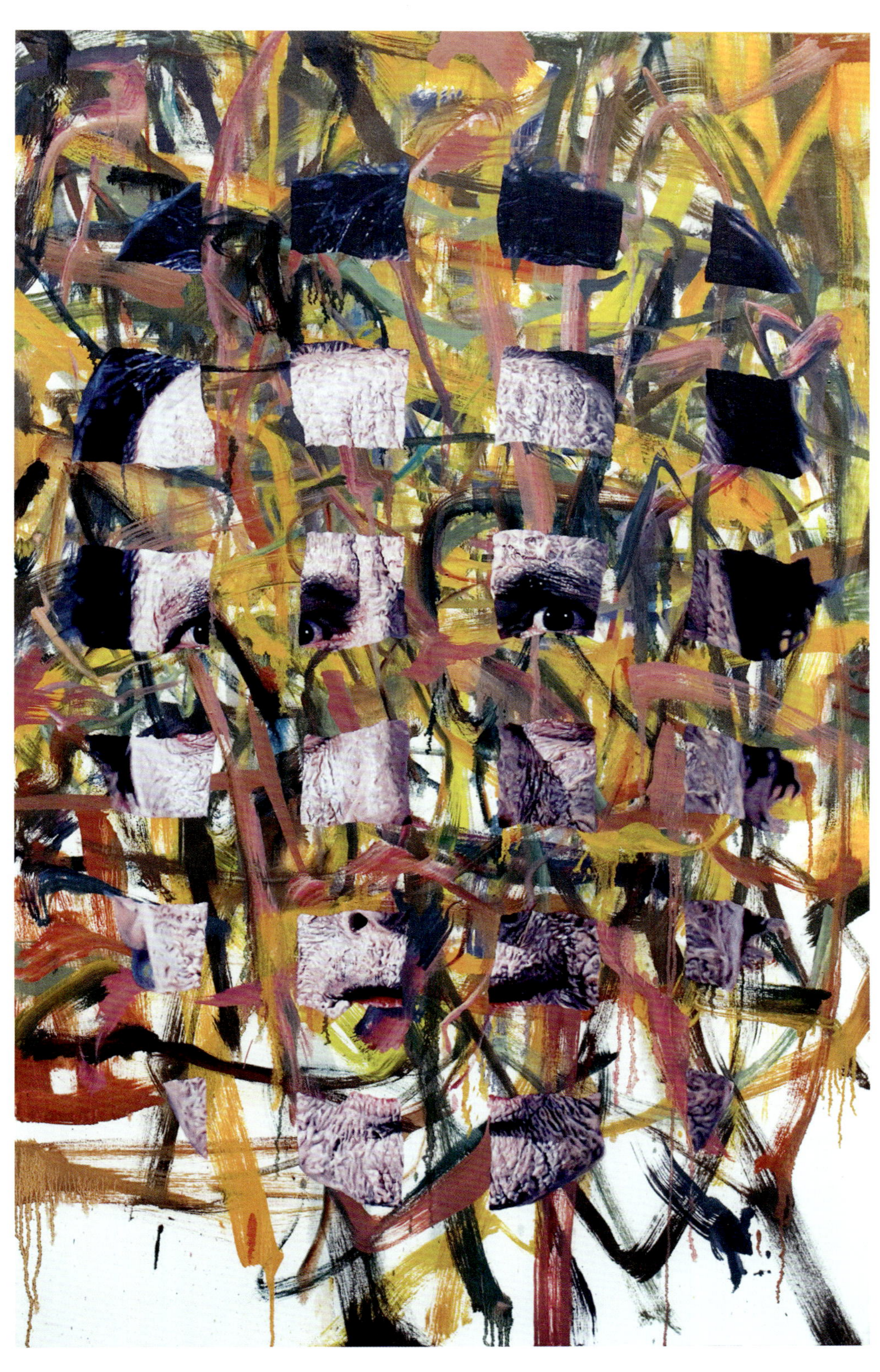

46. Untitled (Ripped up Zombie Face #1)   2009

Oil on canvas
182.9 × 116.8 cm (72 × 46 in)
Private collection

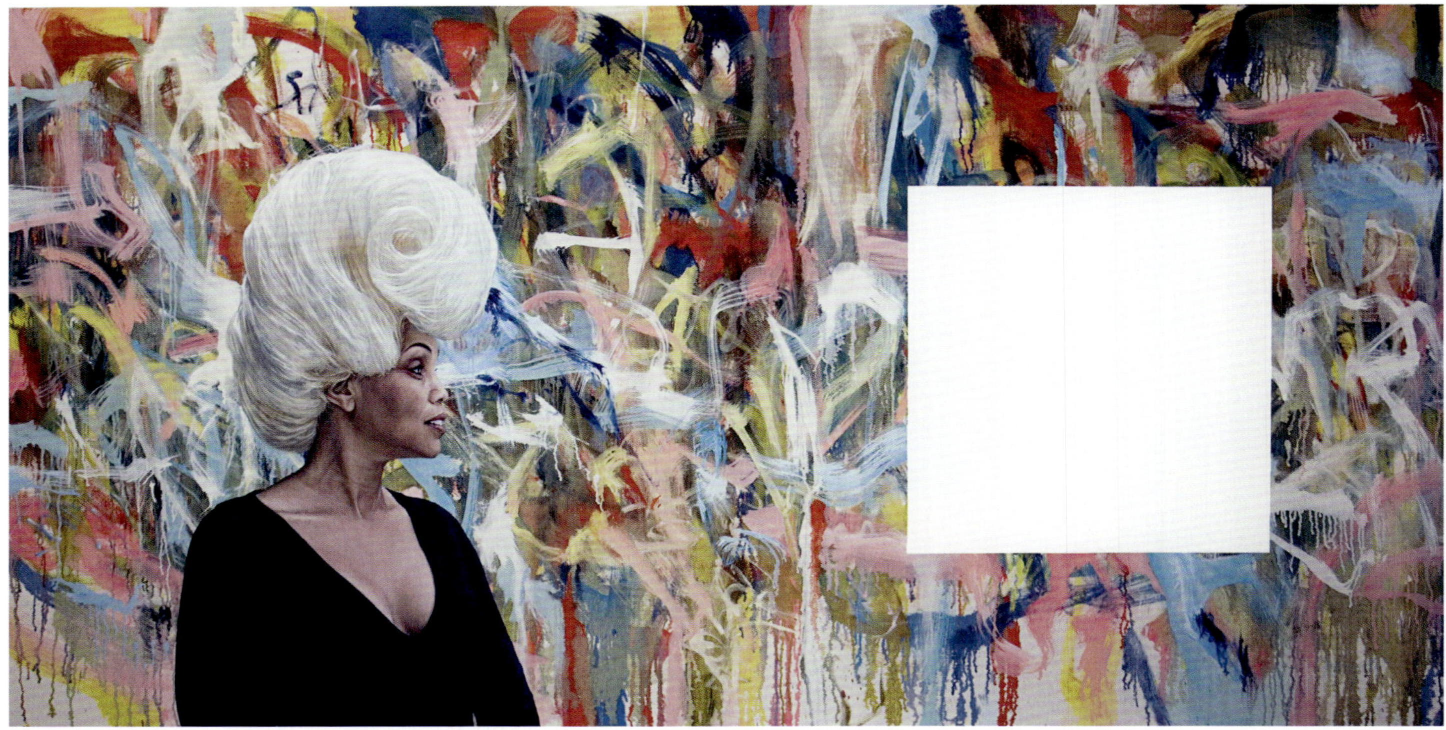

47. Gretchen and Fetal Wig   2012

Oil on canvas; ink and graphite on panel
122.7 × 244.3 cm; 61 × 61 cm (48 × 96 in; 24 × 24 in)
Courtesy Blum & Poe

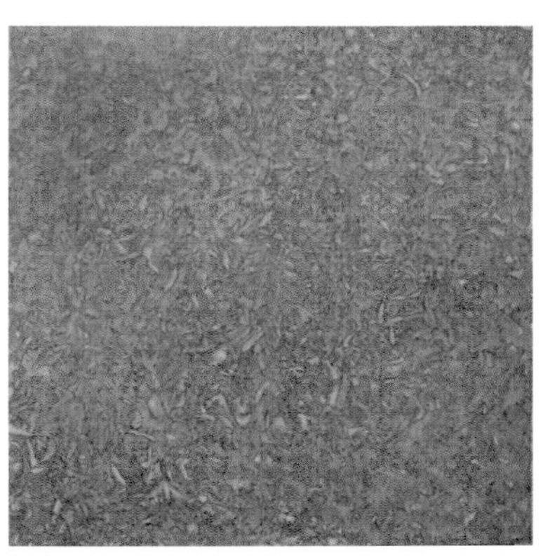

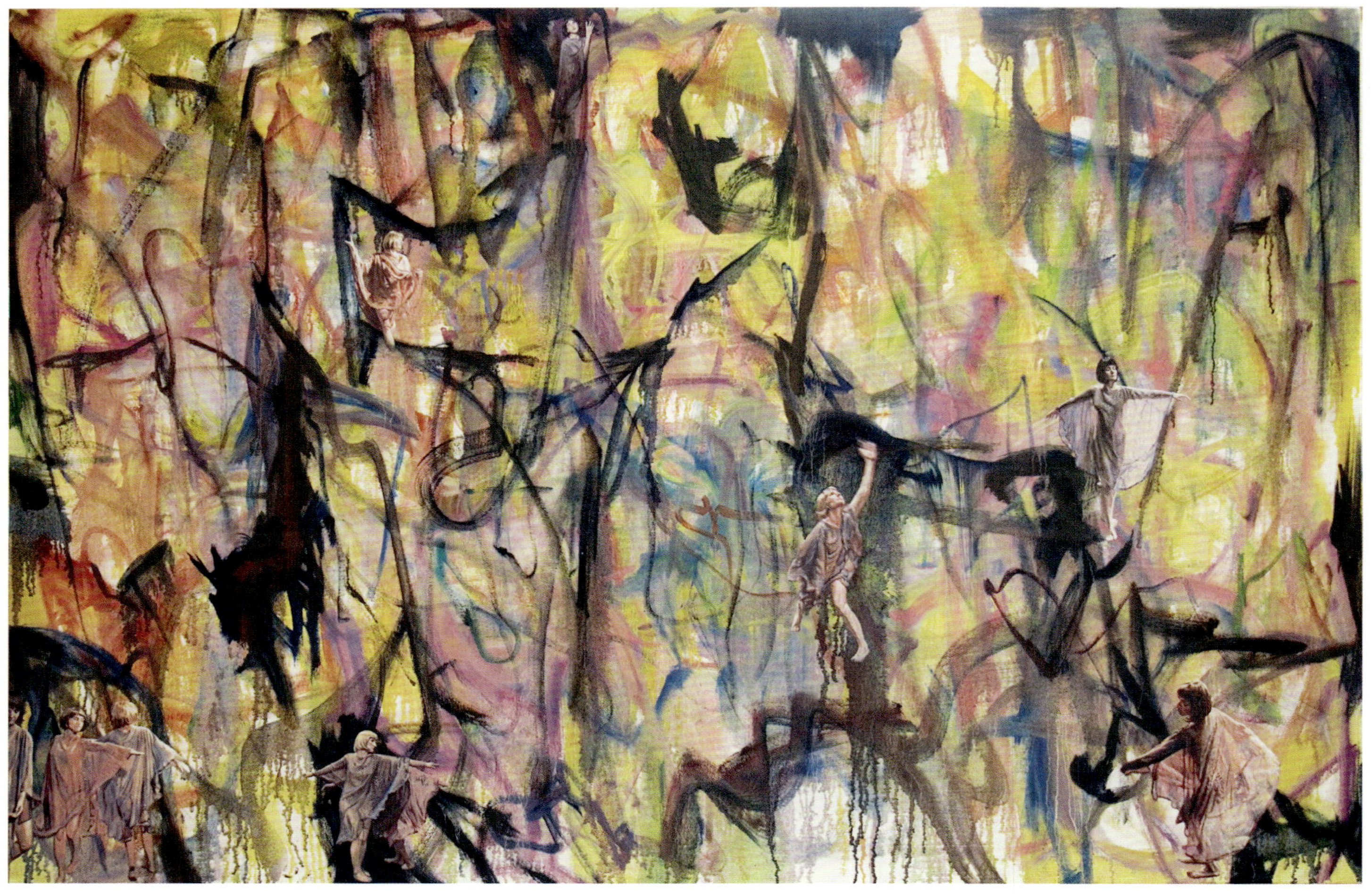

48. Eight and Half Dancers   2012

Oil on canvas
114.9 × 177.8 cm (45¼ × 70 in)
Collection of Patrick Painter

That dynamic unspools in *Untitled (Banyan Tree) 3* (2009) (fig.49), a large work on paper that features a cluster of young banyan trees, realistically rendered in pencil, amidst meandering and overlapping lines, spray-painted from various distances and at various speeds, so that they fade in and out of focus as their widths contract and expand and their shades darken and lighten. The banyan tree, also known as the strangler fig, is an important Oist symbol because it grows toward both heaven and earth. Starting out as a slender, sinuous vine, it eventually strangles the host tree and then completely enwraps it. Octopi and orangutans also figure prominently in the symbology of Shaw's O-focused (if not obsessed) religion, the first for their many-limbed dexterity and the latter for their intelligence and nearly human DNA. The all-seeing eye that hovers above an unfinished pyramid on the United States $1 bill is another symbol integral to Oism, primarily because it is a sign for the illuminati, whose presence, throughout history, is both mysterious and persistent.

Not long after Shaw began making his Oist works, he set his mind to making an Oist opera, in the manner of The Beatles' *Sgt. Pepper's Lonely Hearts Club Band* (1967), Yes's *Tales From Topographic Oceans* (1973) and Genesis's *The Lamb Lies Down on Broadway* (1974). So far, he has outlined the story and some of the music but has not found the time – nor the budget – to get much further than that. Titled *The Rinse Cycle*, his opera is to be set in the 1970s, during the heyday of Prog Rock. Its story unfolds in the 1800s and 1980s – at an Oist university, where a professor has an affair with a student who turns out to be his daughter. Things go bad from there, leading to the fourth apocalypse. Unlike other Oist works, Shaw's unfinished opera and fake religion are coming into existence simultaneously. In the beginning, the story of Oism came first. The works that illustrated the story followed. But with *The Rinse Cycle*, that is no longer the case: the art drives the story and the story unfolds in the art. The relationship between the fabricated narrative and the fabricated objects is reciprocal.

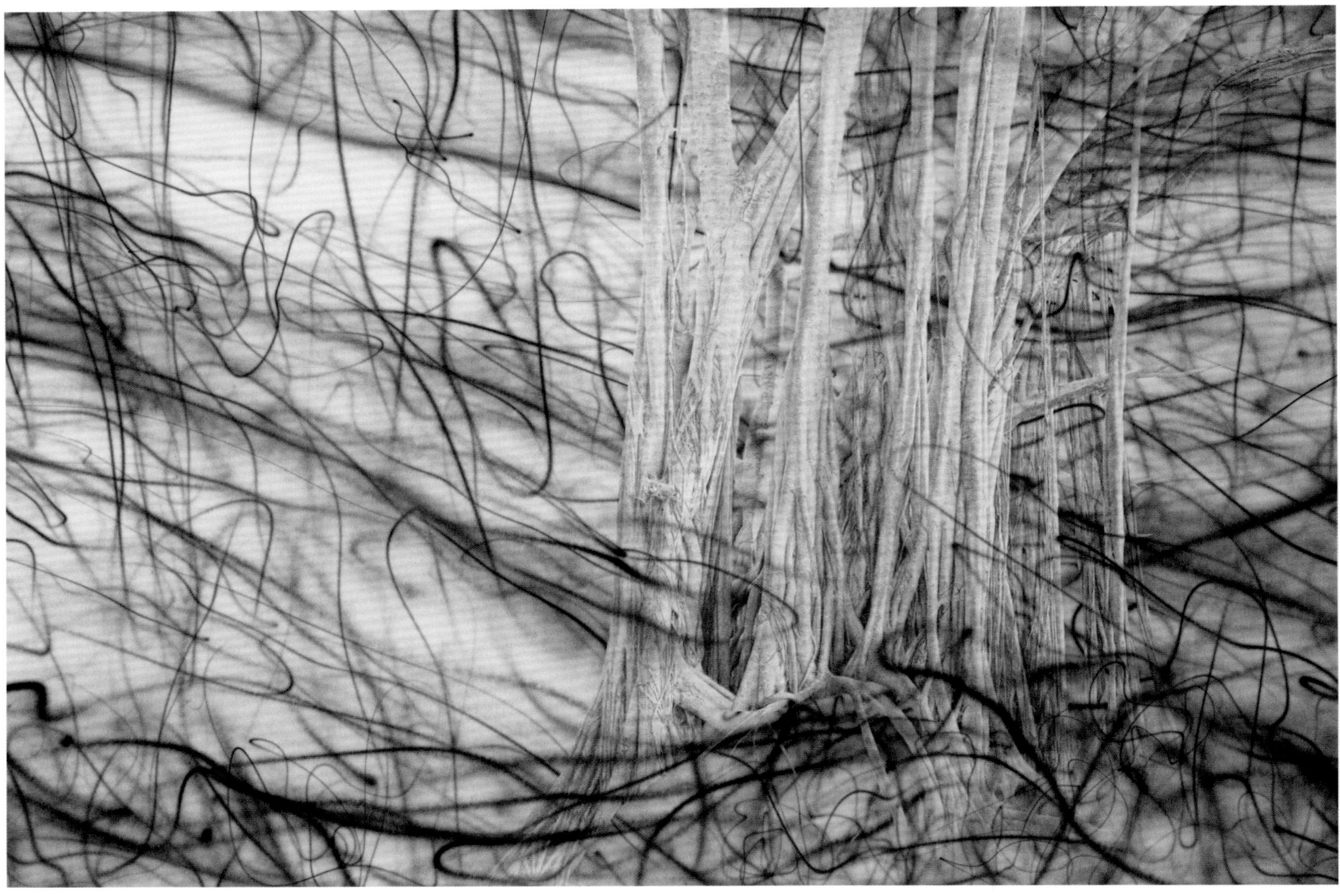

49. Untitled (Banyan Tree) 3   2009

Pencil and aibrush on paper
85.7 × 202.6 cm (33 ¾ × 78 ¾ in)
Private collection, Paris

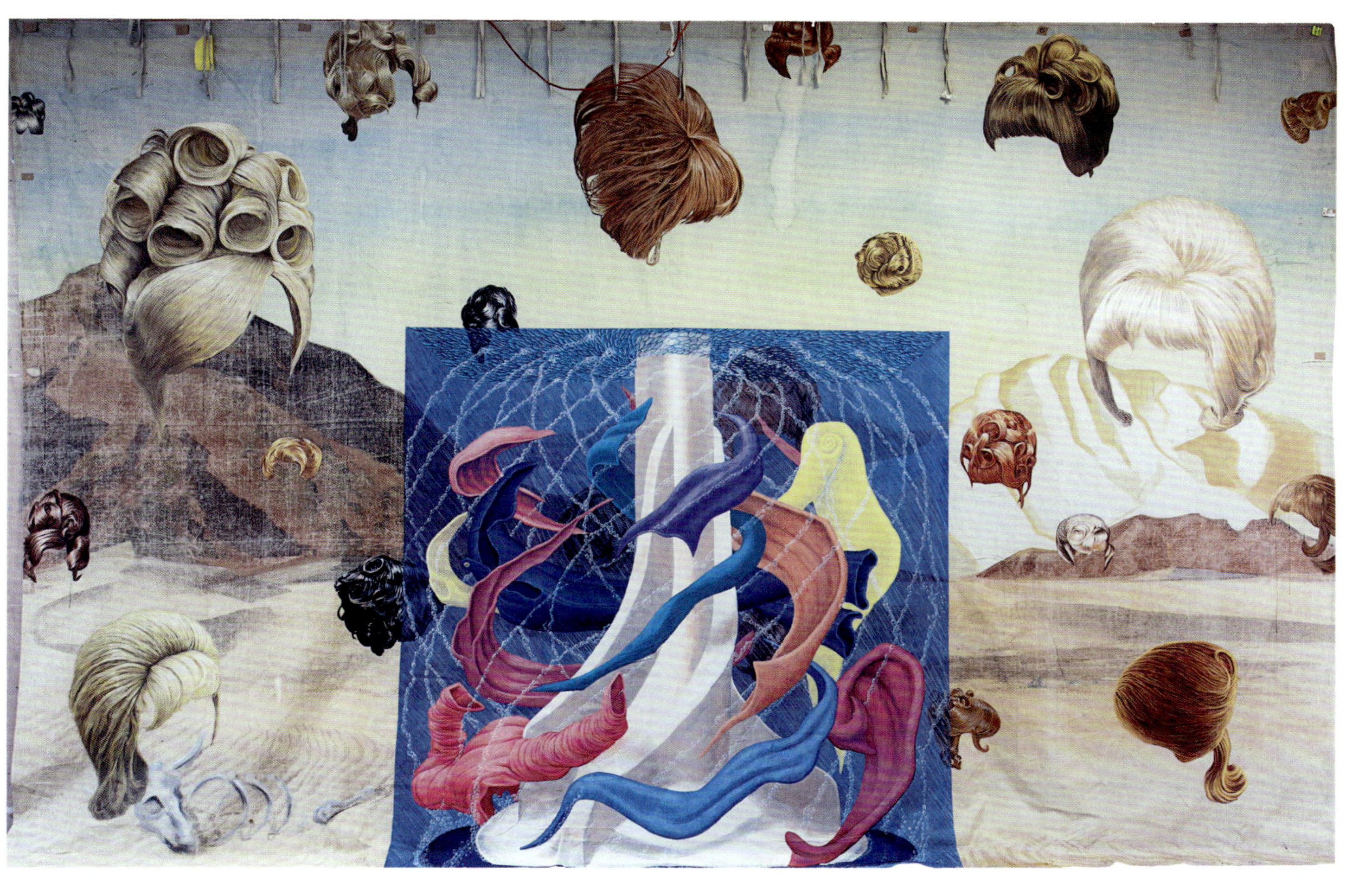

50. Rinse Cycle   2012

Acrylic on muslin
381 × 584.2 cm (150 × 230 in)
Courtesy Metro Pictures

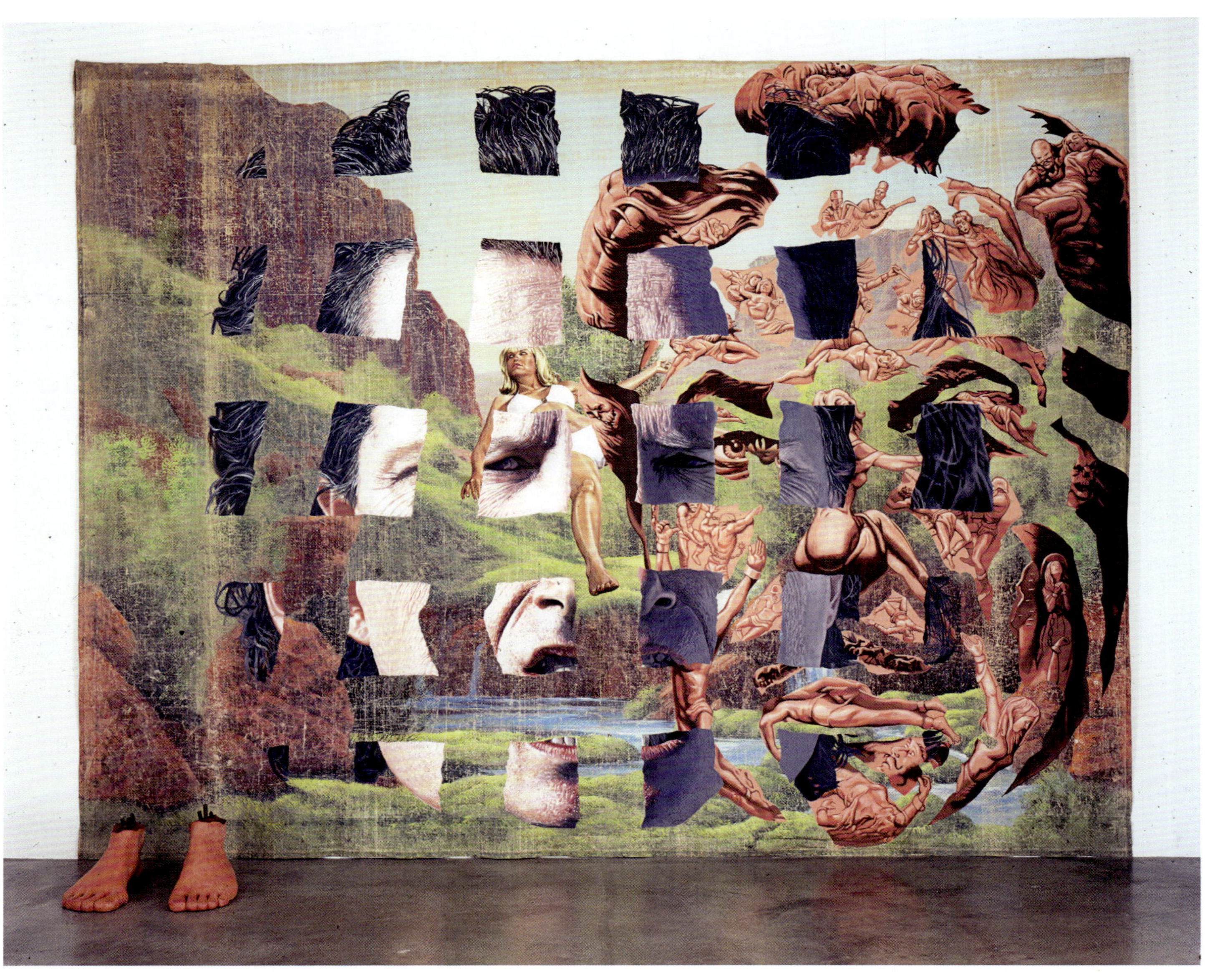

51. Dr. Goldfoot & His Bikini Bombs   2007

Acrylic on muslin; ceramic
364.5 × 484.6 × 91.4 cm (143½ × 190.8 × 36 in)
Private collection

5   Left Behind (2004–12); Cake Paintings and Anatomy Weird-ohs (2008–12)

Two years after Shaw began exhibiting his Oist works, his wife needed a backdrop for a scene in one of the films she was making. Weber enlisted Shaw's assistance. Both scoured the Internet and found a Hollywood backdrop company with a huge 'clearance' section on its site: hundreds of old, worn-out backdrops at bargain-basement prices. Weber selected the backdrop she needed. And Shaw was smitten. At his fingertips was a match made in heaven: the structure (or background) that would form the foundation (or conceptual underpinning) of his next series, *Left Behind*. Like *My Mirage*, his nightly dreams and *The Book of Oism*, the inexpensive backdrops, available at the digital equivalent of a thrift store, provided him with a format against which he could endlessly riff: paint, draw and collage additional illusions that created significant visual dissonance and even greater psychological resonance because of the backdrops they stood out from – like mind-bending non sequiturs, crystal-clear hallucinations and, most important, as if they were the new-and-improved, multi-authored backdrops for a drama so complex and illogical and perplexing that it was not all that different from the reality of American life.

Shaw explained:

A few minutes of perusing [the backdrop website] and I cursed myself, for I knew I had to do something with them. I was attracted to the Americana imagery, and I felt that anything on that sort of scale would have to function as a political cartoon. I was wrapped up in the build-up to the 2004 U.S. election, the Iraq invasion, and thinking a lot about the societal change begun by Reagan and Thatcher, and cemented by Bush Jr., from the ethos and mythos of the New Deal to the fever dream of the neoliberal present.

The title, *Left Behind*, refers both to the best-selling series of books in history, right-wing Christian fantasies about the rapture and coming apocalypse, and the American worker, left behind by globalism, with a weak labor movement and little support from the Democrats. Many have turned to born-again Christianity in lieu of any other hope for the future, which has in turn been exploited heavily by the right wing.[3]

Queen Yma Sumac, in *The End is Here!*, turned out to be more prophetic than
Shaw may have imagined. The same goes for *My Mirage*: Billy's return to religion
anticipated what would happen to a large swathe of the population in the United
States fewer than 20 years later.

The discarded backdrops Shaw rescued from the dustbin of history were
enormous, many measuring 25 x 40 ft (around 8 x 12 m), the smallest about half
that size. They allowed him to use something that was never meant to be anything
more than an illusion – the backgrounds for forgotten scenes from forgotten
Hollywood movies from the 1940s, '50s and '60s – as a means for telling the truth
about the real world: that nostalgia for a past that never existed was beginning to
stand in for a future that would never arrive, partly because politicians preferred
the status quo and partly because the voting public had lost the capacity to
imagine anything different. Shaw thought he might as well see what he could
do about that.

He required a large studio, one much bigger than the extra bedroom, living room
and dining room that he had adapted – or commandeered from his roommates – at his
home in Silver Lake, a cheap '60s apartment building just north of Sunset Boulevard,
across the street from Micheltorena Elementary School. So he rented a big storefront
studio on Figueroa Street, in the no-man's land near the Fourth Street Railroad Yards
and the Los Angeles River. It was only the second studio specifically dedicated to art-
making of Shaw's career. He stayed two years. Then, in 2005, he moved to a studio in
Glendale, which was also adjacent to train tracks. More important, it was four times
the size of his Figueroa studio, and much more nicely appointed. He worked there
until 2012, when he wrapped up work on *Left Behind*.

With the massive backdrops covering the walls and floors of his 5,000 sq-ft (1,500 sq-m)
space in Glendale, Shaw's imagination ran rampant, interrupting bucolic scenes
of the countryside, as well as old-fashioned pictures of small towns and big-city streets
from yesteryear, with gigantic flying mustaches and hovering hairdos, as well as the
interiors of washing machines and vacuum cleaners with octopus-style hoses. The
theatrical backdrops Shaw selected generally pictured expansive vistas and wide-open
spaces, sometimes with ranches, mining towns, shacks and outposts in the middle
distance, or, in the foreground, such generic urban settings as the platforms of railway
stations and the facades of banks, skyscrapers, hotels, libraries, even the United States
Capitol, as well as parks, rivers and suburban streets, usually with a whiff of Americana.

Painted by anonymous artisans when movies were shot in studios, and 'locations'
were changed without leaving the stage, the backdrops looked real when filmed, their
good-enough-to-get-the-job-done illusionism suiting Shaw's affection for workaday
illustration and his distaste for the elitism that often accompanies fine art. In person,
they looked nothing like they did on film. The movie magic vanished, leaving viewers
dwarfed before images whose dimensions made murals seem like easel paintings,
not quite postage stamps but no match for the larger-than-life dimensions of Shaw's

backdrops. Plus, the backdrops were never meant to stand on their own. Without the props that stood in front of them and gave them a greater sense of three-dimensionality, and without the actors whose acting energized them, they felt vacant, leached of life, forlorn – a vacuous, hollowed-out version of history that made waxing nostalgic difficult, if not impossible.

But Shaw also saw that the backdrops were ripe for recycling. If time could be turned around, à la Oism, his gargantuan cartoons might come to life as mirrors of the increasingly absurd world in which they existed. And, like a banyan tree growing around a helpless host, Shaw's painterly additions might transform the backdrops into something far different from the originals: a toehold, in reality, for his hyperactive imagination, which was always searching for ways to weave itself into the fabric of everyday life.

In Shaw's *Left Behind* works, the layering of imagery and the range of references are more nuanced, subtle and sophisticated than in anything he had previously made. That deepening and broadening are accompanied, perhaps paradoxically, by a kind of stylistic streamlining that had not been a part of his repertoire, which, until this series, followed an additive, everything-plus-the-kitchen-sink approach. Rather than piling styles atop styles, medium atop medium, Shaw started to simplify, limiting himself, compositionally, to the creation of vivid, crisply rendered, illusionistic images that he and his assistants painted atop the faded backdrops. Many of the backdrops had been folded and unfolded so many times that much of the paint had crumbled away, leaving the muslin visible, like the graphics on vintage T-shirts. It was as if the expansive dimensions of the backdrops allowed Shaw to spread out and slow down, to cut back on the number of elements without eliminating any of the weirdness his cockeyed realism captured in the world it surveyed. The contrast, between the ghostly backdrop imagery and the vivid pictures he painted atop them, mixed dreamy illusions with graphic realities in ways that made both seem to be both true and false, neither fact nor fantasy but suspended in a nether world between the two – much like the present.

Shaw proceeded through his inventory of theatrical backdrops by fits and starts, neither striving for stylistic consistency nor serial coherence but by mixing and matching his conscious desires and unconscious inclinations in ways that made each piece seem to be its own world – or any number of worlds within worlds. The size of Shaw's *Left Behind* pieces made them difficult, but not impossible, to exhibit. In 2010, the CAPC Musée d'Art Contemporain in Bordeaux, France, presented *Jim Shaw, Left Behind*, which included 18 paintings, three installations and two Oist videos. In 2013, the Museum Boijmans Van Beuningen, in Rotterdam, The Netherlands, took advantage of its space, a converted submarine manufacturing facility, and displayed 15 *Left Behind* works in *XXXL Painting: Klaas Kloosterboer, Chris Martin, Jim Shaw*. Four were shown in Shaw's 2015 survey at the New Museum in New York.

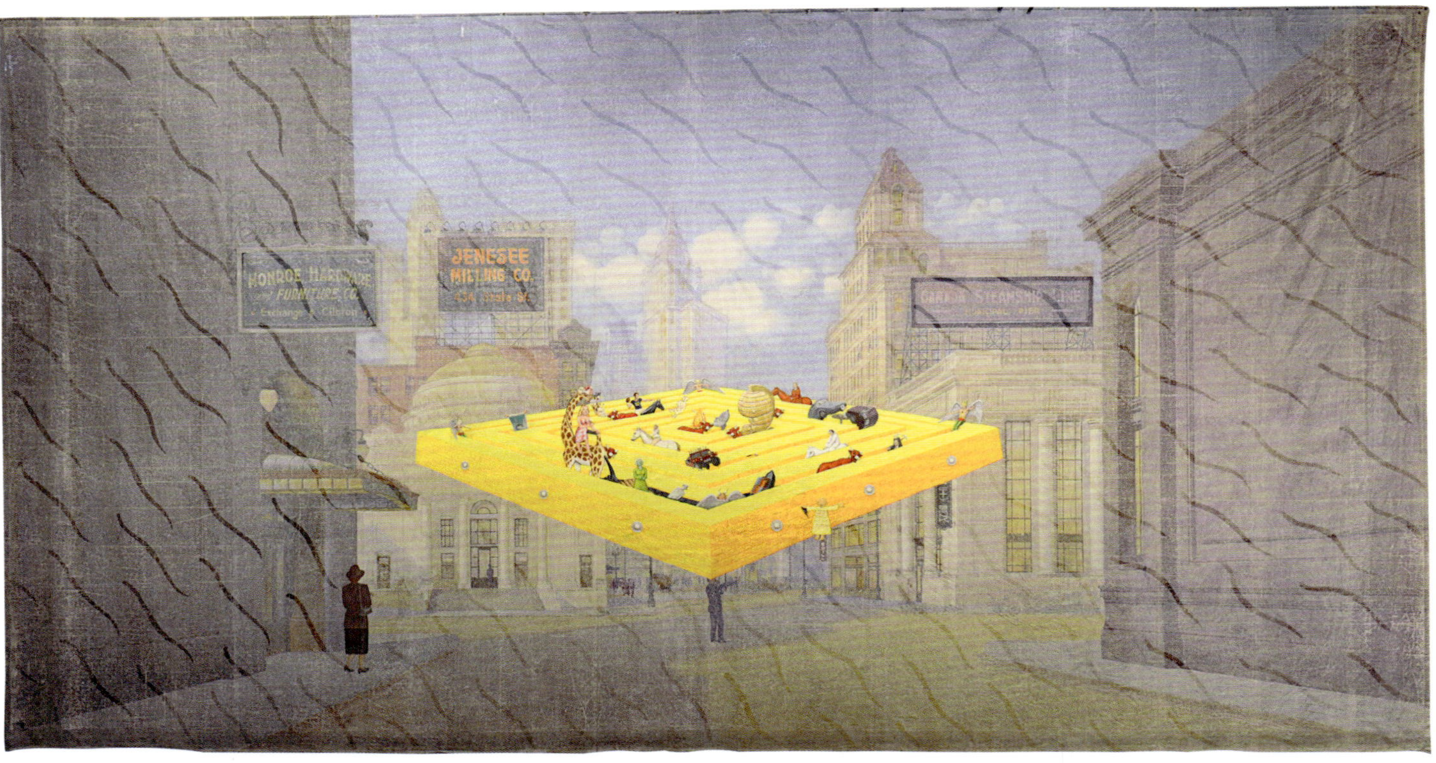

52. Dream Object ("I dreamt of an image of a
yellow walled city with a yellow kid sticking his
finger in the outer wall . . .")   2004

Acrylic on muslin
671 × 1158.2 cm (264 × 456 in)
Collection of Joseph Dalle Nogare Collection, Bolzano

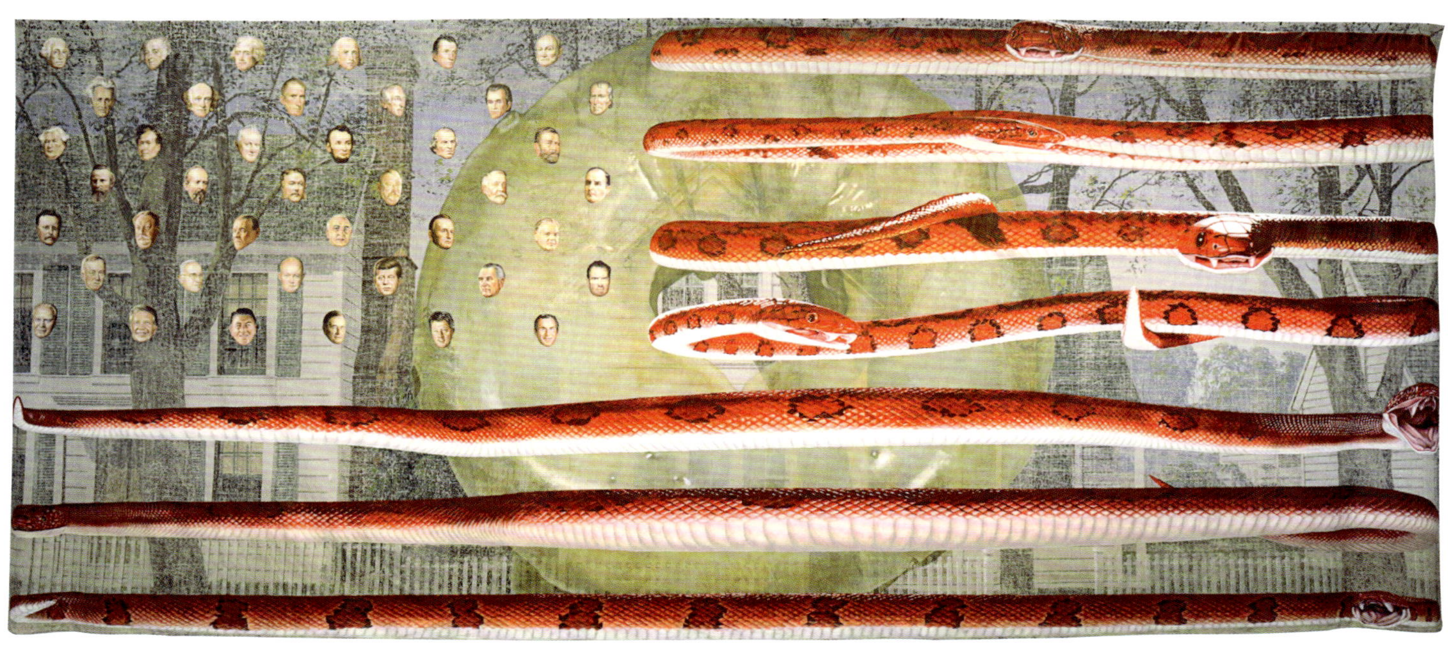

53. Untitled (U.S. Presidents)   2006

Acrylic on muslin
487.7 × 1158.2 cm (192 × 456 in)
Private collection

The first backdrop painting Shaw made came from a dream, making it both a *Dream Object* and a *Left Behind* piece. *Dream Object ("I dreamt of an image of a yellow walled city with a yellow kid sticking his finger in the outer wall...")* (2004) (fig.52) is a three-layered work. The first layer is the backdrop, which depicts an intersection in downtown Rochester, New York – not far from the birthplace of Oism – in what appears to be the 1930s. The next layer is a gauzy veil made up of the repeated silhouettes of snakes, slithering from lower right to upper left, a direction in which no language is read. The third layer depicts a barricaded golden city made of nothing but walls. In the gaps between the seven walls, which were inspired by the Book of Revelation, Shaw has packed portraits of contemporary political figures and celebrities standing in as Biblical figures: Tom Delay, Pat Robertson, Ayn Rand, Ronald Regan and Bill Gates as the Horsemen of the Apocalypse; Britney Spears, in a Lynndie England pose, as the Whore of Babylon; Barbara Bush as Medusa on a raft; George W. Bush as a sinking statue; Alan Greenspan as the Fourth Beast from Daniel; the superhero Hawkman as the four animal-headed angels from the Book of Revelation; and the Yellow Kid, a character from one of the first cartoons printed in American newspapers, as a figure that embodied, for Shaw, the role tabloid journalism has played – and continues to play – in starting wars: media mogul William Randolph Hearst fanning the flames of aggression that led to the Spanish-American War and Fox News cheering on the United States' invasion of Iraq. Together, the superimposed images leave viewers before a world in which the facts neither made complete sense nor could be dismissed as nonsensical: they existed in the nether land of ambiguity.

Likewise, *Untitled (U.S. Presidents)* (2006) (fig.53) superimposes an image of the Stars and Stripes atop an enormous, transparent, frosting-covered donut, which is superimposed atop a backdrop depicting three suburban houses. Shaw's rendition of the American flag – its stripes comprised of red corn snakes and its stars by the disembodied heads of US presidents – suggests that something is amok in the land of the free and the home of the brave. But he does not point fingers or place blame, preferring to embody, in his painting, the anxiety, disquiet and impending sense of doom simmering beneath the surface of political life in the United States.

A different sort of layering takes place in *Dr. Goldfoot & His Bikini Bombs* (2007) (fig.51) and *Ticker-Tape Laocoon* (2008) (fig.54). The first is more fractured, like Shaw's *Untitled (Ripped Up Zombie Face #1)* (fig.46). The latter is among the most spatially coherent works Shaw has made. He describes the first:

In this mural my ripped up self-portrait floats over three layers. The first is a desert landscape that corresponds somewhat to the landscape in Duchamp's *Etant Donnes*, on top of which is painted a girl in a bikini in the same pose as Duchamp's nude. On top of that is a portrait of Vincent Price derived from the ad for *The Masque of the Red Death*, in which his face is formed from various bodies in states of distress. This image has been separated into component parts.[4]

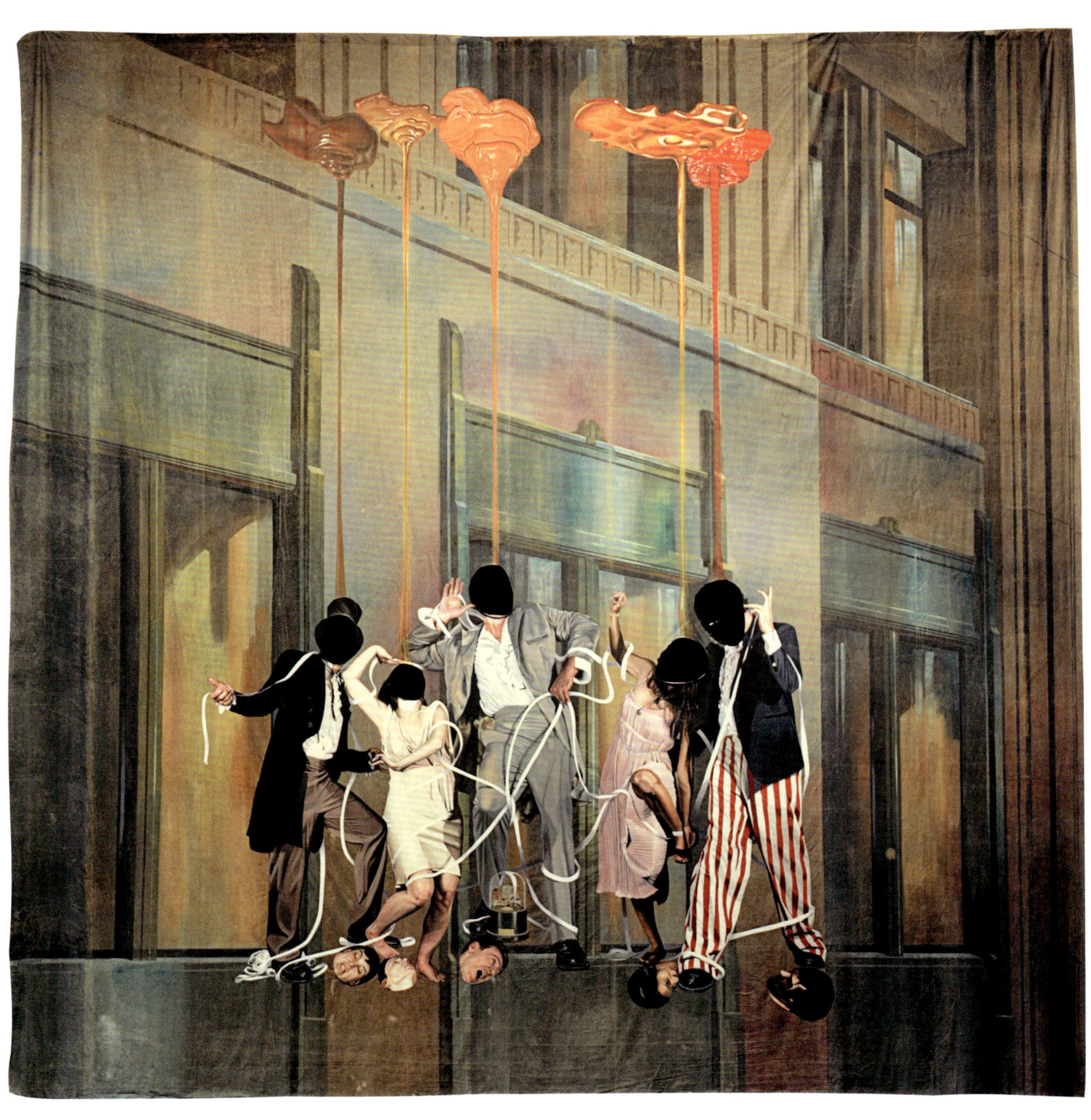

54. Ticker-tape Laocoon   2008

Acrylic and oil on muslin
762 × 744.2 cm (300 × 293 in)
Private collection

On the floor in front of the approximately 12-x-16 ft (3.5-x-5-m) painting stands a pair of feet, made of clay and iron, which refers to Daniel's interpretation of Nebuchadnezzar's dream in the Old Testament. Shaw's tableau derived from his interest in the infamous and unsolved 'Black Dahlia' murder of Elizabeth Short in 1947, its relation to the Los Angeles art world, his guilt about using body parts in his work, and, mostly, his doubts about his own artistic integrity, which made him wonder whether he was making art because he needed to or because there was a market for it – which was new to him, but would not last long, with the economic crash of 2008 just around the corner. *Dr. Goldfoot & His Bikini Bombs* stands out as one of the few works in which Shaw took himself as his subject, focusing on his thoughts and anxieties rather than his dreams.

In contrast, *Ticker-Tape Laocoon* looks outward. Painted on a relatively undamaged backdrop, its space is more uniform and consistent with the space a viewer's body occupies. Its larger-than-life-size figures, in masquerade ball costumes, strike the pose of Laocoon and his sons, as they were attacked by snakes sent by the gods, as punishment for trying to warn the Athenians of their enemies hidden in the Trojan Horse. After painting his rendition of the classic tragedy, Shaw removed the heads of his five figures by cutting ovals out of the muslin backdrop. He then glued the cutout heads under each figure's upraised foot – as if all of the figures were vanquishing themselves, being both winners and losers of an imaginary economic battle (tickertape was the symbol of Wall Street, before the world went digital). The holes atop their shoulders recall the painted plywood props tourists sometimes stand behind to have their photos taken at sightseeing destinations, to show others, back home, how their travels allowed them to 'go local', or to pretend to do so, without really believing it – or wanting to.

The cutout heads led Shaw, the next year, to make freestanding pieces that were also two-dimensional. Propped up by wooden struts, like the hand-painted 'flats' in school plays, his custom-shaped paintings depict a cast of characters very much like the ones that appear in his *Presence sculptures*: Biblical, mythical, historical and contemporary personages, from album covers, political cartoons, paintings, sculptures and newspapers. *Labyrinth: I Dreamt I was Taller than Jonathan Borofsky* (2009) (fig.58) had the presence of a deconstructed – or blown-apart – *Presence sculpture*, its imagery detached from a volumetric form and dispersed in space. Shaw originally installed his multipart piece in front of two murals, one by Picasso and the other by Dalí, at L'Abattoir, in Toulouse, France. Shaw's ability to paint like a chameleon, changing styles and techniques in the blink of an eye, makes the posthumous collaboration look like pre-planned teamwork: an adventure in absurdity too surreal to believe yet too realistic to be dismissed. Six years later, Shaw re-installed his freestanding pieces, replacing the paintings by Picasso and Dalí with two of his own works: *Judgement* and *The Moon* (both 2015) (fig.57 and fig.56). The dissonance was undiminished, catching visitors in the undertow.

The spatial coherence of *Ticker-Tape Laocoon* also appears in Shaw's *Left Behind* paintings that do double-duty as Oist works. In *Octopus Vacuum* (2008) (fig.55), the mustaches, hoses and women dressed in courtly costumes all seem to be in the same tree-filled landscape – not superimposed on one another or cut-and-pasted into a

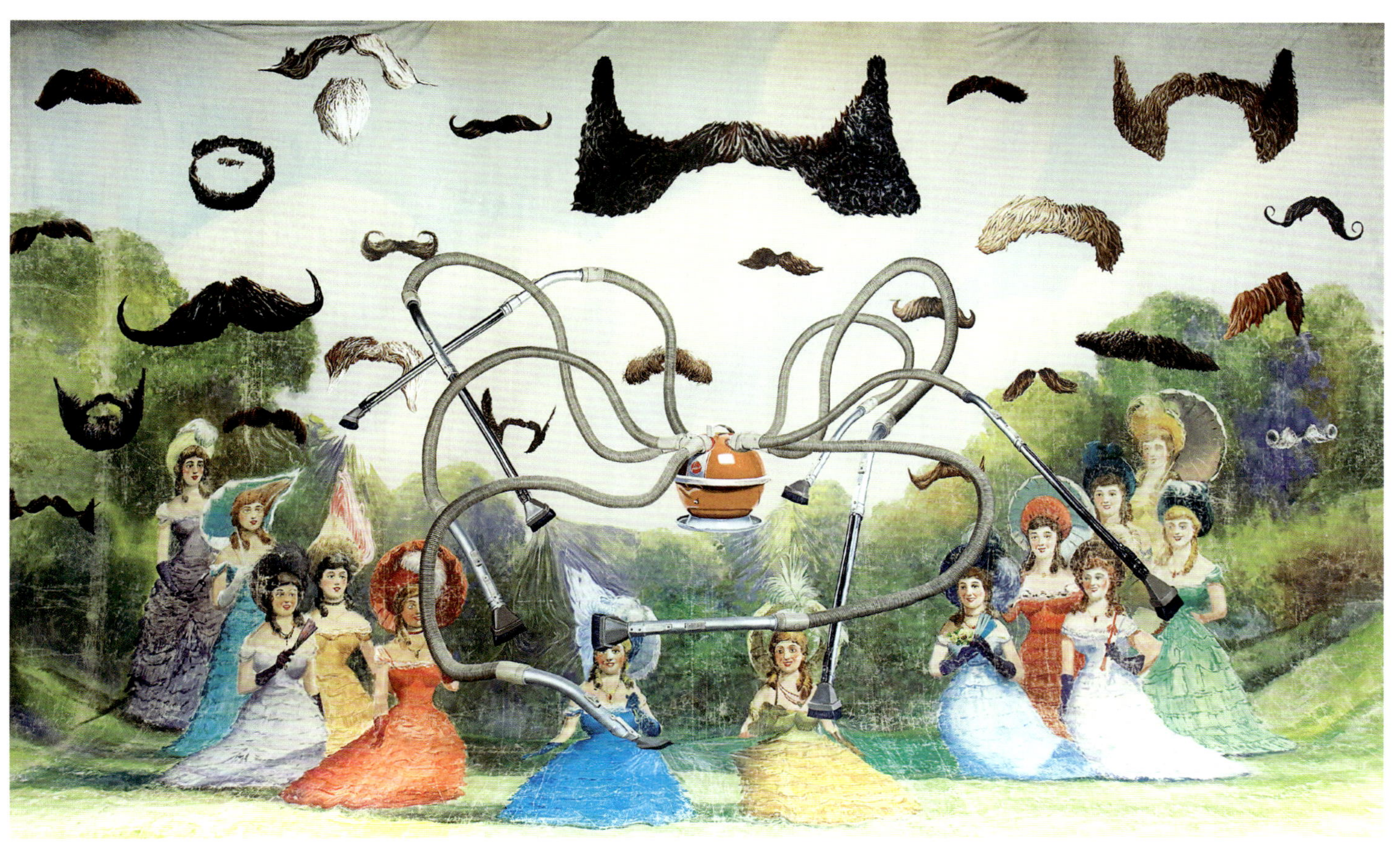

55. Octopus Vacuum   2008

Acrylic on canvas
492.3 × 717.6 cm (193⅘ × 282½ in)
Courtesy Praz-Delavallade

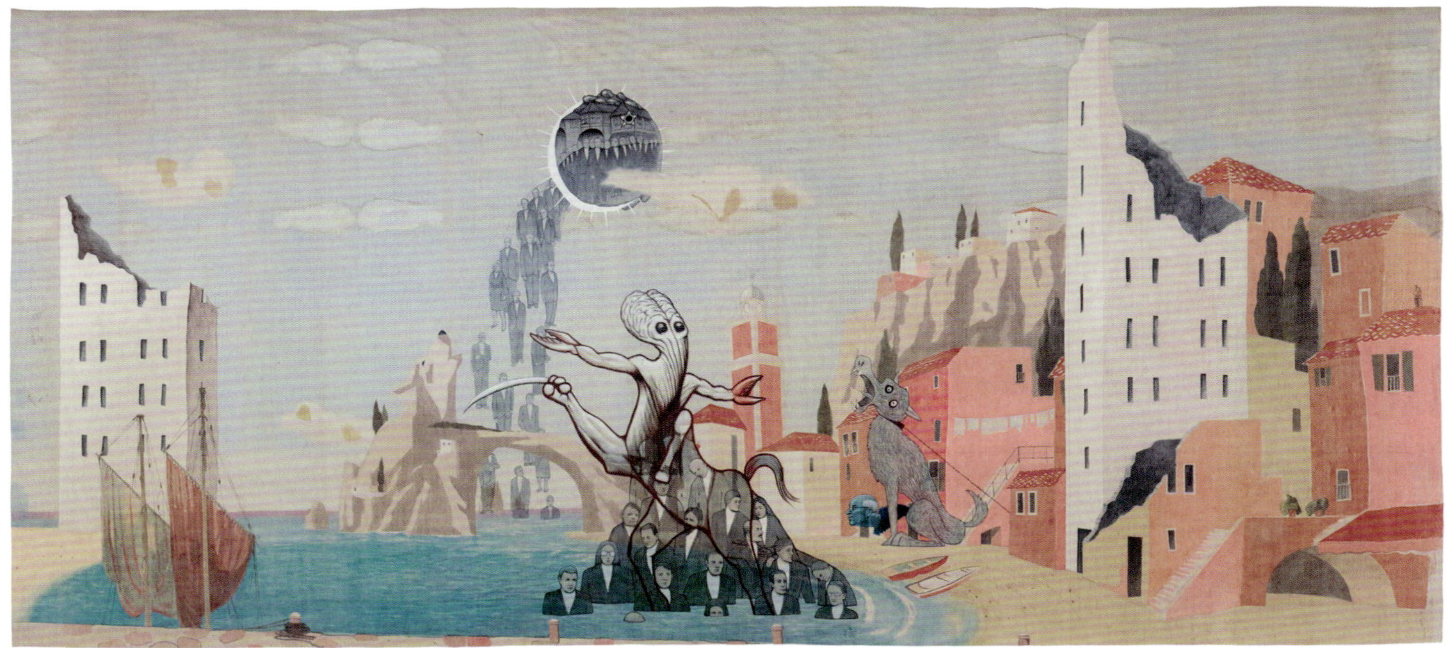

56. The Moon   2015

Acrylic on muslin
731.5 × 1524 cm (288 × 600 in)
Courtesy Blum & Poe and Metro Pictures

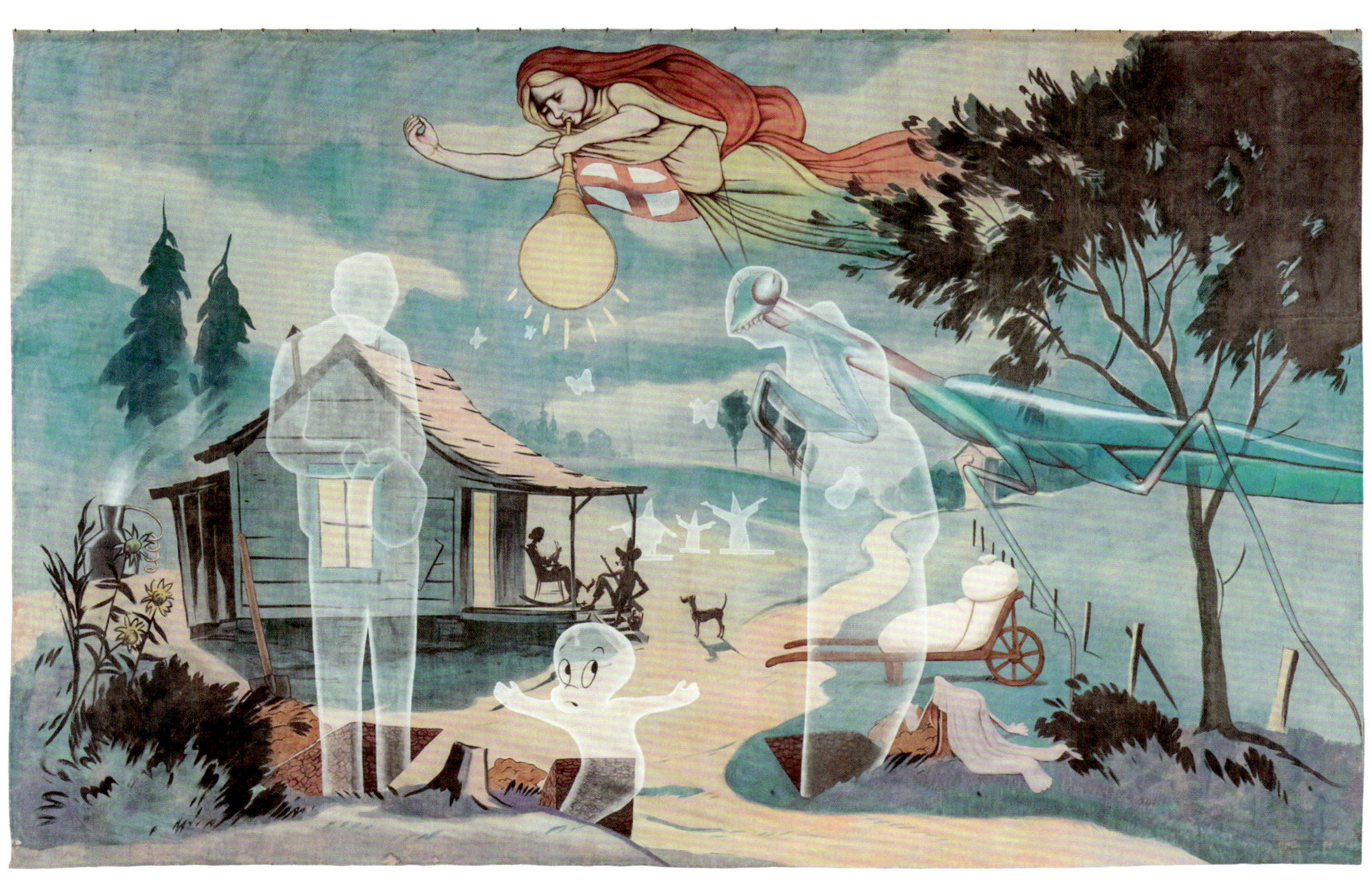

57. Judgement   2015

Acrylic on muslin
609.6 × 980.4 cm (240 × 386 in)
Courtesy Blum & Poe and Metro Pictures

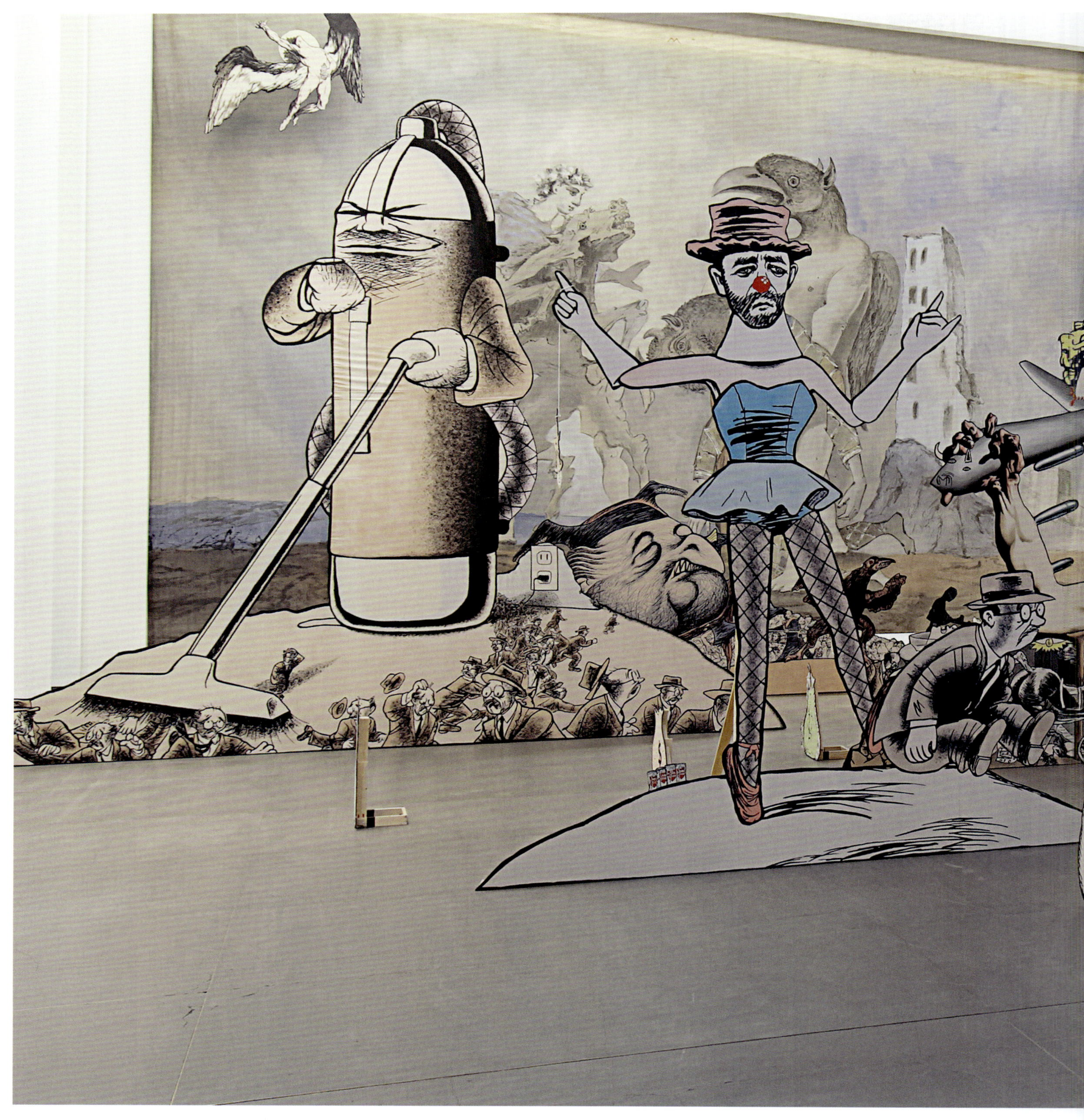

58. Labyrinth: I dreamed I was taller than Jonathan Borofsky (installation view) 2009; Background: Pablo Picasso's stage backdrop for the play *Le 14 Juillet* (1936); Salvador Dalí's stage backdrop for the play *El Sombrero de Tres Picos* (1949)

Acrylic on muslin stretched on plywood; acrylic on muslin
6.10 × 11.34 m (20 × 37⅓ ft)
Collection Eric Decelle

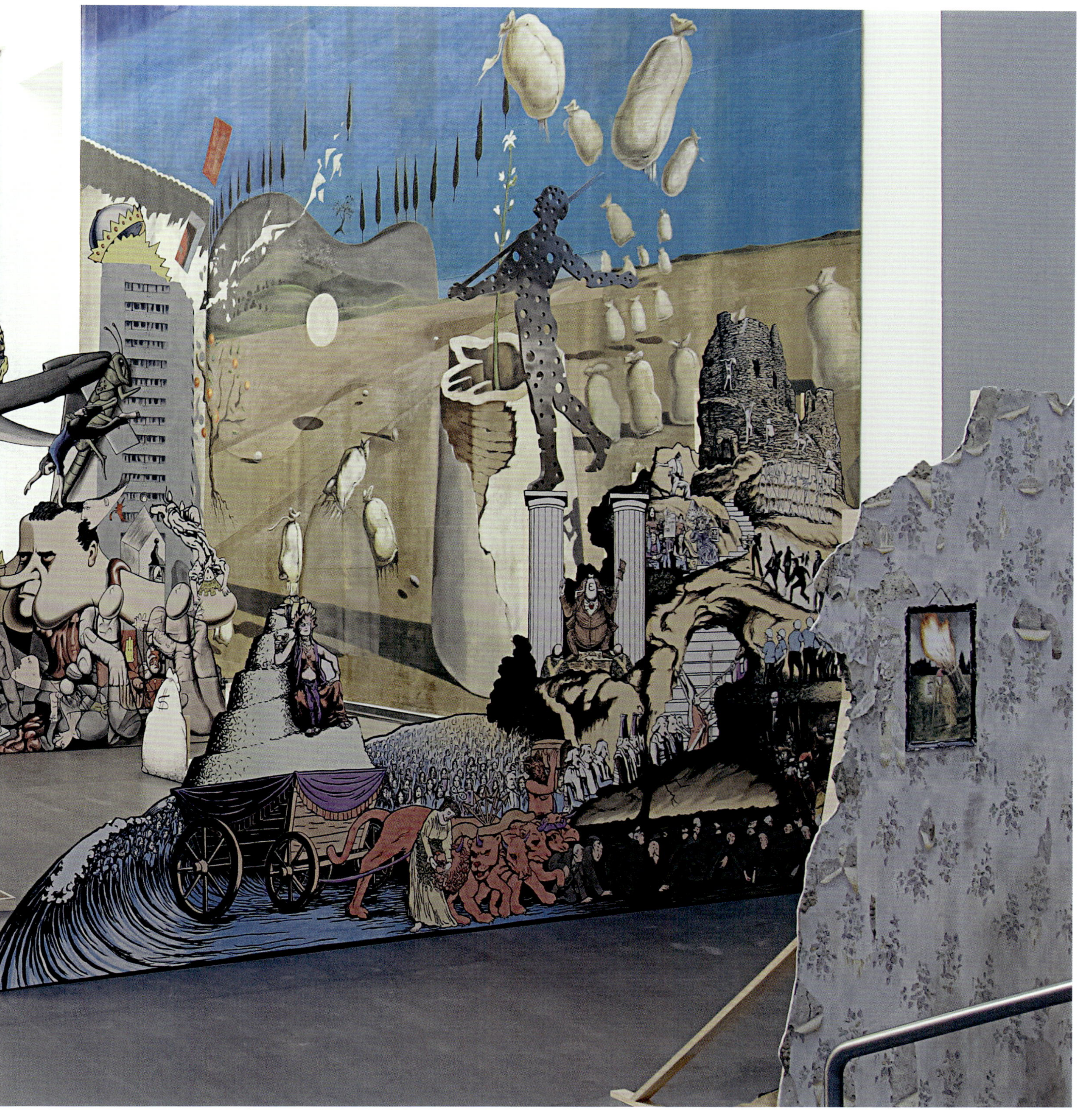

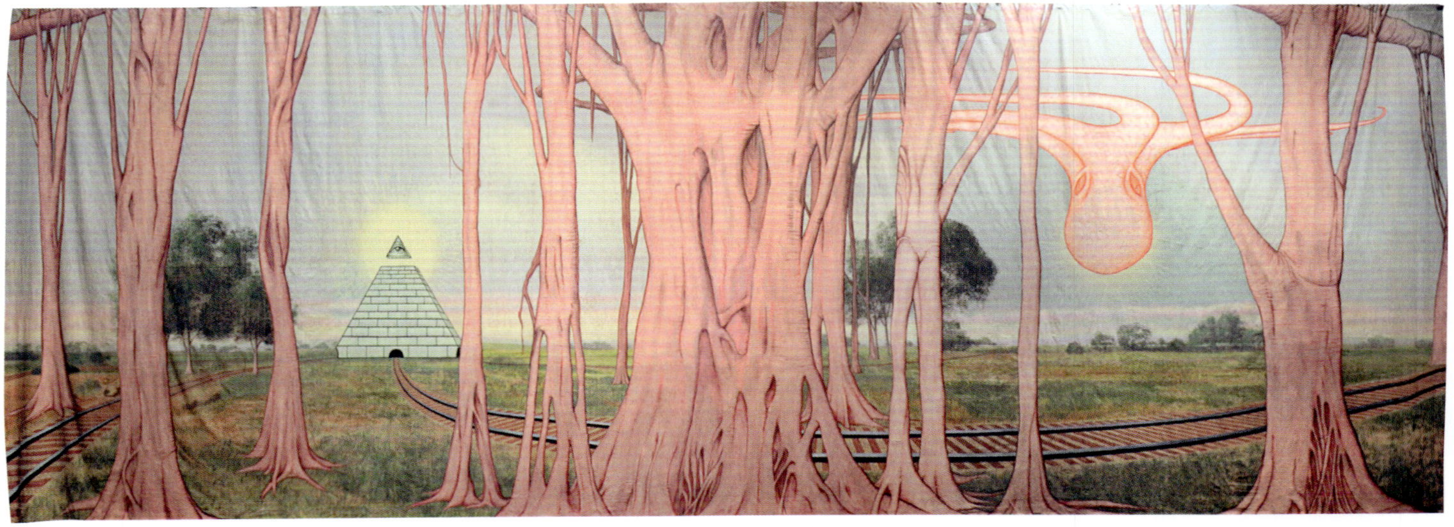

59. D'red Dwarf, B'lack Hole   2010

Acrylic on muslin
500.1 × 1481.8 cm (196⁹⁄₁₀ × 583²⁄₅ in)
Museum Boijmans van Beuningen, Rotterdam

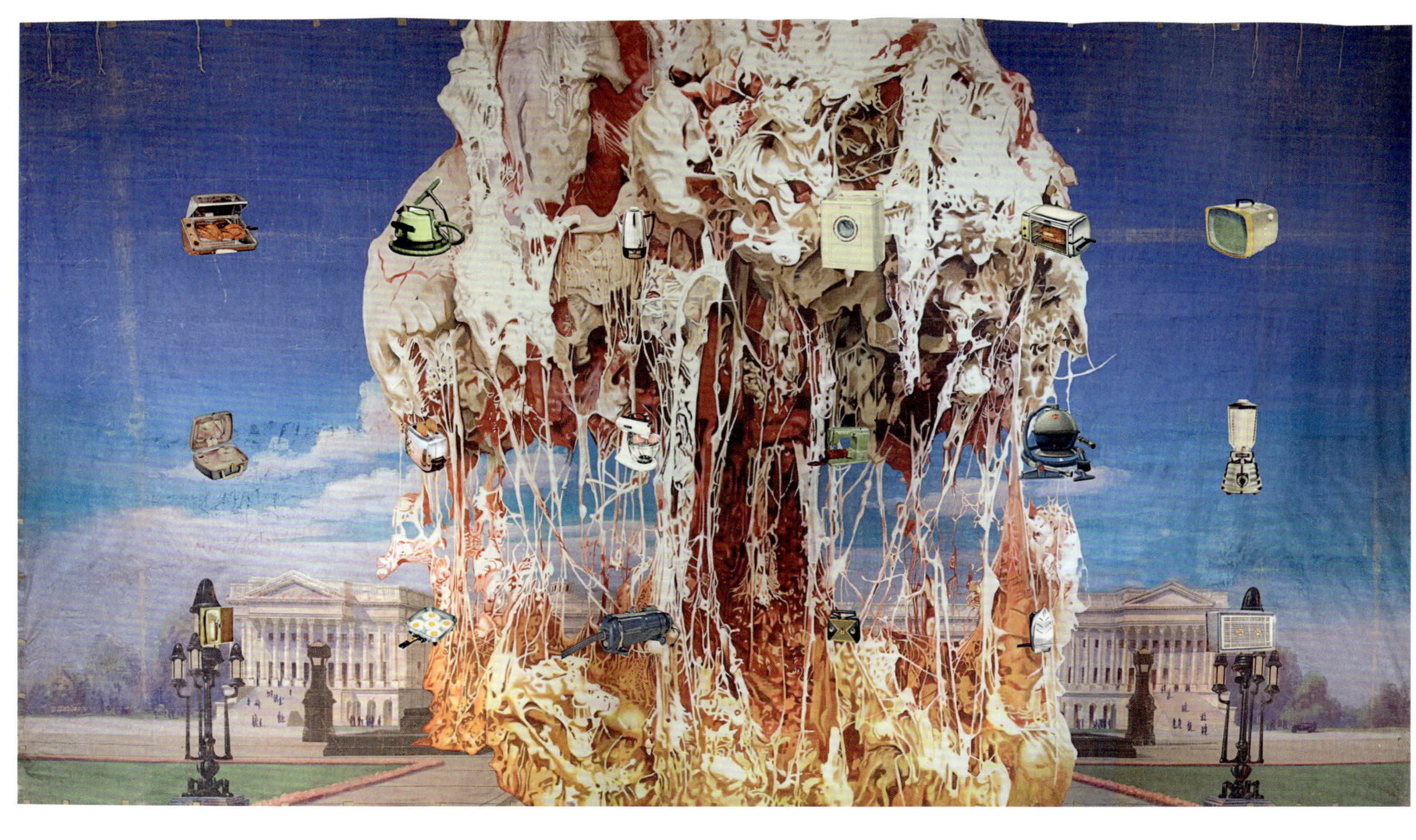

60. Capitol Viscera Appliance Mural   2011

Acrylic on muslin
500 × 1016 cm (196 ⅞ × 400 in)
Courtesy Simon Lee Gallery

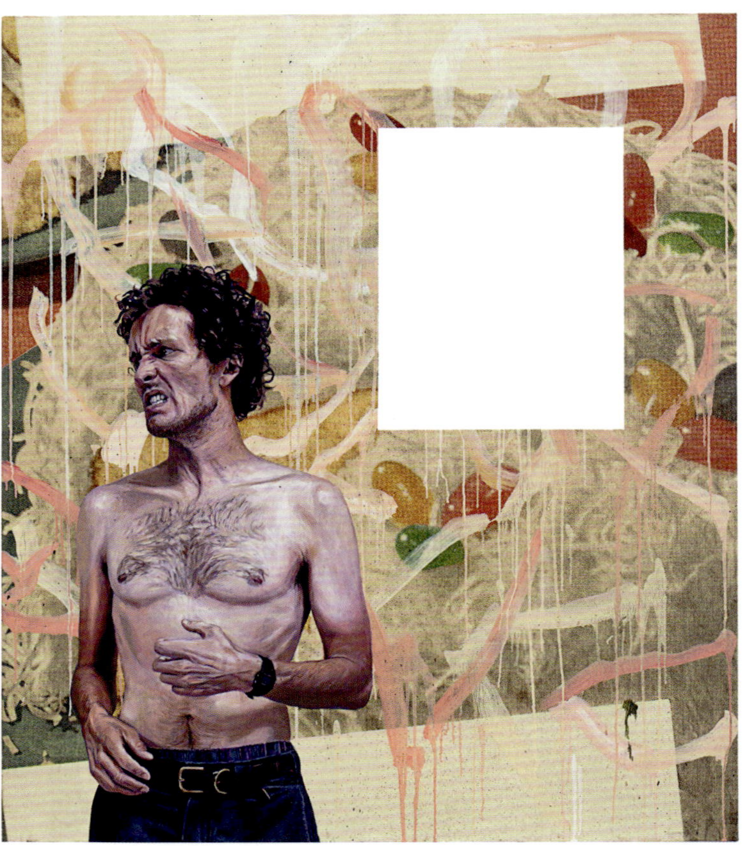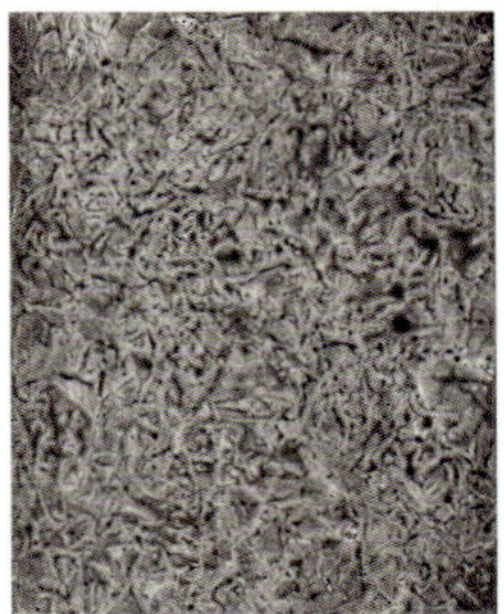

61. Cake (Daniel in Disgust)   2011

Oil on digital inkjet print and acrylic and ink on panel painting
111 × 99 cm; 40.6 × 33 cm (43¾ × 39 in; 16 × 13⅛ in)
Private collection

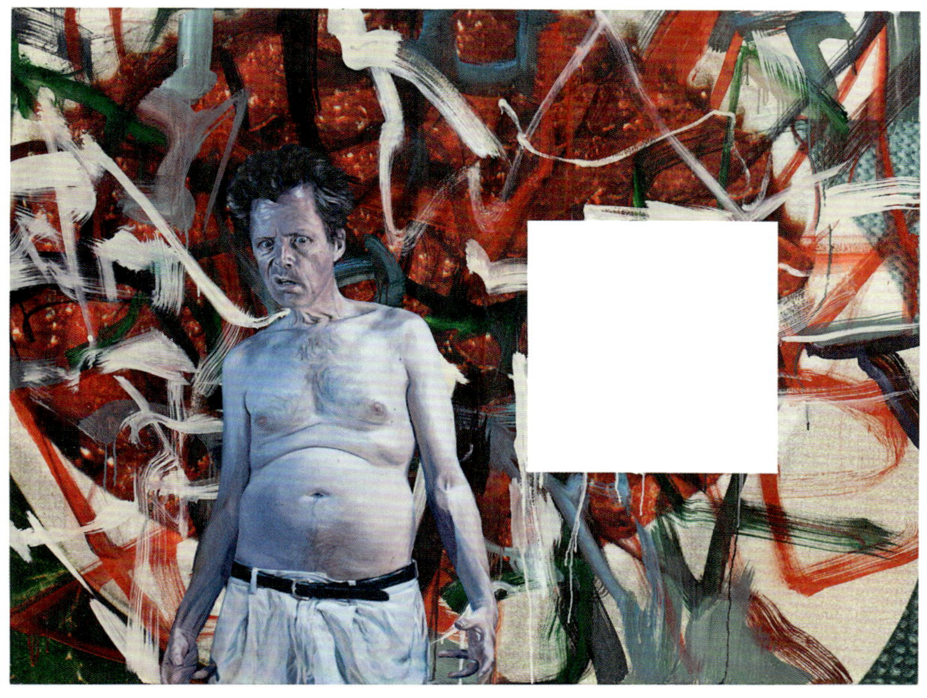 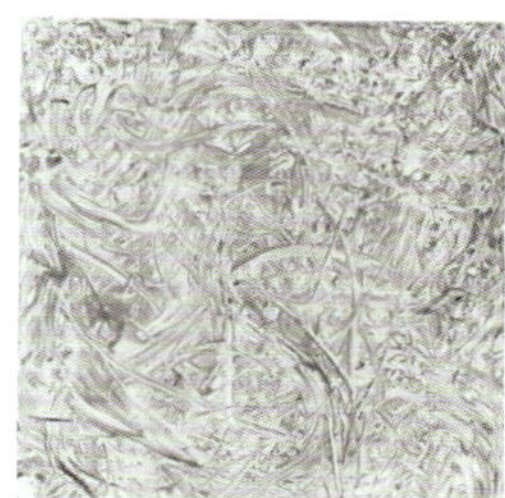

62. Cake (Jim Anger Frustration)   2011

Oil on digital inkjet print and acrylic and ink on panel painting
95.3 × 129.5 cm (37½ × 51 in)
Private collection

fractious space, but all part of a unified illusion. The same is true of the pyramid, all-seeing eye, railroad tracks, banyan tree and upside-down octopus in *D'red Dwarf B'lack Hole* (2010) (fig.59). Likewise, the bluer-than-blue sky of *Capitol Viscera Appliance Mural* (2011) (fig.60) prevents the grid of realistically rendered household appliances from appearing to pop off the picture plane while leaving plenty of room for the mushroom cloud/banyan tree/expanse of meat to occupy center stage.

While Shaw was making Oist and *Left Behind* paintings, he was also painting on raw canvas, combining different techniques and media in works that harked back to the *Distorted Face* paintings he made just before and after graduate school. Shaw's *Cake Paintings* and *Anatomy Weird-ohs* did not begin with the idea that either would be a series. Each started out as an experiment, an exploration with no grand plan – or any plan at all. But several steps were involved, much like the layering that was taking place in his *Left Behind* paintings.

Each of Shaw's *Cake Paintings*, including *Cake (Daniel in Disgust)* (2008) (fig.61) and *Cake (Jim Anger Frustration)* (2011) (fig.62), consists of a large rectangular panel from which he has cut out a rectangular section and set it to the side, forming an unbalanced diptych. On the large panel Shaw has printed a blown-up close-up of a piece of cake. On top of that, he has used oil paint to make de Kooning-esque gestures and Pollock-ish drips. Atop both he has superimposed a realistically rendered image of a shirtless man (his assistant, Daniel Hope, or himself), expressing an extreme emotion. The portrait component came from photographs shot by a photographer in Shaw's studio as he directed both model and photographer. On the extracted rectangle, Shaw has drawn, in pencil, densely webbed abstractions in which he has hidden realistically drawn faces and figures. The combination of digital printing, abstract painting, figurative painting, pencil drawing and quasi-sculptural tableaux-making echoes what Shaw did in *My Mirage*: combine diverse techniques and media in a quasi-encyclopedic overview of his repertoire. But this time, style and subject are more compressed, more condensed, more Shaw – less an homage to his heroes than an emblem of what he does best: bring seemingly unrelated elements together to tell stories that make some kind of sense while never letting you forget that they are only a tiny fraction of the possible stories that might be told.

A similar sort of back-and-forth animates Shaw's *Anatomy Weird-ohs* (figs 64 and 65). Each riffs off of the eight-volume book series *The Ciba Collection of Medical Illustrations*, by Frank H. Netter. Netter was an American surgeon and painter who made 2,300 paintings over his 25-year career. Most illustrate various ailments of the human body and mind. Netter's goal was to teach other physicians how to make accurate diagnoses; to read, as accurately as possible, the external signs of internal illnesses. In Shaw's comic paintings, various bodily organs become cartoon characters – google-eyed creatures struggling to express whatever ails them, whether physical illness, mental distress, psychological trauma or even moral outrage. That was not all that different from what Shaw was up to in his studio, or what anyone else might be doing as they struggled to make sense of society, particularly as it was shaping up in the United States.

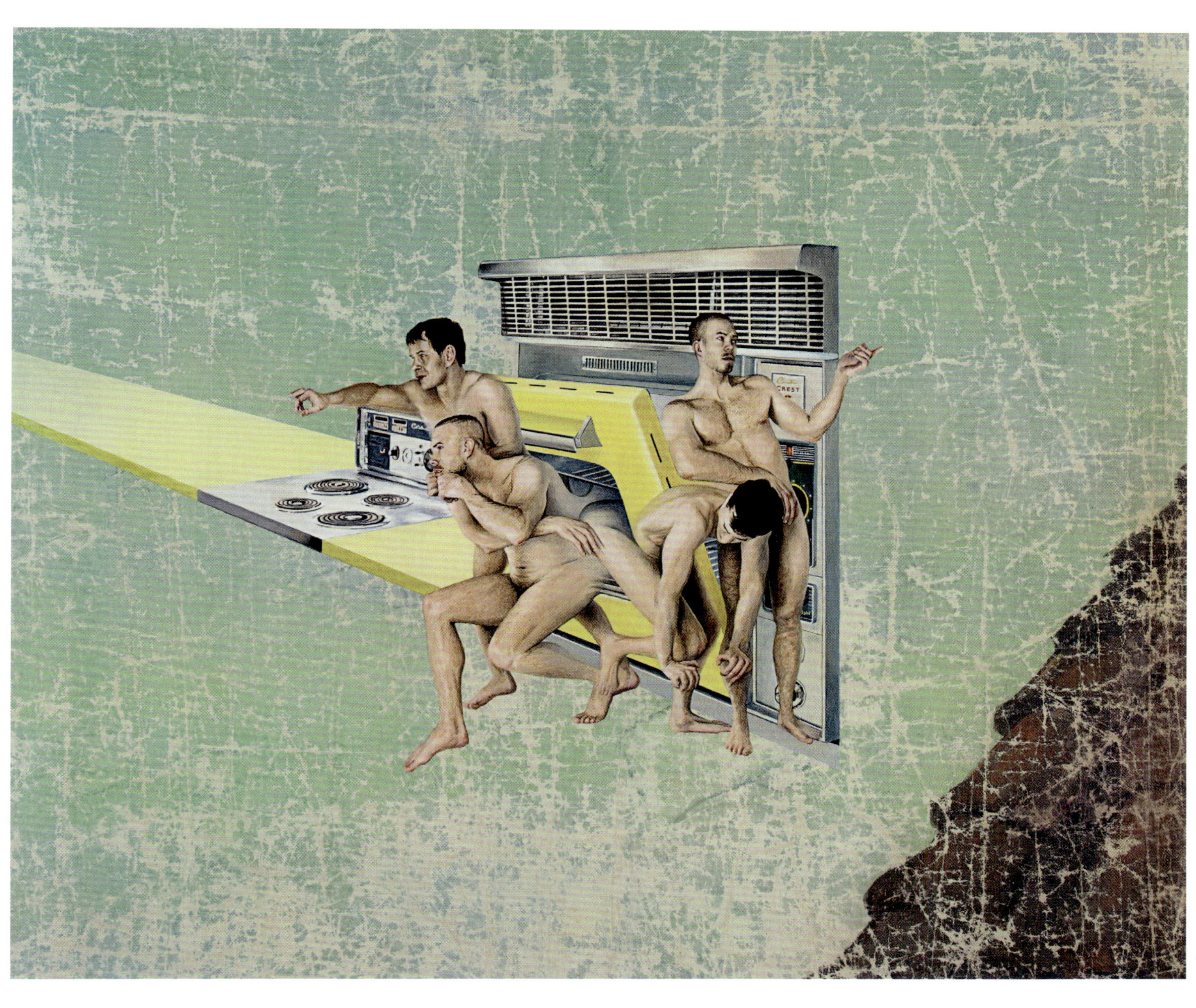

63. The Built In Twins   *2018*

Acrylic on muslin
104.5 × 129.8 cm (41¹⁄₁₀ × 51¹⁄₁₀ in)
Courtesy Simon Lee Gallery

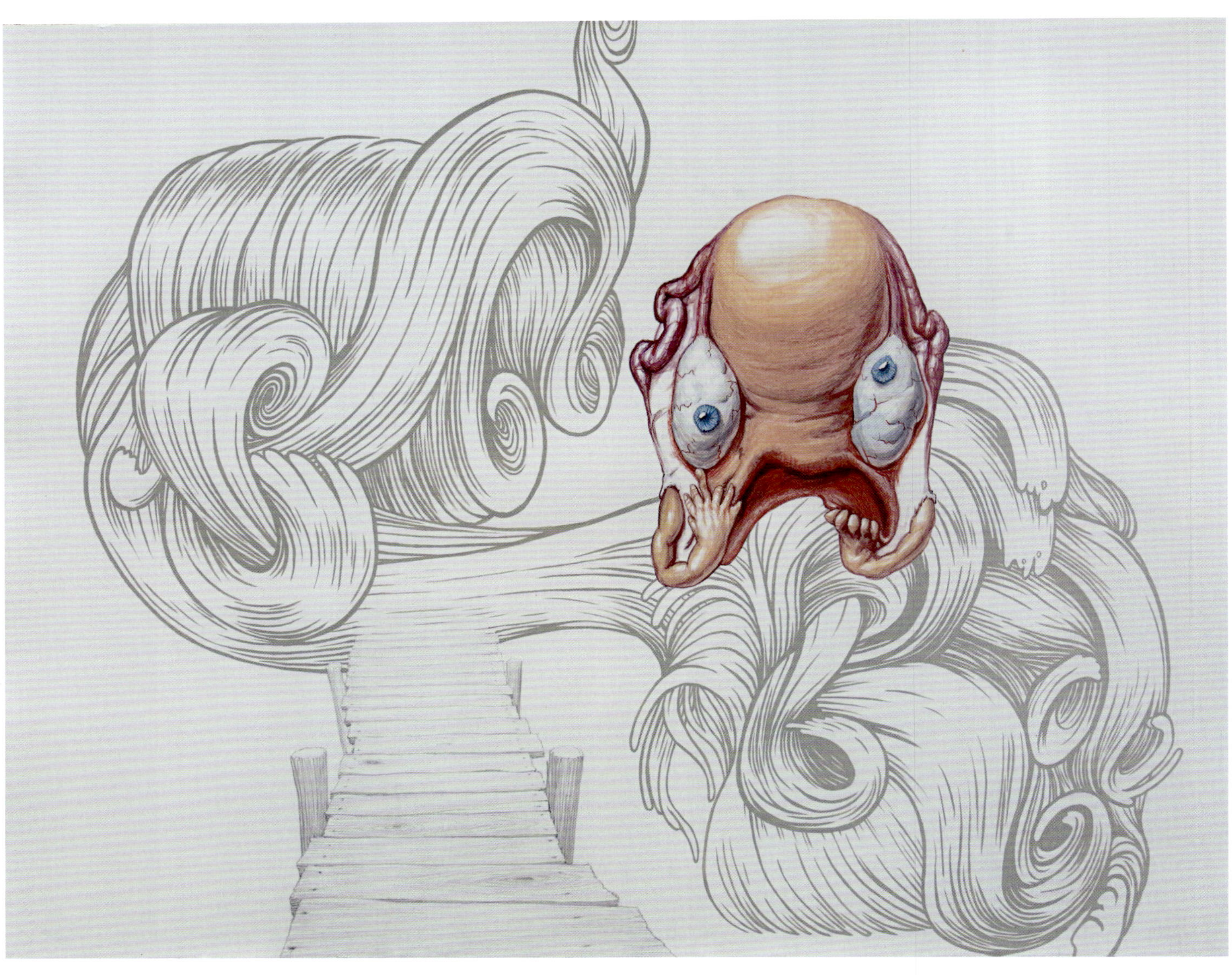

64. Anatomy Weird-oh 2011

Acrylic, graphite and ink on paper
56.2 × 76.2 cm (22½ × 30 in)
Courtesy of the artist and Praz-Delavallade

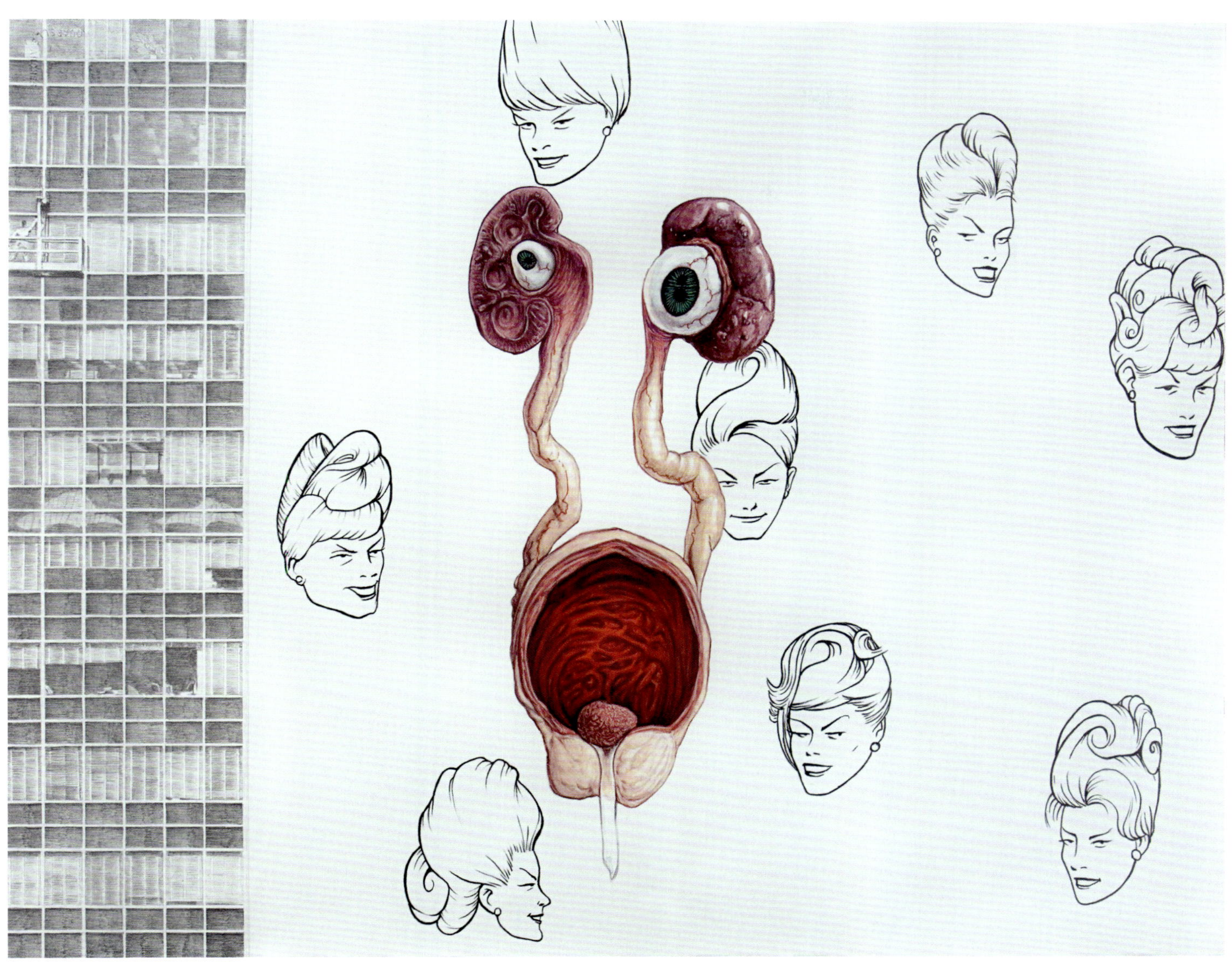

65. Anatomy Weird-oh   2011

Acrylic, graphite on ink on paper
57.2 × 76.5 cm (22½ × 30⅛ in)
Courtesy of the artist and Praz-Delavallade

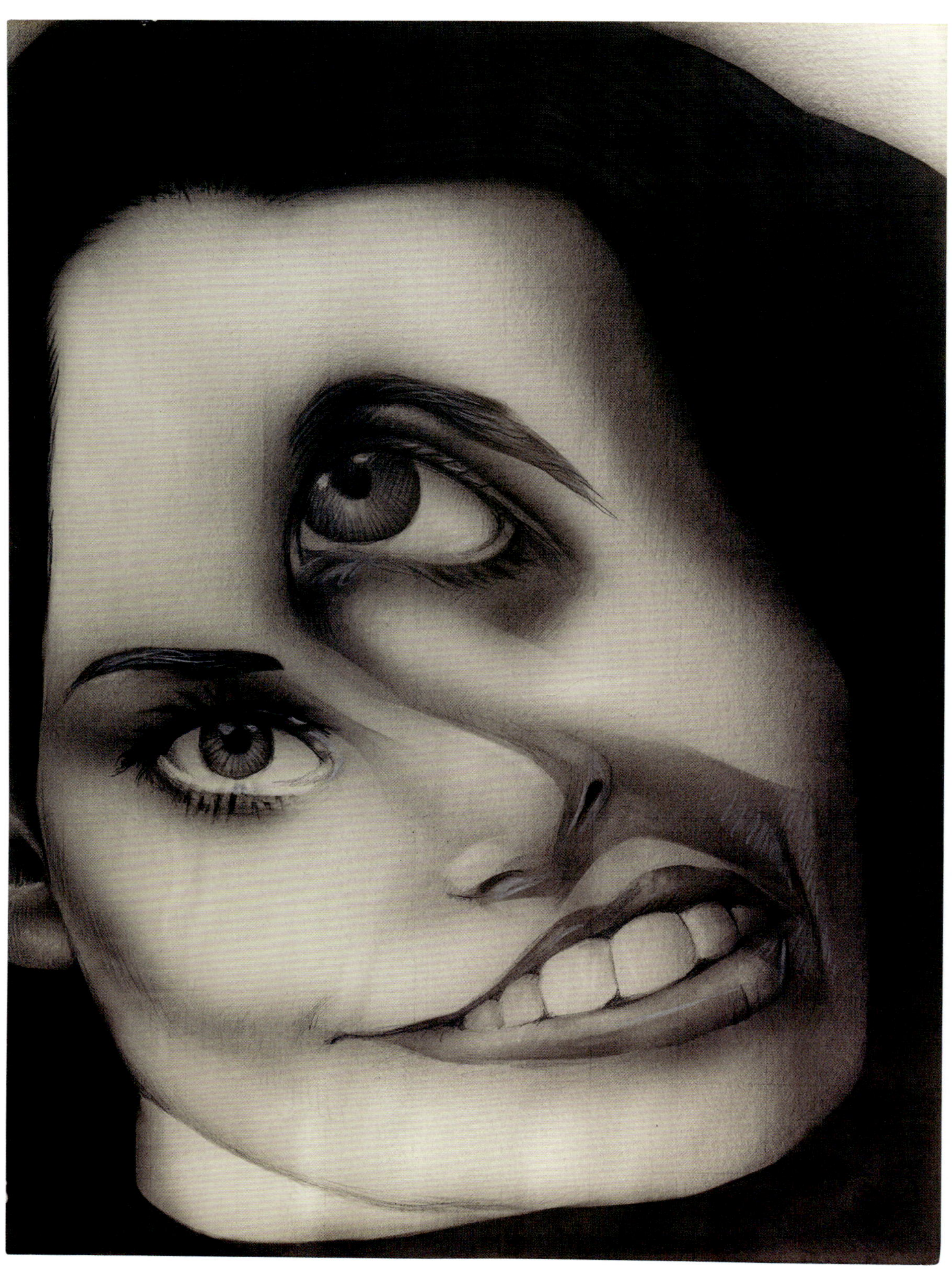

66. Untitled (Distorted Faces series)   1984

Graphite, airbrush and Prismacolor on paper
35.6 × 27.4 cm (14 × 10⅘ in)
Private collection

In the post-crash world of 2012, Shaw felt that his Glendale studio was ridiculously large, so he moved to a strip-mall in Altadena, 14 miles from downtown Los Angeles and directly north of Pasadena. His new studio was closer to the Spanish-style house on Highview Avenue that he and Weber had purchased in 2010, with plans to convert its garage into her studio and its house into his studio. Eventually, Weber discovered that she preferred to work at home, so she set up her studio there and Shaw took over the Highview house and garage. In the meantime, he spent two years in the strip-mall, where he made his last *Left Behind* paintings, folding them over and working on one section at a time, before moving into the Highview house, where he and his assistants have worked since.

Also in 2012, Shaw started to cut some of the muslin backdrops he had collected into rectangular sections and stretch them over wooden bars. That was not the first time he had made paintings. But it would be the first time he stuck to that format for so long – continuing to the present – and so straightforwardly. Although painting played an important role in his *Cake Paintings*, *Anatomical Weird-ohs*, *Irregularly Shaped Canvases* and *Presence sculptures*, it was one media among others – always drawing (in pencil and ink), often sculpting (whether three-dimensional or in low-relief) and sometimes digital printing. It was as if Shaw had been ambivalent about what he did as an artist (illustrate scenes and stories that he found or made up) and what he did as a painter (use brushes and liquid pigments to give bodily presence to those elusive, often hallucinatory visions). Shaw's ambivalence about painting's autonomy, if not purity, can be seen in *Split Head* (2012), *Untitled (Giant Face Paintings)* from 1992, and *Untitled (Distorted Faces)* (figs 66 and 67) from 1979 and 1984, in which he used spray-paint, colored pencil and graphite to make portraits as if seen in funhouse mirrors, the mutant faces linking the queasy feelings of the sitters with the queasiness they elicited in viewers.

Similarly, working on backdrops allowed Shaw to engage painting obliquely. With a brush, he painted additions to preexisting scenes. Never starting from scratch, with a blank canvas, he made adaptations, not sui generis creations or out-of-nothing inventions. That matched what he had been doing in all of his major bodies of work: telling Billy's coming-of-age-tale (by presenting an encyclopedic overview of his own artistic influences); drawing dreams (that had already happened); making objects (out of what appeared in those drawings); and cobbling together a religion (which served as the backdrop for works in a wide variety of media). In a sense, all of Shaw's multi-year projects made art take a back seat to other elements that drove the endeavor.

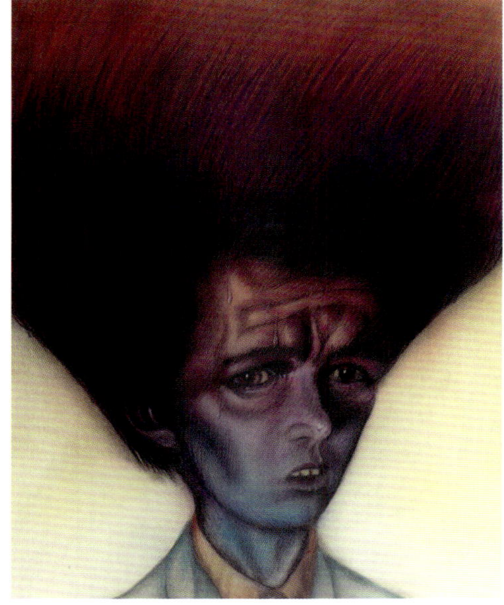

67. Untitled (Distorted Face #4)   1984

Graphite, airbrush and Prismacolor on paper
35 × 26.7 cm (13⅘ × 10½ in)
Private collection

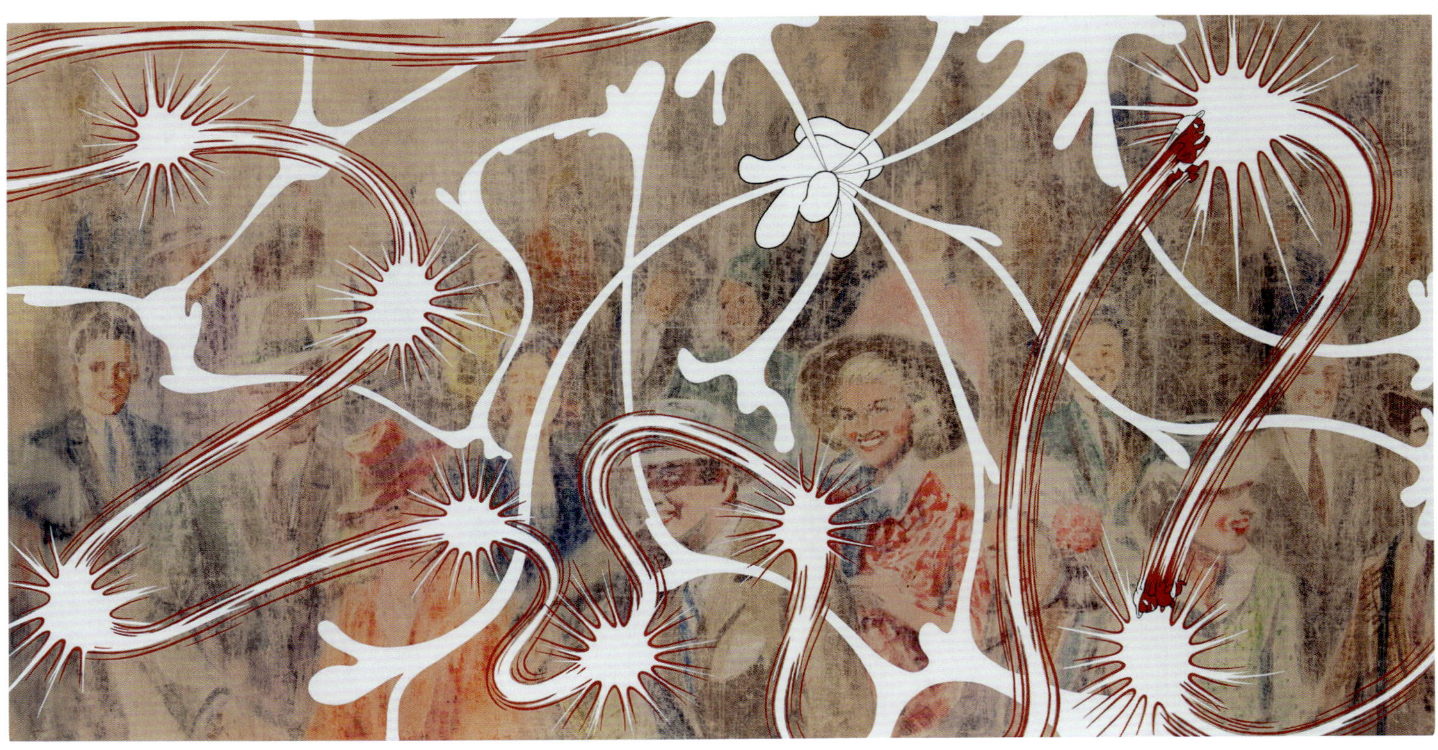

68. Crowd, Devil, Sploosh   2013

Acrylic on muslin
121.9 × 243.8 cm (48 × 96 in)
Collection of Jeffrey Pechter, Venice, CA

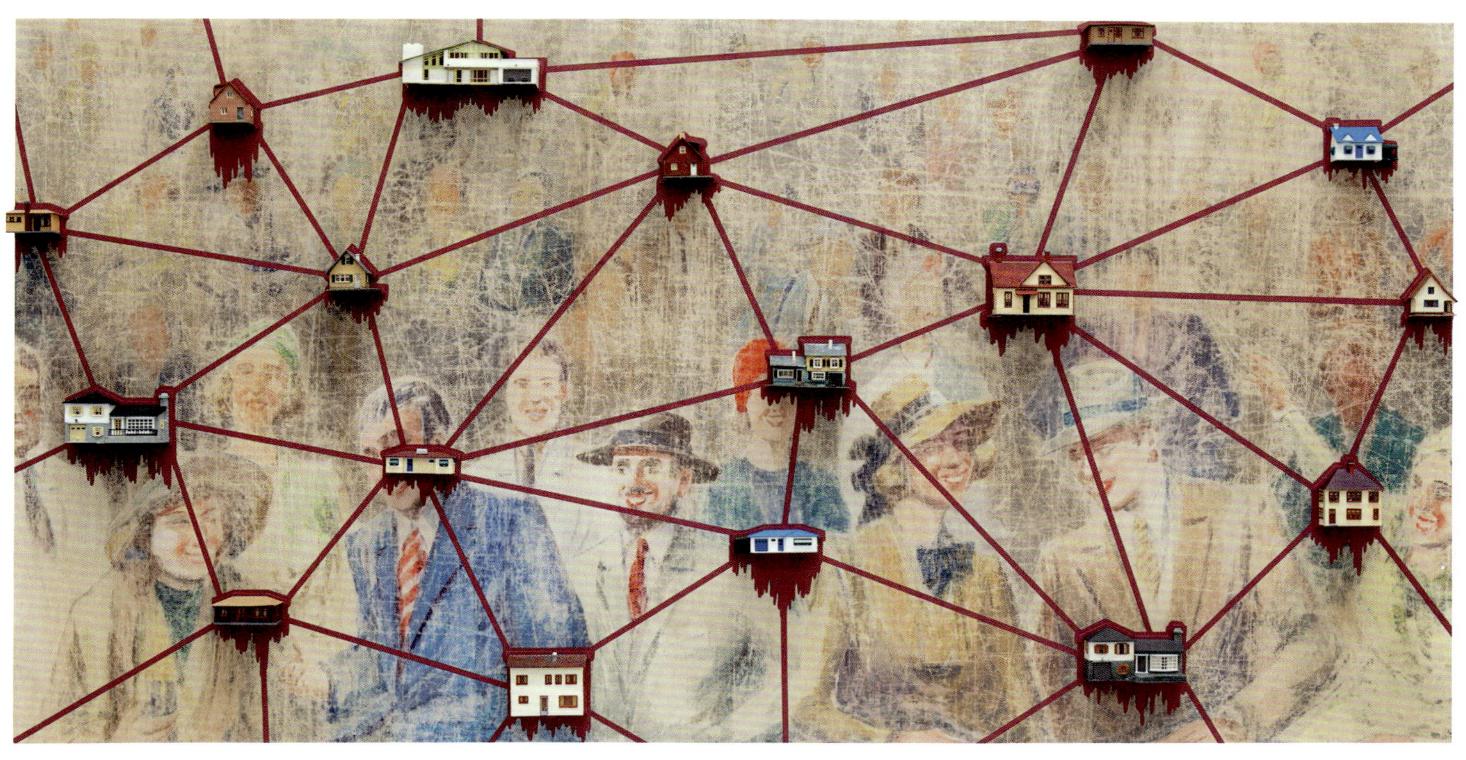

69. Crowd, House, Web   2013

Acrylic, plaster model homes and magnets on muslin
121.9 × 243.8 cm (48 × 96 in)
Courtesy Blum & Poe

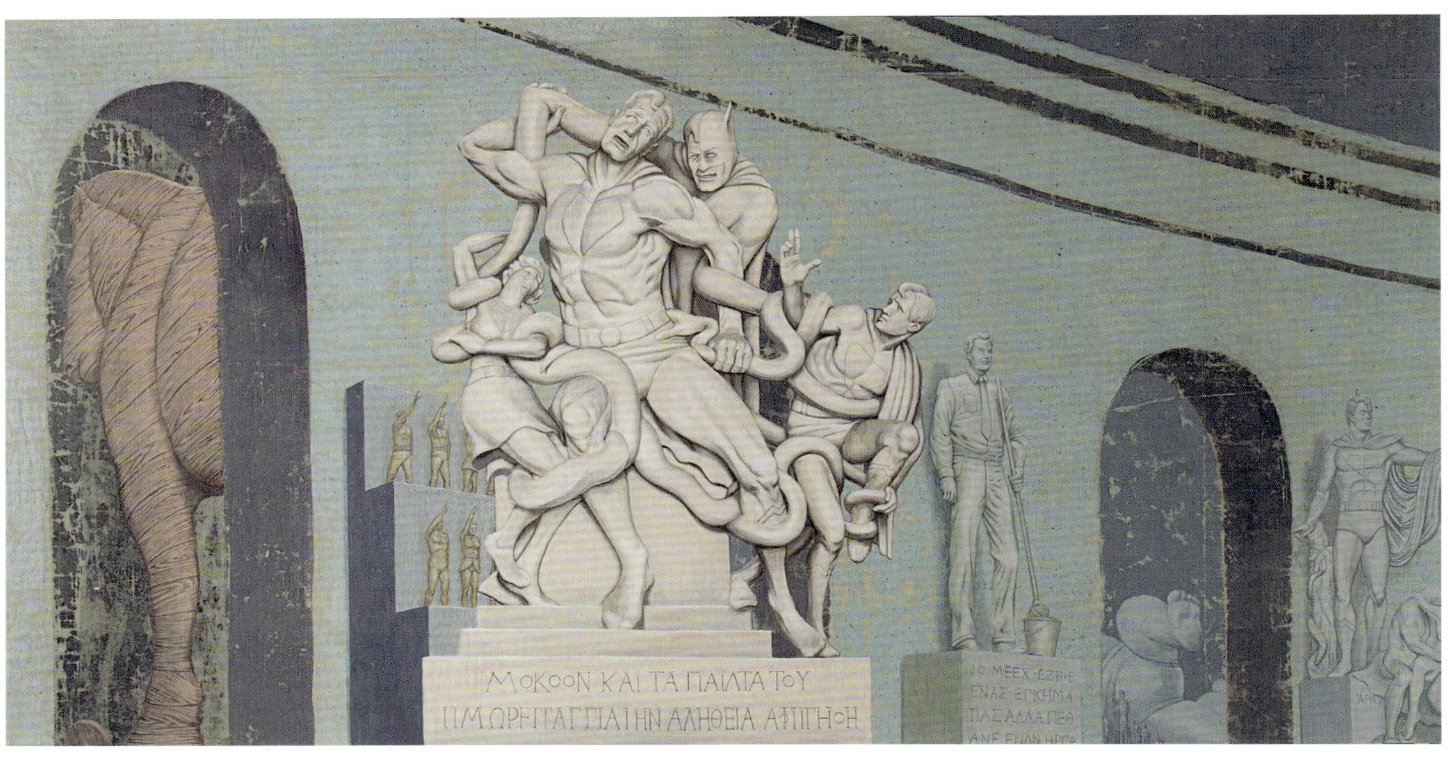

70. Hall of Remembrance   2015

Acrylic on muslin
121.9 × 243.8 cm (48 × 96 in)
Private collection

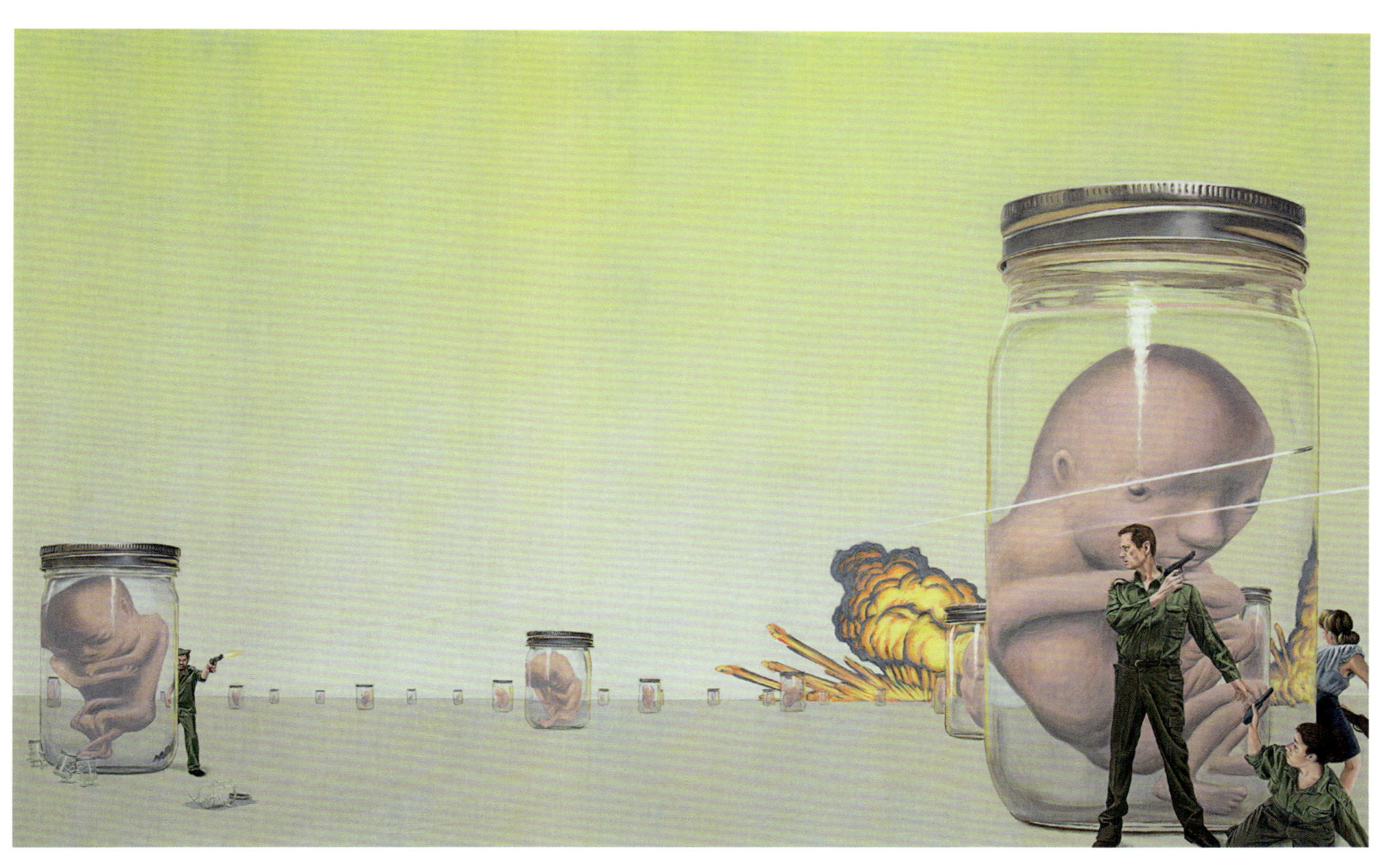

71. Fetuses   2015

Acrylic on muslin
91.4 × 152.4 cm (36 × 60 in)
Courtesy of the artist and Praz-Delavallade

It was as if he had been creating situations in which he could be both client and contractor – the one paying to get a job done and the one hired to do the job. It does not take a great leap of the imagination to see that Shaw was much more comfortable being the latter, working – with his hands, in the studio making things out of stuff – than he was being the boss, coming up with ideas, overseeing the production and evaluating the merits of the works. That 'conceptual' part of art-making was not hardwired into his DNA. But, being a pragmatist, and never one to complain, he accepted its necessity and made the best of it, going to great lengths to work like an illustrator illustrating someone else's stories in a world that presumed art was best when it was 'original' – when it told its own stories and, even better, when it was all about itself. Shaw managed to make powerful works by going through the side-door, sneaking into the sanctum of painting without using the front entrance.

Working on previously painted swathes of stretched muslin made it easier for him to get past his antipathy for blank canvases. He states plainly, 'I don't like white. I have a problem with it.'5 But as Shaw proceeded, the importance of the subjects and settings previously painted on the theatrical backdrops diminished – literally got left behind. Sometimes Shaw stretched sections from which so much of the paint had crumbled away that only the barest traces of an image could be seen. At others, he used sections with no imagery, just abstract expanses of modulated colors or muted, nearly monochrome fields. At still others, the images he added covered most of the surface, making it impossible to know what was originally there. All gave Shaw more space to do his own thing, to paint pictures unconstrained by pre-established setups.

If Shaw's ambivalence about being an artist (and making paintings) lessened in his stretched muslin paintings, that new-found clarity went hand-in-hand with his realization that he did not have to invent any kind of supporting backstory to make his works conceptually legitimate; capturing even a fraction of the absurdity of the world they inhabited would be enough to give them force and traction. Shaw's lifelong interest in conspiracy theories, fringe religions, overlooked oddities and the slippery relationship between fact and fiction found its partner in the political landscape of 21st-century America, where reality was getting so weird and surreal that his once over-the-top propositions about aliens and politicians and religions began to look a lot less far-fetched – if not perfectly reasonable, certainly as effective a way to tell the truth as any other in a world in which the very idea of truthfulness was under fire, up for grabs, threatened with extinction. In Shaw's words:

> I just think that there is a great deal of insanity in the world, but a lot of it is
> societal, a lot of it's based on sociopathic corporate culture. Then you have
> the truly insane schizophrenics, some of whom just live in a bubble and may
> have been shamans in a different time and place. I guess I'm trying to become
> something like that. I'm trying to open up the channels to whatever . . . In this
> sense Blake would be a kind of strange ideal . . . He died in poverty but he was

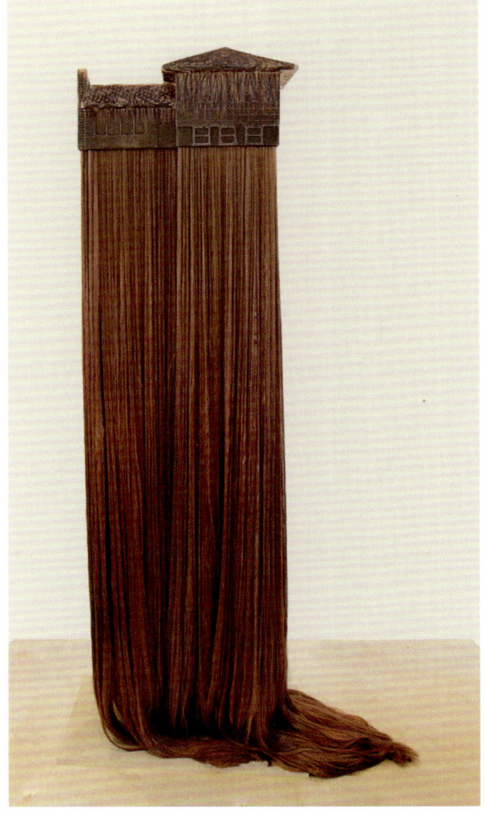

72. Hair House #2   2014

Epoxy resin, synthetic hair, plexiglass, fiberglass, welded steel, wood
185.4 × 50.8 × 27.9 cm (73 × 20 × 11 in)
Private collection

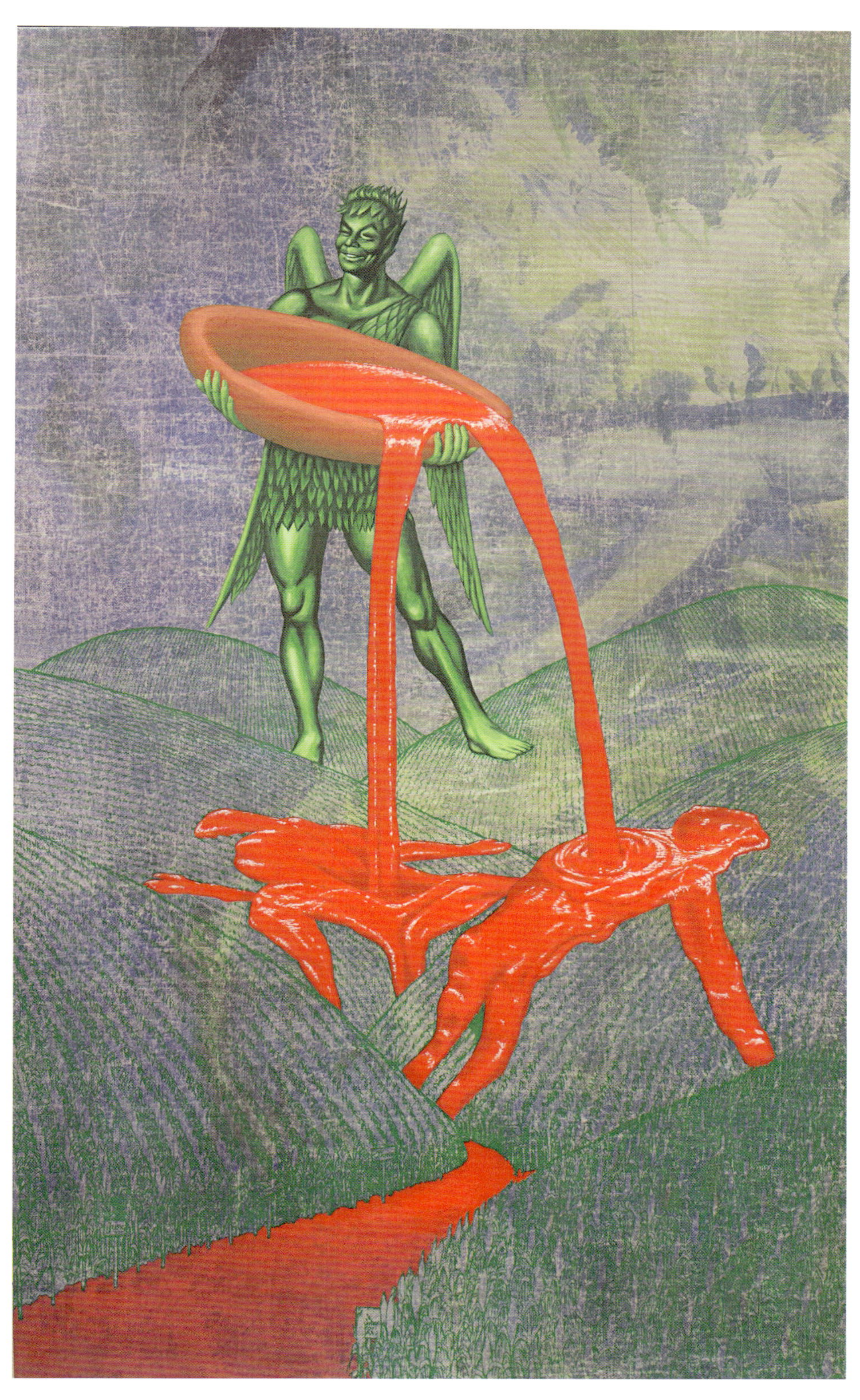

73. The Third Angel   2015

Acrylic on muslin
182.9 × 114.3 cm (72 × 45 in)
Courtesy Simon Lee Gallery

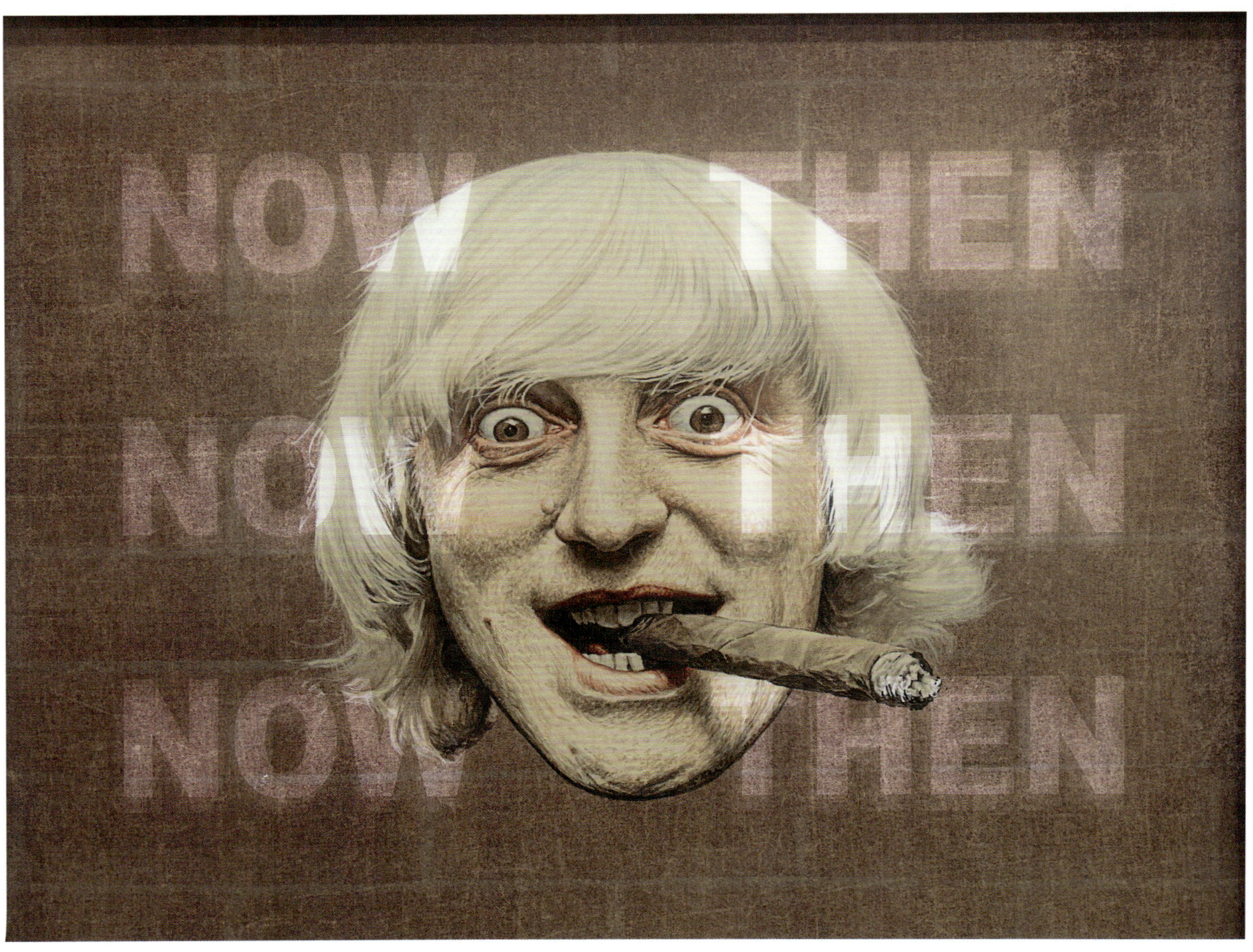

74. Beware the Eyes That Hypnotize   2017

Acrylic on muslin with vinyl text overlay; plexi and wood frame
48.3 × 63.5 cm (19 × 25 in)
Private collection

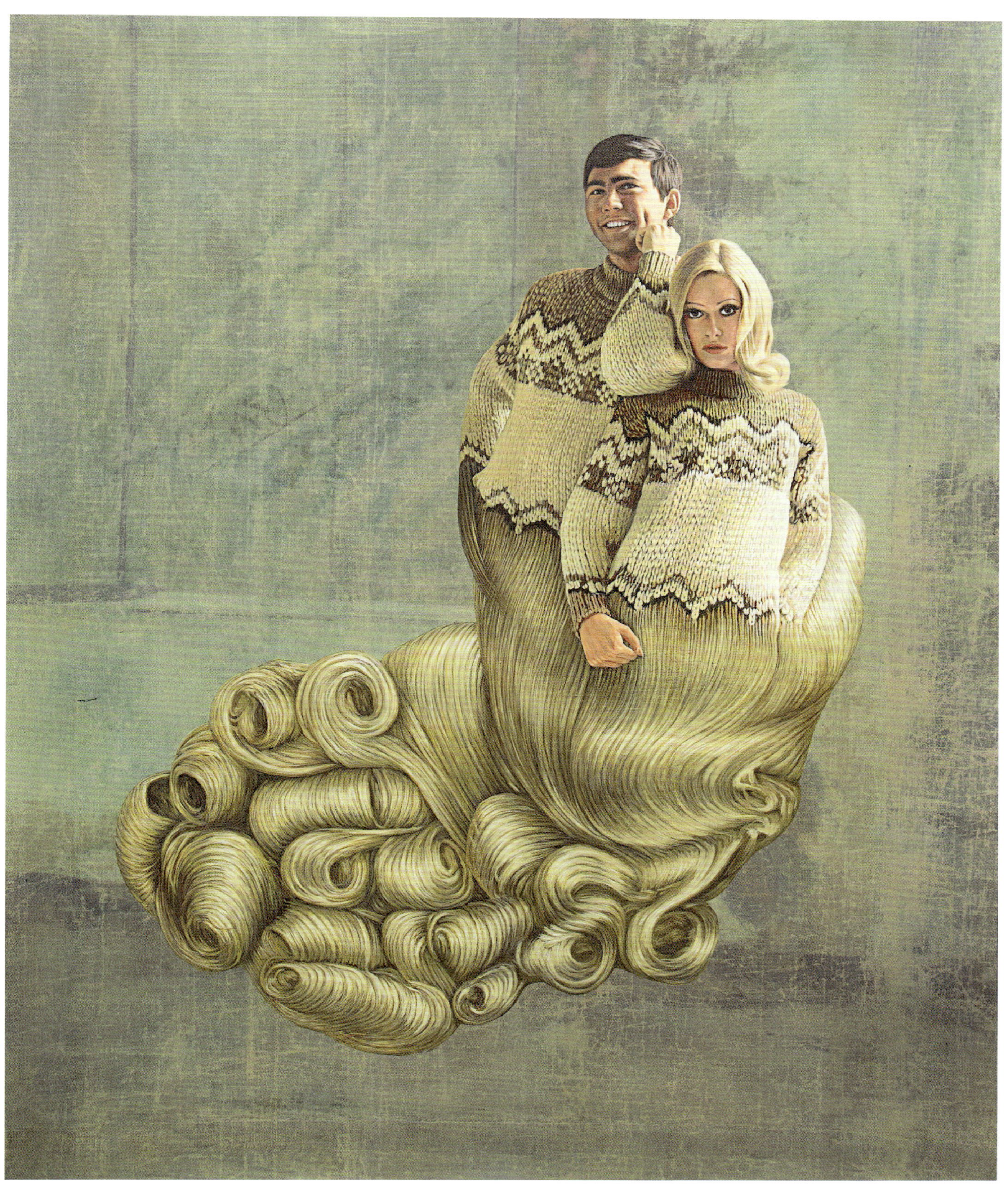

75. **The Ties That Bind**   2017

Acrylic on muslin
167.6 × 157.5 cm (48 × 62 in)
Collection of Maurice and Paul Marciano

107

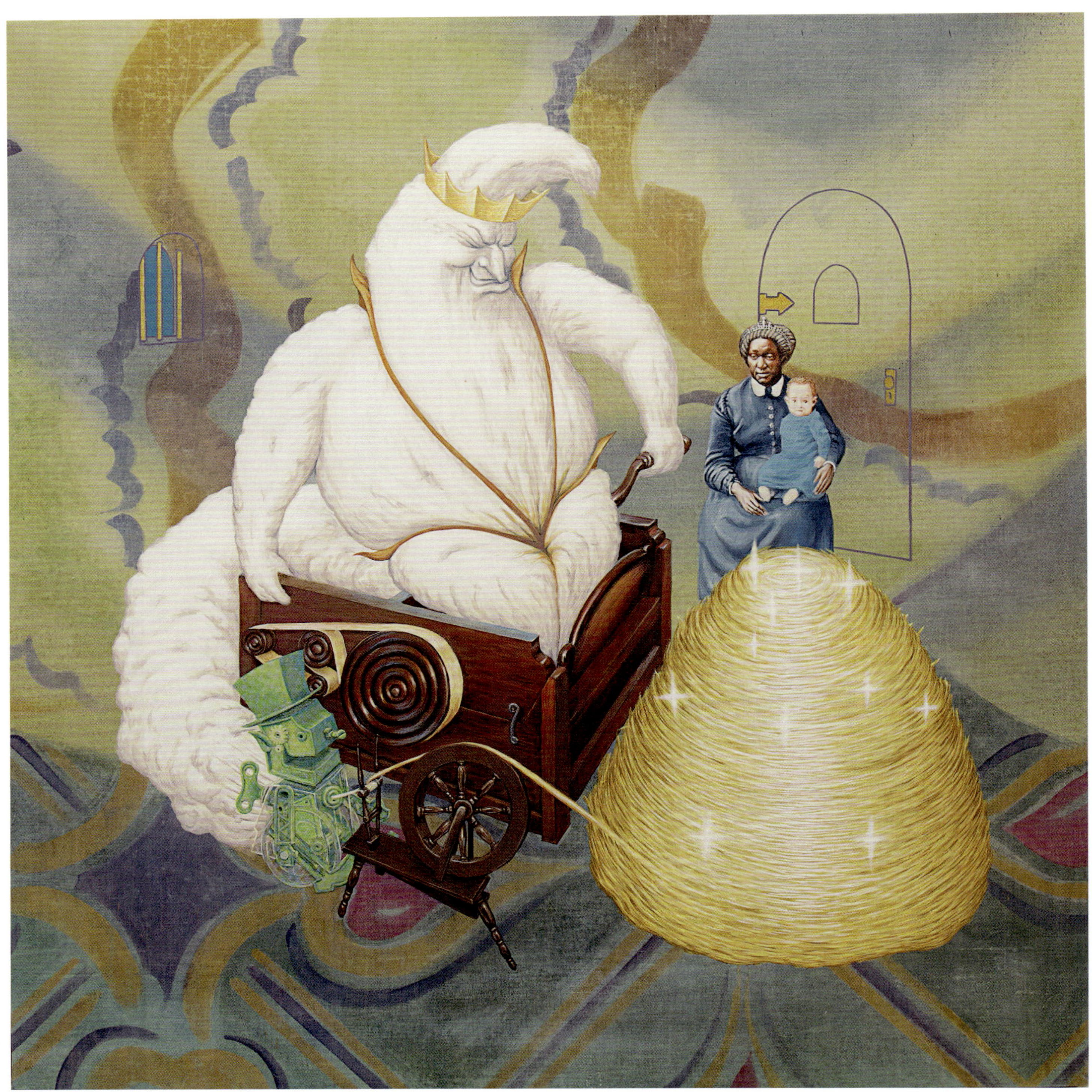

76. King Cotton   2015

Acrylic on muslin
121.9 × 121.9 cm (48 × 48 in)
Private collection, Lebanon

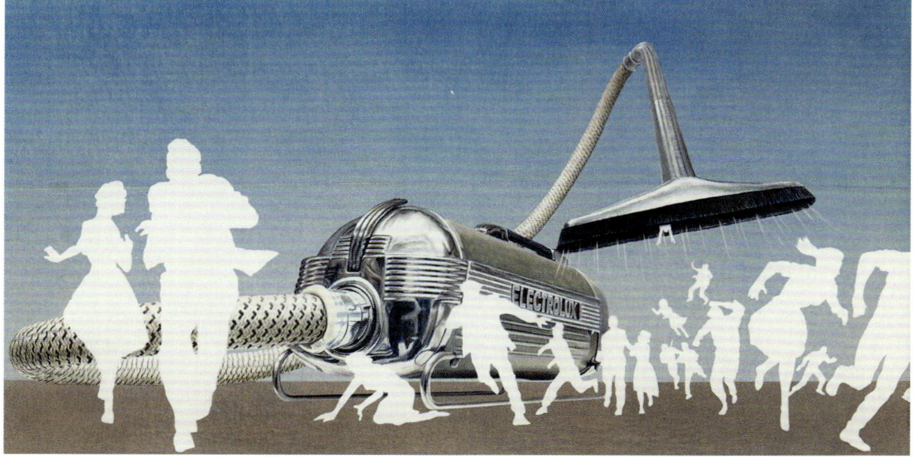

a great visionary, a kind of fiery prophet of doom. I'm not a genius like him or like
Rudolf Steiner, but at least I can at some level try to emulate them.[6]

In a nation presided over by a reality TV has-been/double-dealing real-estate mogul
who holds court on Twitter, Shaw's stretched muslin canvases not only hold their
own against the maddening parade of preposterousness that spills from the endless
news-cycle, they also fight back. They turn the insanity inside out, creating confusion
not to get individuals to betray their own interests, but to get us to figure things out
for ourselves, to see the vileness of the increasingly stage-managed democracy in the
United States for what it is and to do something about it.

The link – between open-ended aimlessness and self-discovery, or anarchistic
rambling and self-determination – can be seen in the variety of subjects Shaw has engaged
in his stretched muslin paintings. This group of works is not a series. It is a loose cluster
of works that may, one day, coalesce into two or three or four series, but, since 2012, has
remained undefined, like a laid-back alliance organized only in terms of its materials
– muslin and paint – and not in terms of idea or theme, such as a mirage, a dream or a
religion. That looseness has allowed Shaw to skip from topic to topic, using painting as a
free space for the freewheeling, stream-of-consciousness associations that are his specialty
and modus operandi. Touching on 19th- and 20th-century politics, Biblical and Greek
myths, outdated advertisements and old-fashioned cartoons, as well as modern art history
and contemporary pop culture, Shaw's stretched muslin paintings play fast and loose with
the idea that a body of work is supposed to be limited to a single set of issues.

Shaw refers to some of his stretched muslin paintings as 'Man-Machine' paintings.
One of these is *Official Portrait #2 (Man Machine)* (2018) (fig.78), which depicts a
19th-century robber baron made anonymous by the upside-down drill press that has
replaced his face. Offshoots of this group include *The Sheep Machine* (2018) (fig.79)
and *Mechanical Mother and Son* (2018) (fig.80), both of which take viewers back to the

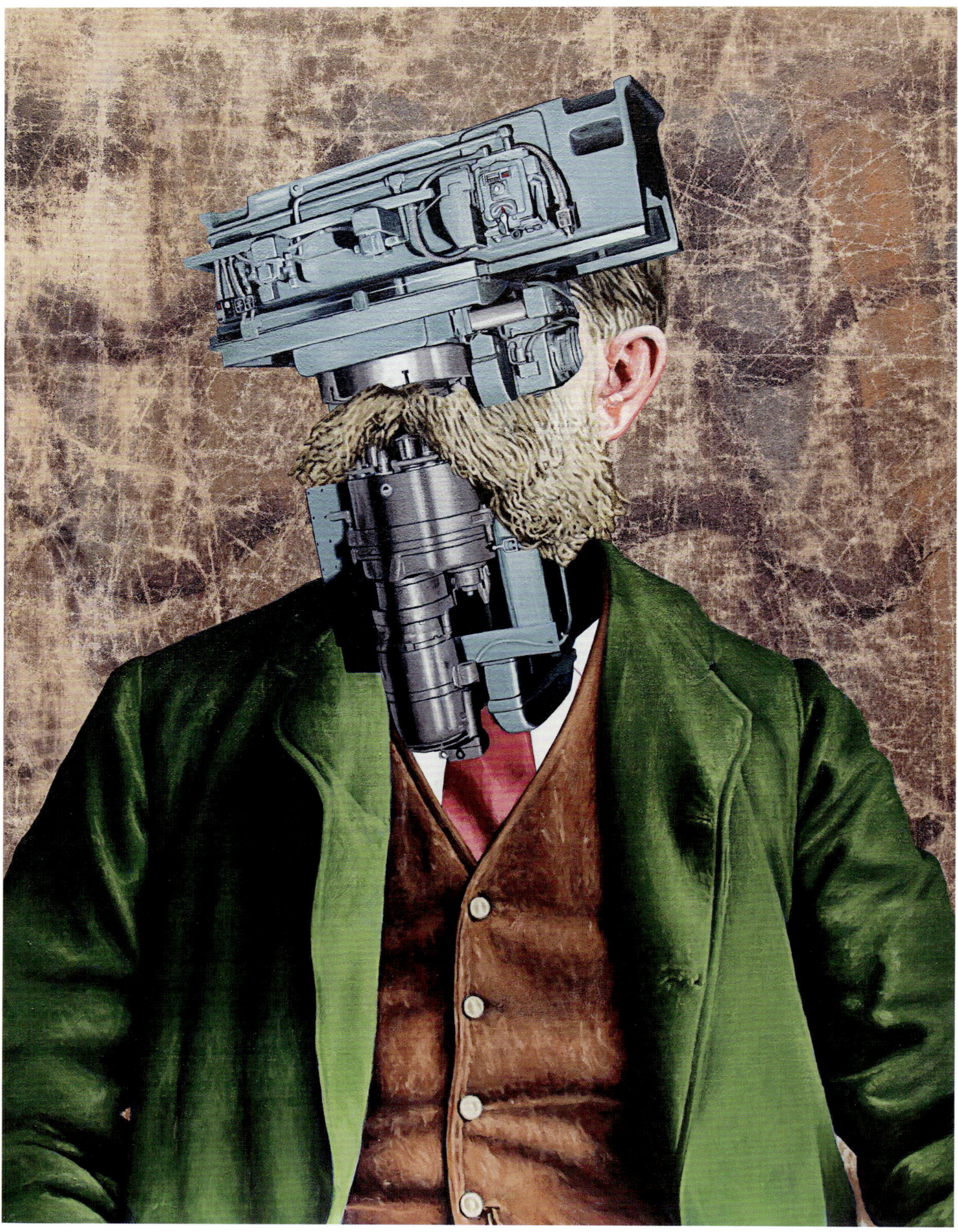

78. Official Portrait #2 (Man Machine)   2018

Acrylic on muslin
71.1 × 56 cm (28 × 22 in)
Private collection

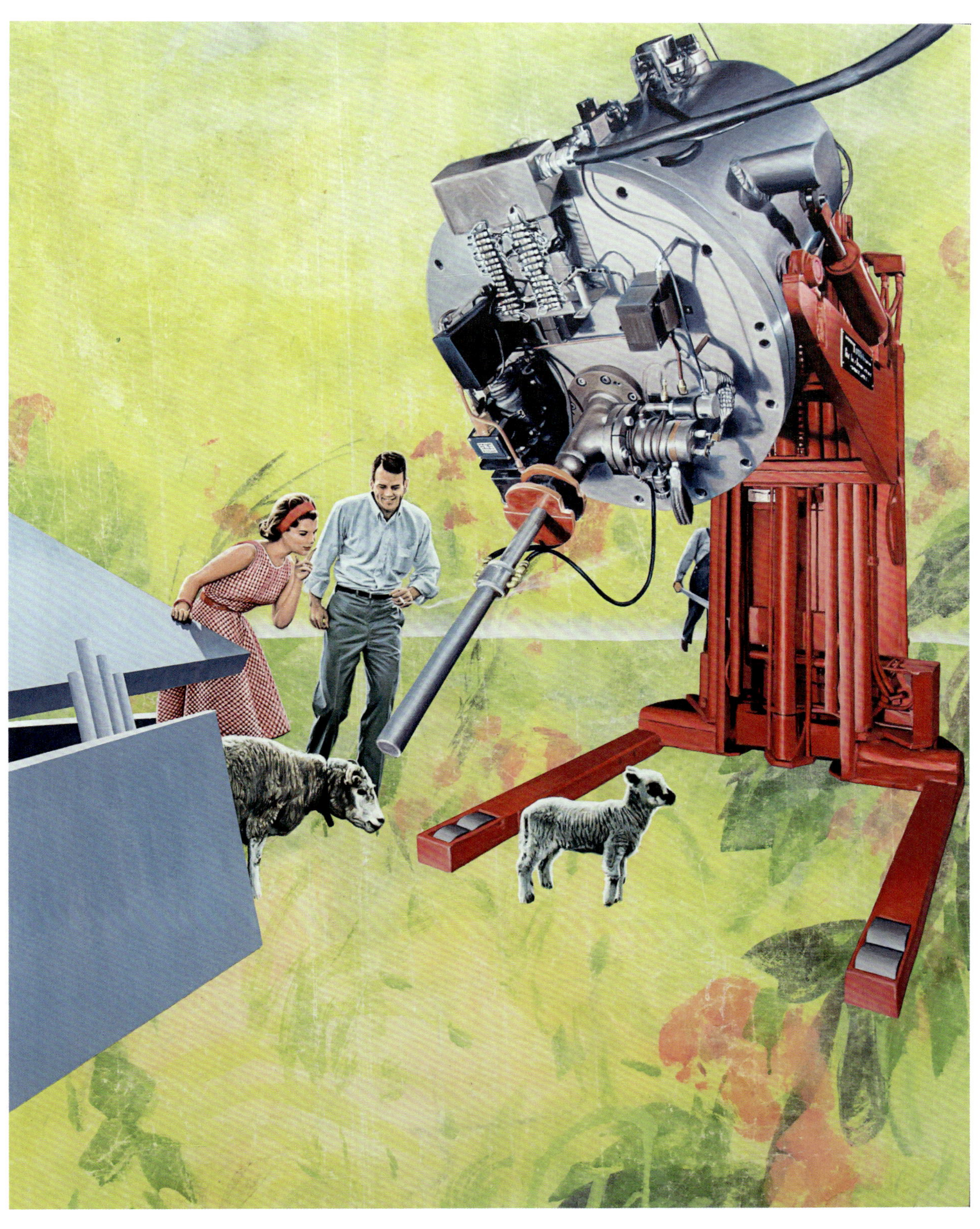

79. A Couple, Sheep, and Machine   2018

Acrylic on muslin
114.3 × 94 (45 × 37 in)
Courtesy Blum & Poe

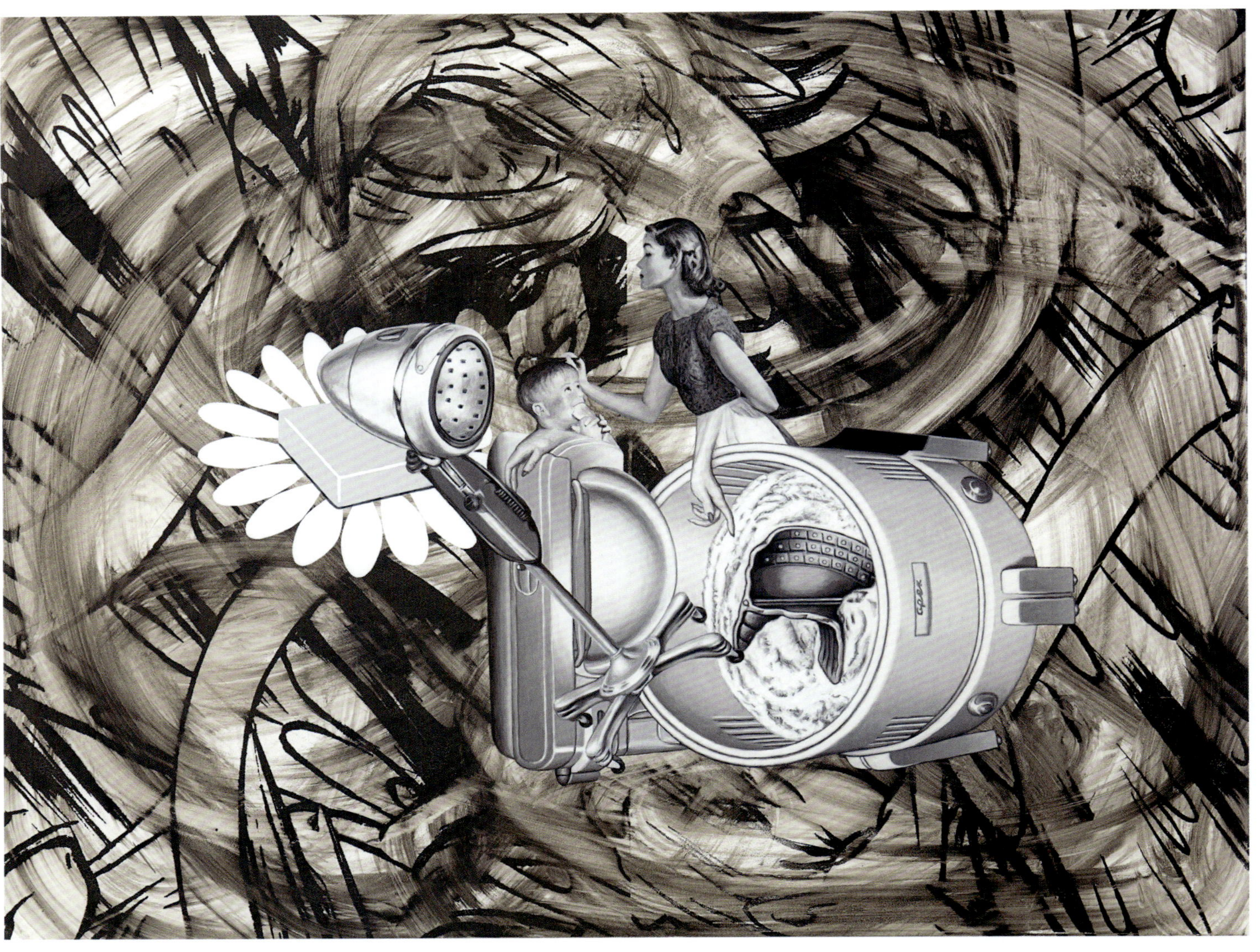

80. Mechanical Mother and Son   2018

Acrylic on board
76.2 × 101.6 cm (30 × 40 in)
Courtesy Blum & Poe

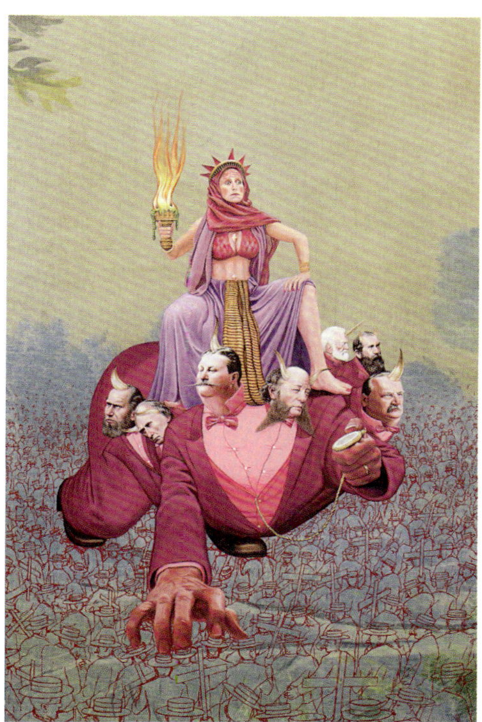

81. *Whore of Babylon + Robber Barons*   2015

Acrylic on muslin
182.9 × 121.9 cm (72 × 48 in)
Theodoros Karathodoros collection

time of Shaw's childhood to suggest that postwar prosperity was more menacing than it was made out to be, both when it was new and, more recently, as it has become a nostalgic, politically tinged fantasy.

Shaw calls another cluster of images 'Men's Facial Hair' paintings. These include *The Octopus* (2015) (fig.82), a portrait of Leland Stanford as a railroad tycoon whose tentacles extend all over the American West, and *The Cremation of Care* (2016) (fig.83), a portrait of Charles Crocker, whose company, Central Pacific Railroad, built the westernmost section of the nation's first transcontinental railroad. Shaw painted the latter in the style of Jan Toorop (1858–1928), a Dutch-Indonesian painter who combined symbolism and art nouveau. In Crocker's portrait, Shaw riffed off of Toorop's sinuous figures, smuggling into their streamlined elegance references to behind-the-scene deals made at The Bohemian Club in San Francisco and to the souls of Chinese and Irish laborers, who were exploited to death as the transcontinental railroad made its owners rich.

A third, and growing, cluster of works is referred to by Shaw as his 'Oligarch Paintings'. These include a two-part piece, *Decapitated Okapi 1* and *Decapitated Okapi 2* (2014) (fig.84), and *Whore of Babylon + Robber Barons* (2015) (fig.81). In the right panel of the diptych, Shaw has isolated, in the manner of his *Fake Dream Drawings*, the decapitated head of an okapi, a mammal indigenous to the Democratic Republic of the Congo and, in Oism, a version of the Anti-Christ. In the left panel, the okapi's body stands naturally, its missing head having grown back, Hydra-style, into an eight-headed beast. The mutant creature has the presence of an upside-down, ass-backwards octopus, its head replaced by the striped backside of the okapi and the tips of its tentacles sprouting the heads of 19th-century politicians, bankers and industrialists, including James Gordon Bennett, William M. Tweed, Leland Stanford, Henry Clay Frick, J.P. Morgan, William Jennings Bryan and Henry Huttleston Rogers. In *Whore of Babylon + Robber Barons*, the Statue of Liberty appears to have come to life as a belly dancer who is both shocked and appalled to find herself astride a seven-headed, ten-horned beast, like the one from the Book of Revelation, as it crawls over a crowd of men at a political convention. The seven-headed beast is also a group portrait of the men who controlled the United States in the Gilded Age, in the late 19th century, when income disparity was at its highest point in American history (until now, when economic inequity is so extreme that it makes the rapacious greed of the robber barons look modest). From left to right, Shaw has portrayed Allan Pinkerton, Anson P. Morrill, 'Diamond Jim' Fisk, Cornelius Vanderbilt, Grover Cleveland, Jason 'Jay' Gould and Andrew Carnegie.

As always with Shaw, those three groups of paintings are outnumbered by uncategorizable outliers, wickedly independent pictures that invite double takes – and then some.

In *Seven Deadly Sins* (2013) (figs 85 and 86), Shaw has transformed the facade of a home and its white-picket-fenced yard into a backdrop for seven meticulously rendered vignettes. Each of his representations of the deadly sins combines a misbegotten mélange of references. One melds, in miniature, Théodore Géricault's

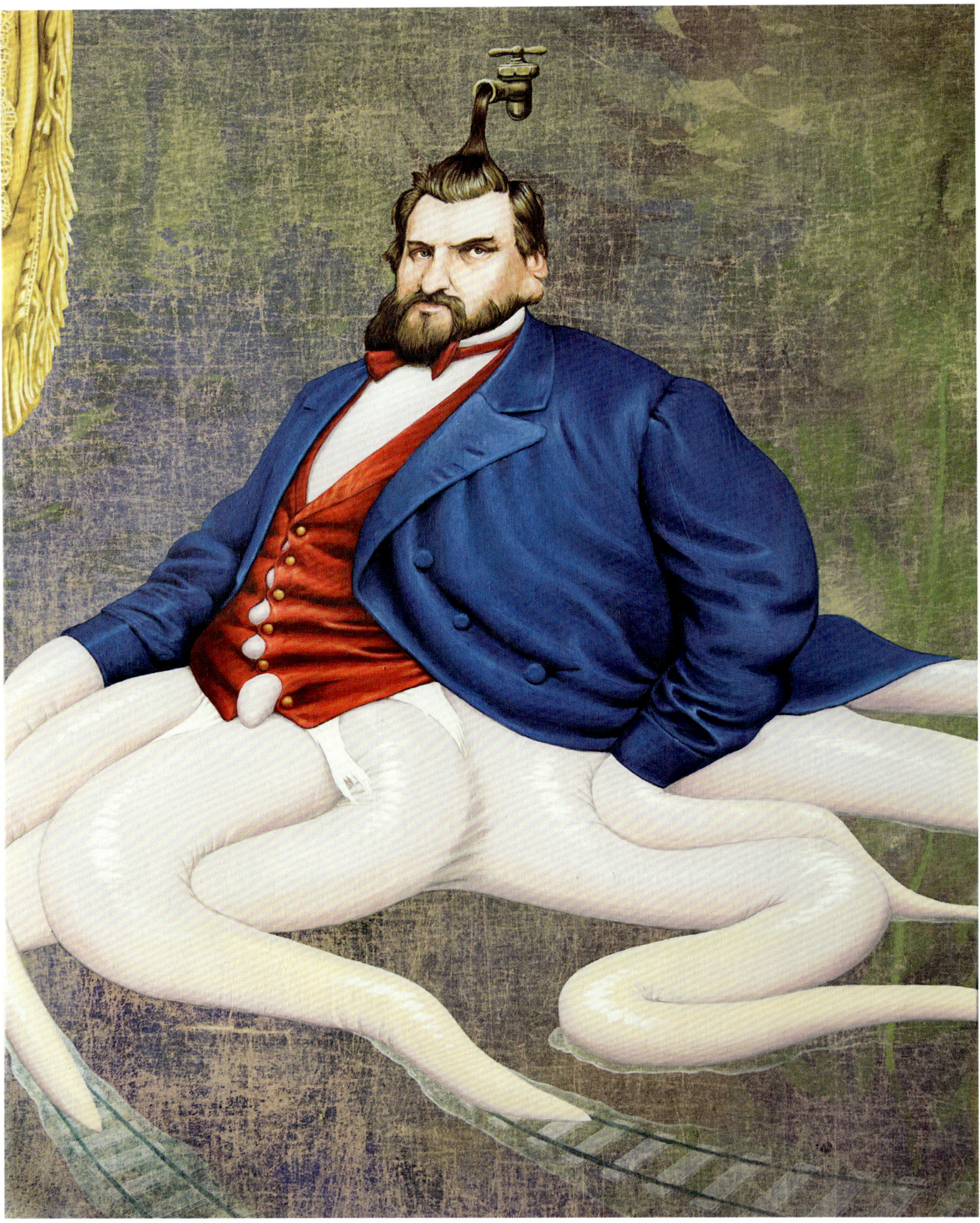

82. The Octopus   2015

Acrylic on muslin
167.6 × 96.5 cm (48 × 38 in)
Private collection

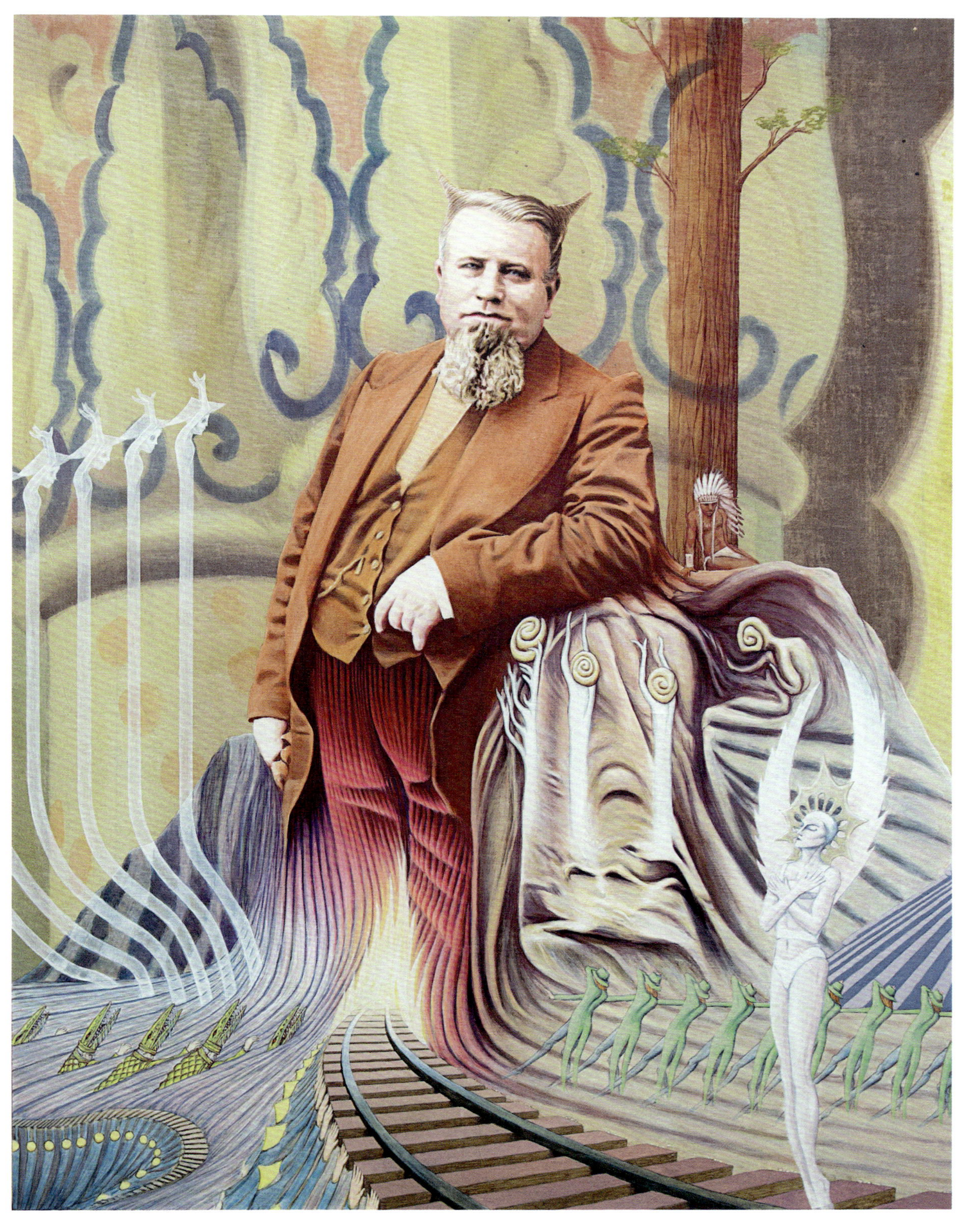

83. The Cremation of Care   2016

Acrylic on muslin
167.6 × 96.52 cm (48 × 38 in)
Courtesy Metro Pictures

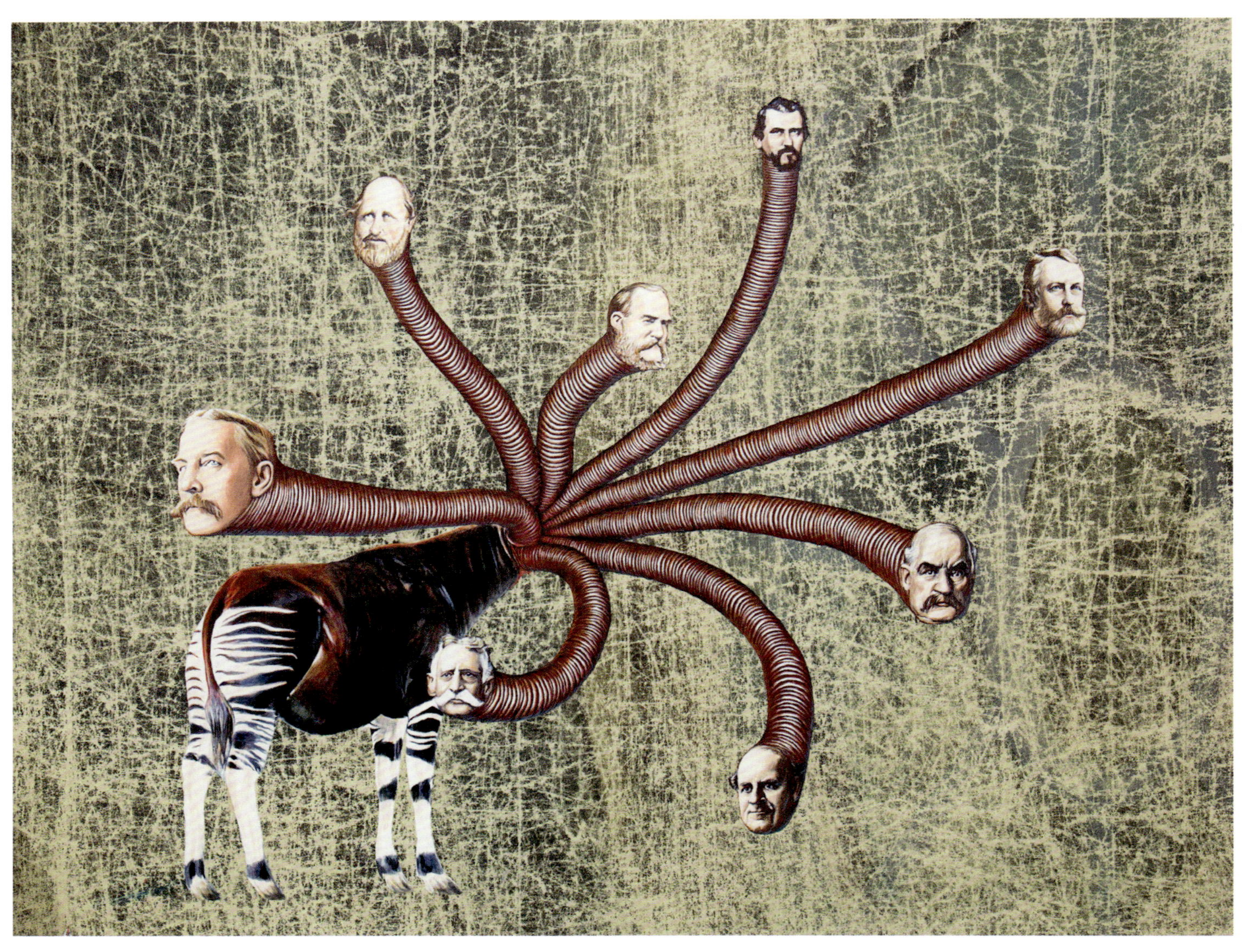

84. Decapitated Okapi 1;
Decapitated Okapi 2 (diptych)

2014

Acrylic on muslin
Left panel: 61 × 121.9 cm (26 × 48 in);
Right panel: 61 × 66 cm (24 × 26 in)
Courtesy Simon Lee Gallery

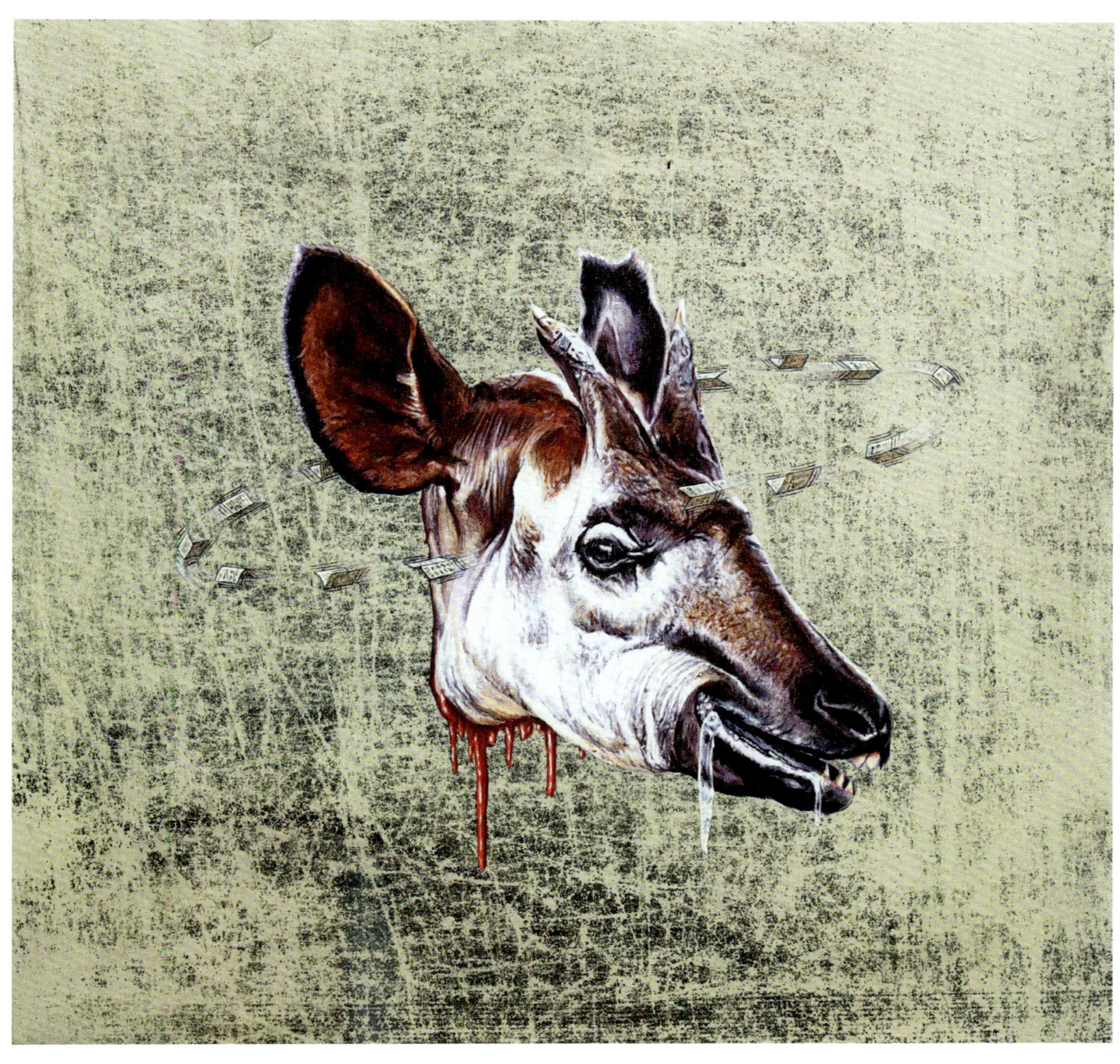

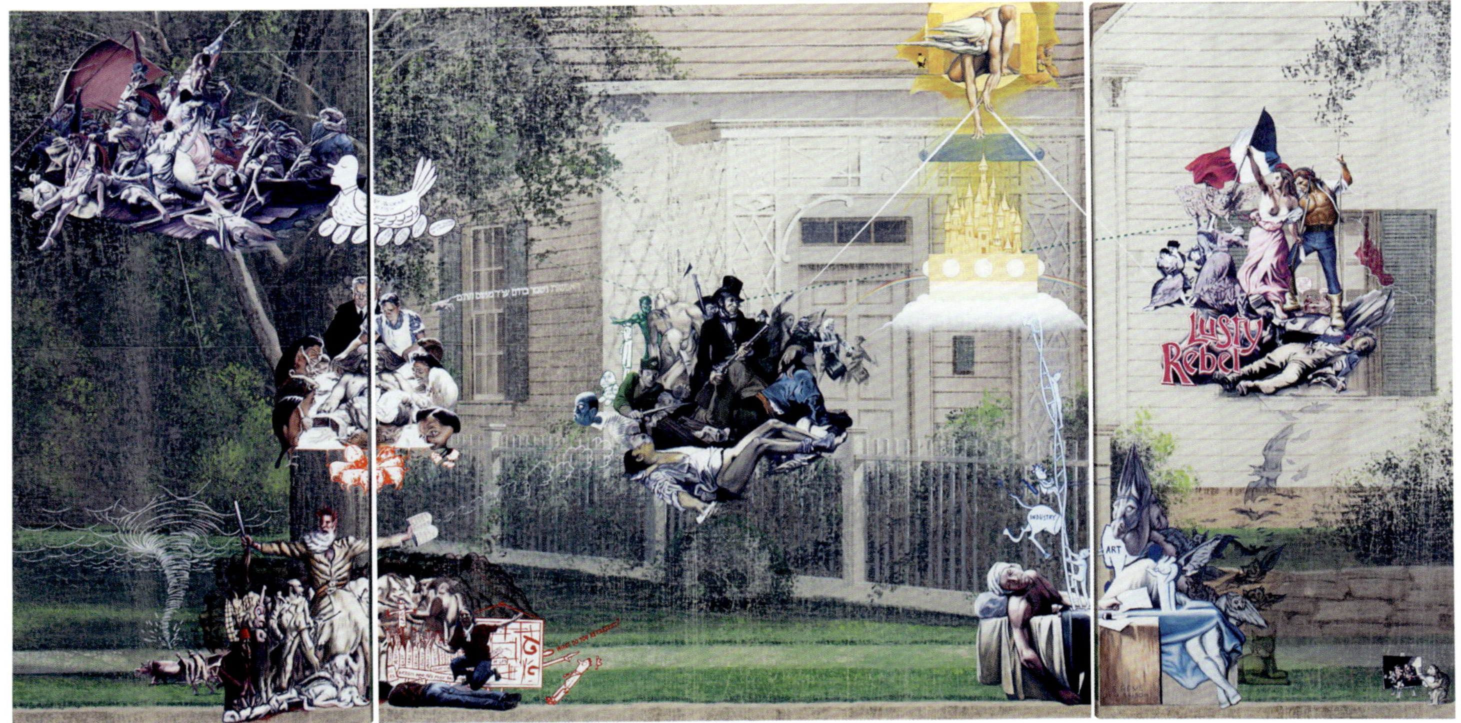

85. Seven Deadly Sins   2013

Acrylic on muslin
243.8 × 492.8 cm (96 × 194 in)
Courtesy Blum & Poe

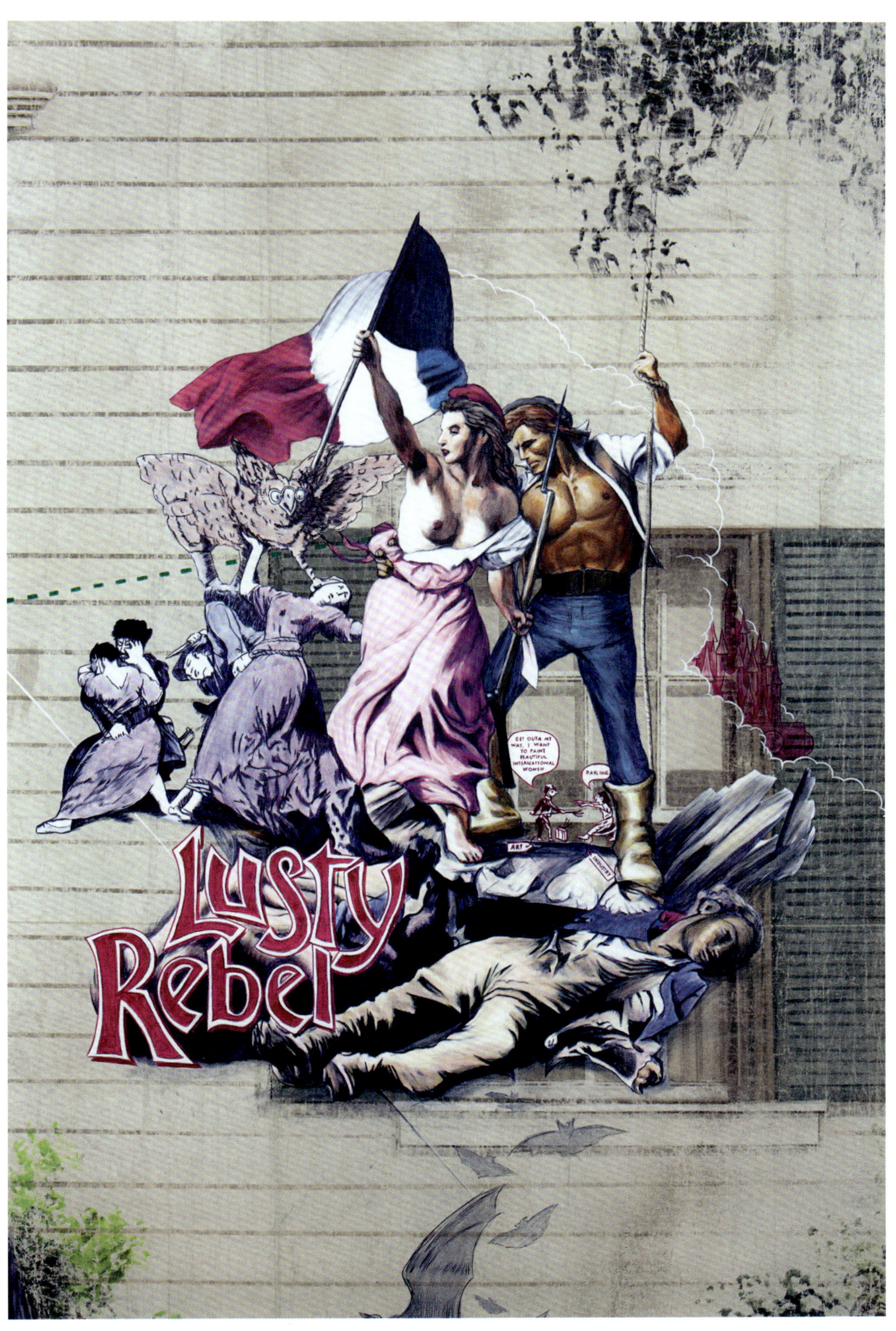

86. Seven Deadly Sins (detail)   2013

Raft of the Medusa (1818–9) and Emanuel Leutze's *Washington Crossing the Delaware* (1851), emblems of failure and success, as well as suffering and misery, redemption and its absence. An Ad Reinhardt cartoon also appears, depicting an abstract painter as a chicken that lays golden eggs. In the gluttony vignette, Shaw mashes together Norman Rockwell's Thanksgiving picture of a feasting family and Rembrandt's *The Anatomy Lesson of Dr. Nicolaes Tulp* (1632). Turning an all-American holiday into a grisly gore-fest, the melded masterpieces acknowledge the artistic cannibalism at work in Shaw's art.

Similar sorts of self-consumption take place in other works. *The Rhinegold's Curse* (2014) (fig.87) is among Shaw's most complex reflections on the pains of art-making. Riffing off of *The Rhinegold*, the first of the four musical dramas that make up Richard Wagner's *The Ring of the Nibelung*, Shaw's three-panel painting is also inspired by Kurt Weill and Bertolt Brecht's *The Threepenny Opera*, first performed in 1928, and *Burning of the Midnight Lamp*, a 1967 song by the English-American rock trio, the Jimi Hendrix Experience. Wagner, Brecht and Hendrix appear in the upper left of the adapted backdrop, portrayed, as characters are in a *Superboy* comic book, as giant wax candle heads. Shaw's painting meditates on the obsessive-compulsive nature of his work habits. Like *Dr. Goldfoot & His Bikini Bombs* (2007) (fig.51), it transforms a landscape with a waterfall, lake and Lorelei-style cliffs into the setting for a story about manic activity and the inescapability of suffering. This time, the landscape is a workshop where gnomes hear the siren song of duty as they work diligently, mining precious metals and struggling to spin straw into gold, like the miller's daughter in *Rumpelstiltskin*. The lamp, held by an upraised hand, duplicates the posture of the figure in Duchamp's *Étant Donnés*, who also appears in *Dr. Goldfoot & His Bikini Bombs*.

In *St. George and the Dragon* (2015) (fig.89), an ouroboros does double-duty as an infinity symbol, suggesting that the end is here and that there is no end to it. Inside the two loops of the Möbius-strip-style serpent, Shaw has painted his mental picture of *The Conqueror*, a 1956 film produced by Howard Hughes, directed by Dick Powell and starring John Wayne as Genghis Khan and Susan Hayward as the Tartar princess Bortai. Superimposed on the movie-star portraits are single-color images of US Marines raising the flag on the Japanese island of Iwo Jima, and an exotic dancer from the film, dancing exotically. The film was shot in 1954 in St. George, Utah, 137 miles downwind of Yucca Flats, Nevada, where 11 nuclear bombs had been exploded above ground in a 1953 test, contaminating the movie set with nuclear fallout. Truckloads of radioactive sand were shipped back to Hollywood, so that the scenes shot there would match those shot in the desert. Studio executives were aware of the risk but did not take it seriously. Of the 220 people who made up the cast and crew, 91 developed cancer and 46 of them died because of it. Shaw's picture of Hollywood's underbelly is a grim memento mori, a dark reminder that even though movies are illusions they can be deadly.

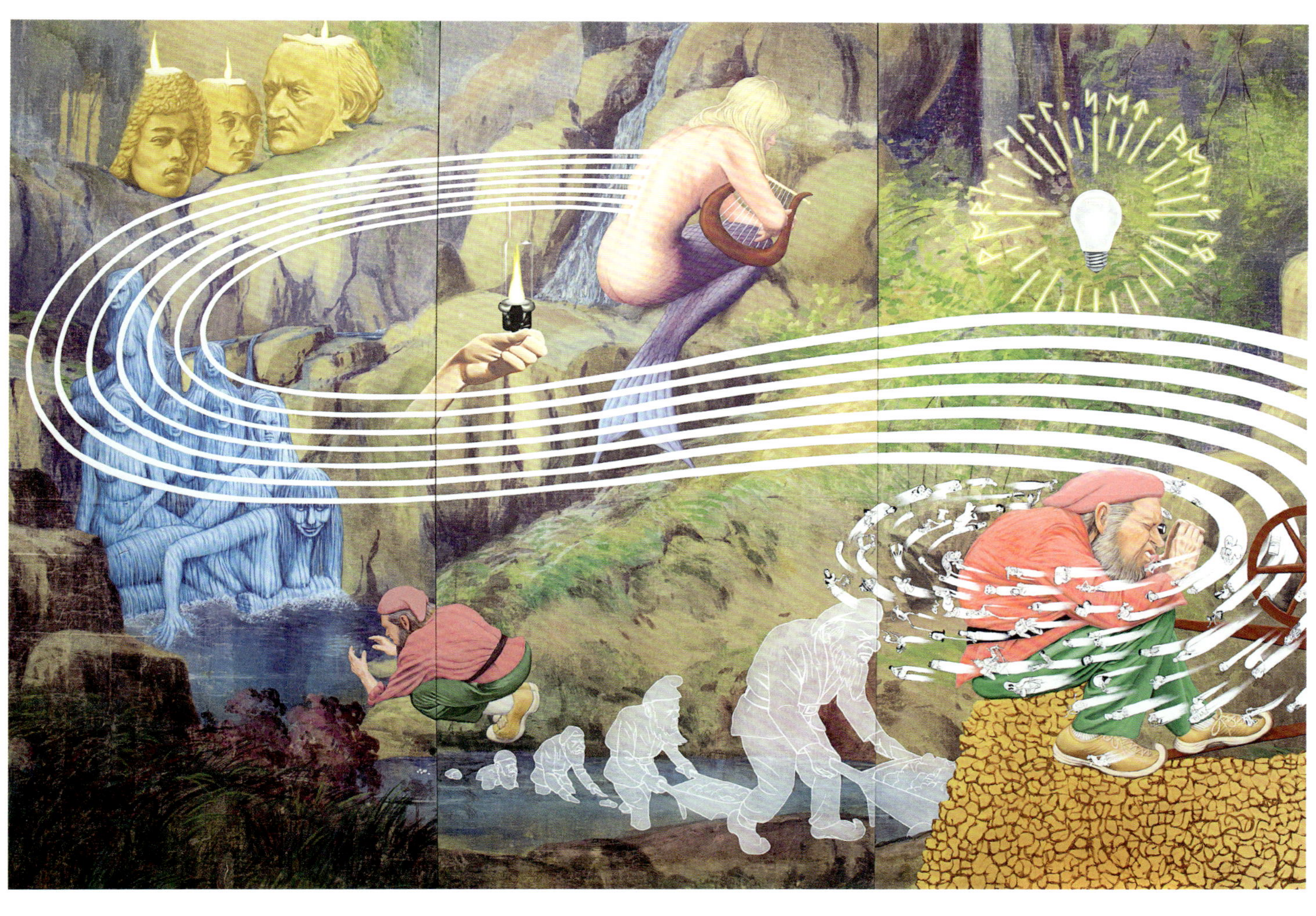

87. The Rhinegold's Curse   2014

Acrylic on muslin
243.8 × 365.8 cm (96 × 144 in)
Courtesy Metro Pictures

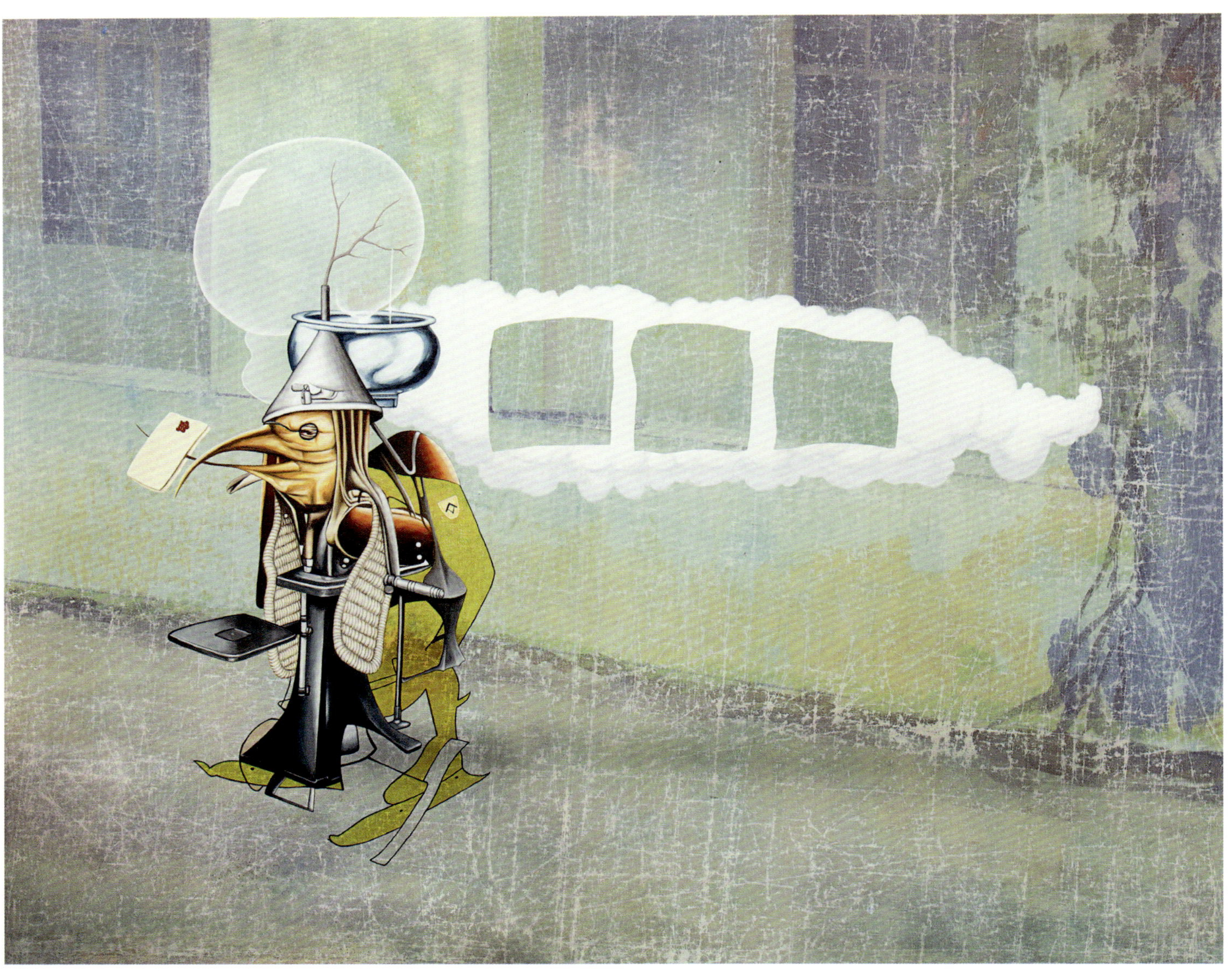

88. The Milk Separator   *2017*

Acrylic on muslin
121.9 × 157.5 cm (48 × 62 in)
Courtesy Blum & Poe

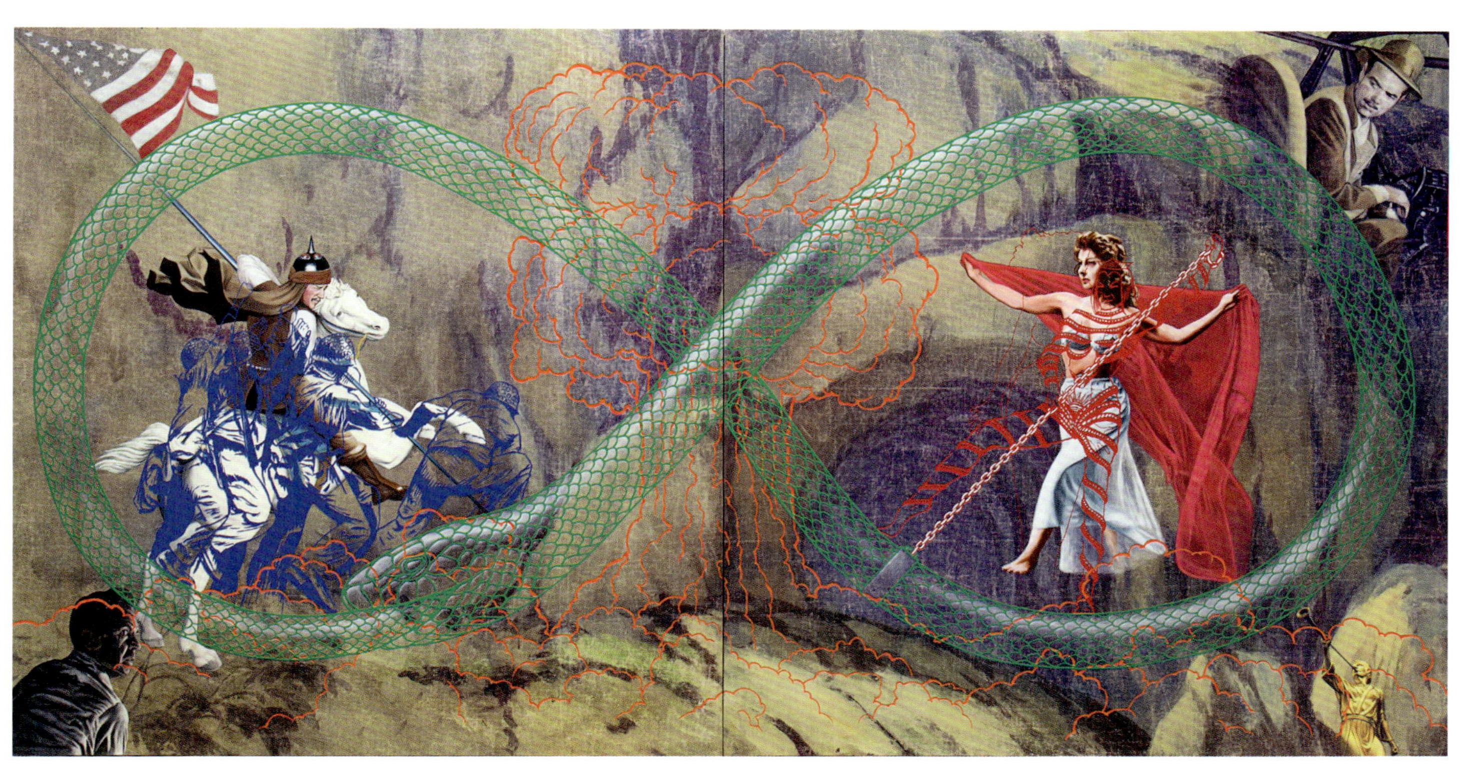

89. St. George and the Dragon   2015

Acrylic on muslin
167.6 × 335.2 cm (66 × 132 in)
Private collection, Paris

Coincidentally – or not – Shaw painted *St. George and the Dragon* the same year his survey exhibition opened at the New Museum in New York, which he titled, along with the 266-page catalog that accompanied it, *The End is Here*. Shaw recycled the title of his graduate pamphlet, sans the exclamation point, as if to say, 'no need for hyperbole, the survey and catalog are simply stating the facts, matching the unreality of reality with the way I see it, honestly and truly.'

In other stretched muslin paintings, contemporary political corruption – particularly behind-the-scenes deal-making – comes into focus more explicitly than it had in any of Shaw's previous works. In *All the President's Men* (2018) (fig.91), Shaw depicts Roger Stone (who worked on the campaigns of Richard Nixon, Ronald Regan, Robert Dole, Jack Kemp and Donald Trump, and is currently under indictment for lying, obstruction of justice and witness tampering) as an Aztec priest who has just placed a sacrificial heart on the chest of Paul Manafort (who was Trump's campaign manager and is now in prison, convicted of tax fraud). Lined up are mafia bosses and mid-level mobsters (including Carlos Marcello, Sam Giancana, Santo Trafficante and Mickey C. Cohen); Watergate burglar Frank Sturgis; mafia lawyer and confidante of Nixon, Bebe Rebozo; labor union leader Jimmy Hoffa (who mysteriously disappeared in 1975); and Jack Ruby (nightclub owner who assassinated Lee Harvey Oswald in the basement of the Dallas police station two days after Kennedy was assassinated). Each holds the heart of a sacrificed human. In the background is a resort in the Bahamas where the mafia moved its casinos after Fidel Castro kicked them out of Havana. Nixon got a cut of the tolls from the only bridge to the island casinos – as payback for favors that are not on the books.

To Serve Mankind (2018) (fig.90) portrays conservative billionaire Robert Mercer and his daughter Rebekah as visiting aliens and the couple in Grant Wood's *American Gothic* (1930). Peter Thiel, co-founder of PayPal, makes a cameo as a pixie-size Metaluna Mutant from the 1955 sci-fi film *This Island Earth*. Both Mercer and Thiel parlayed their entrepreneurial success into political power. Mercer used the money he made as the co-CEO of Renaissance Technologies to support the Brexit campaign, Breitbart News and Donald Trump. Thiel funded Hulk Hogan's lawsuit against *Gawker*, which bankrupted the company and put its blog out of business, and supported Trump's presidential run. AssBurgers, the name of the burger stand in the painting, is what Shaw saw in his mind's eye the first time he heard someone say 'Asperger's syndrome'. That developmental disorder is characterized by significant difficulties in social interaction, particularly in terms of non-verbal communication. For Shaw, painting is all about non-verbal communication. And, at least since Iron Butterfly's mistranslation of 'In the Garden of Eden', Shaw has valued misunderstanding as a way of coming to see the reality that lies beyond appearances.

Similar slip-ups – or coincidences – animate *Good N Plenty* (2018) (fig.92), in which Uncle Sam battles a piece of cake that is also a werewolf, both posed in the manner of the protagonists in the 1943 horror movie *Frankenstein Meets the Wolf Man*. Similarly, *Tragedy Display* (2018) (fig.93) features a crowd of 1950s Americans admiring a Second World War

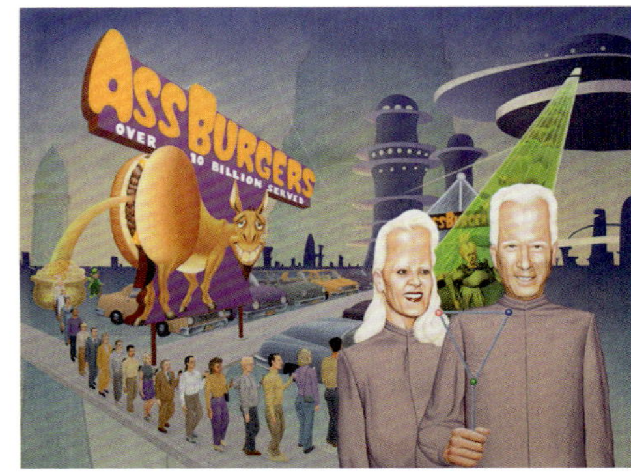

90. To Serve Mankind   2018

Acrylic on muslin
137.2 × 182.9 cm (54 × 72 in)
Private collection

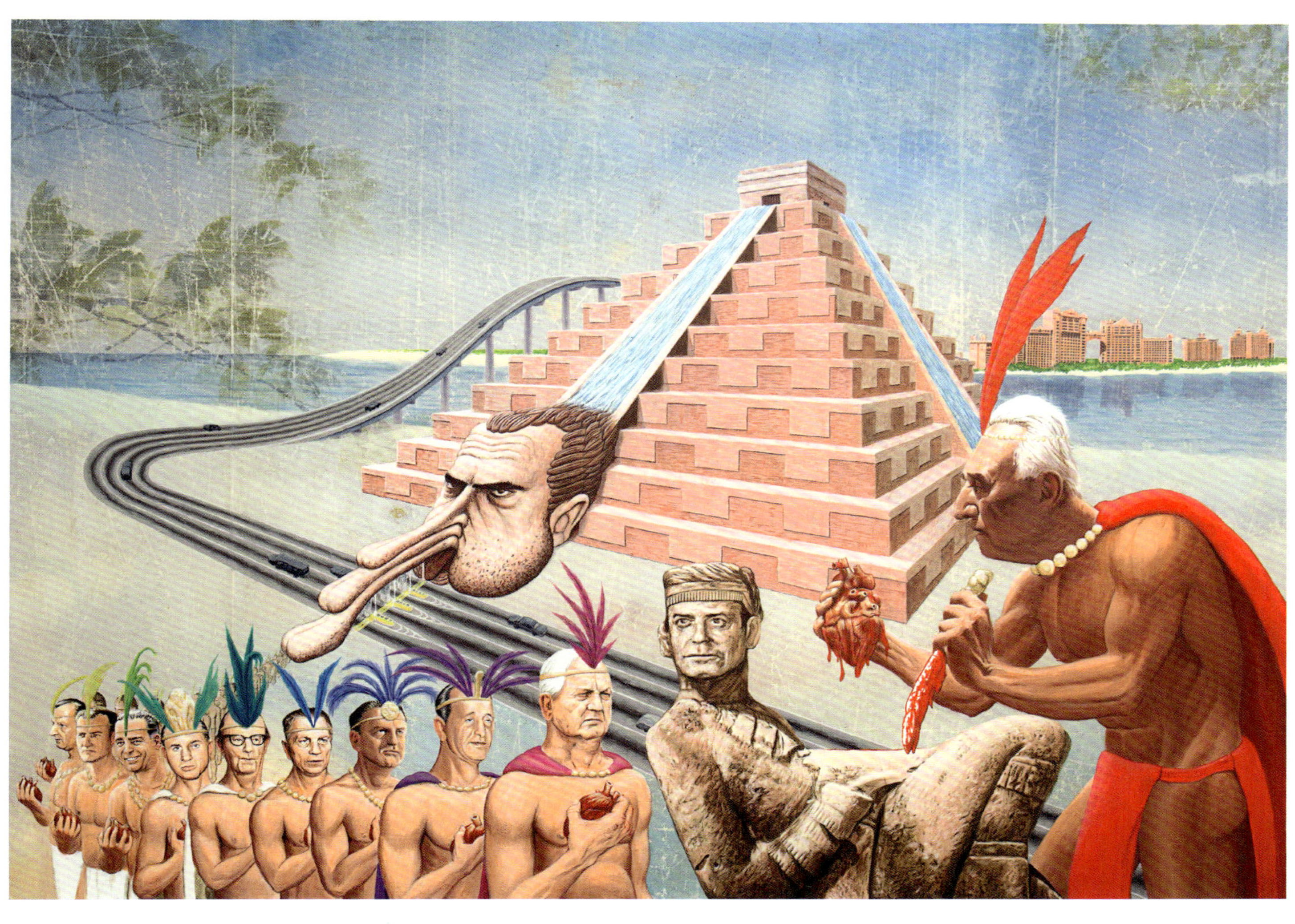

Acrylic on muslin
121.9 × 177.8 cm (48 × 70 in)
Private collection

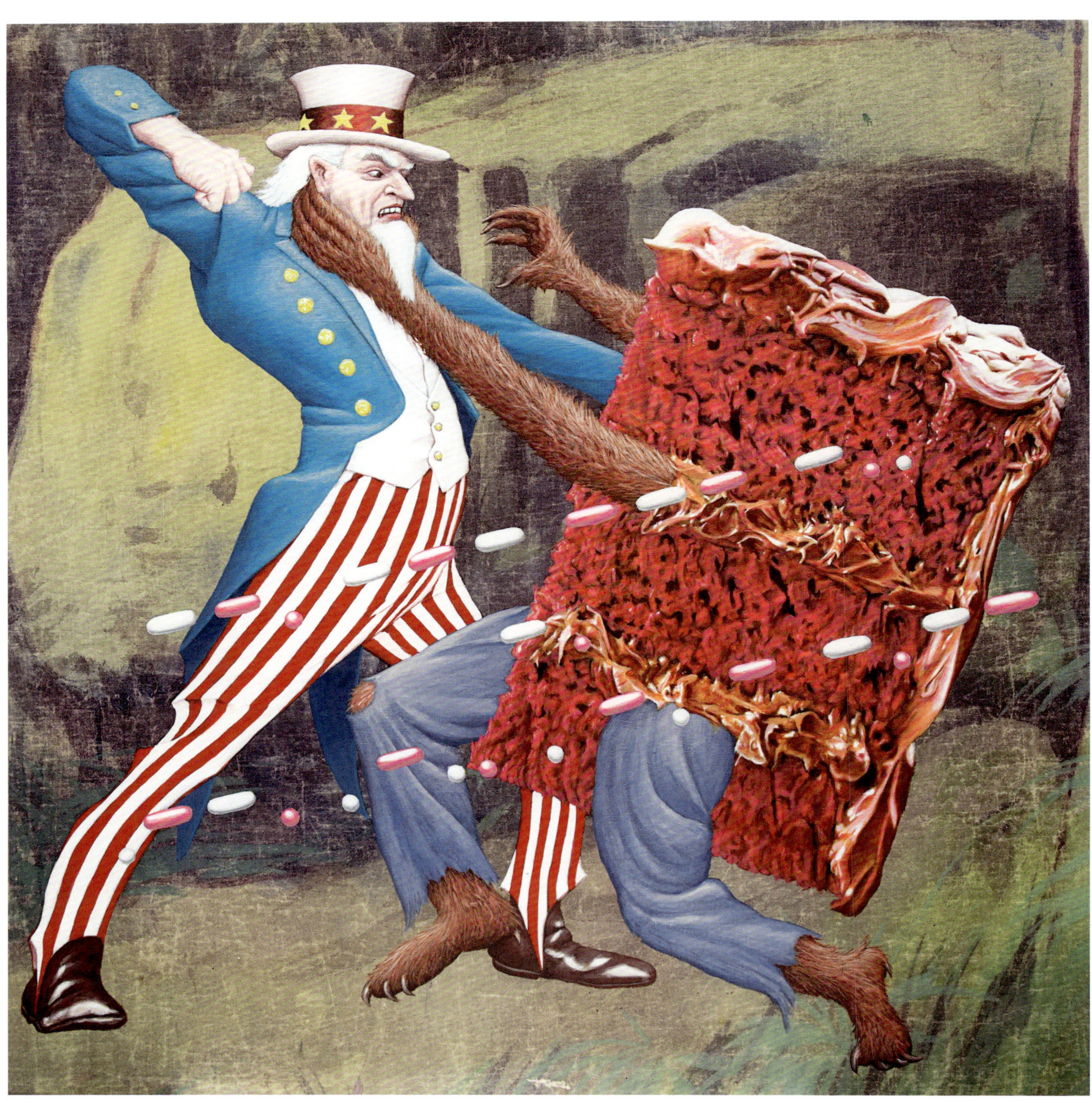

92. Good N Plenty   2018

Acrylic on muslin
91.4 × 91.4 cm (36 × 36 in)
Private collection

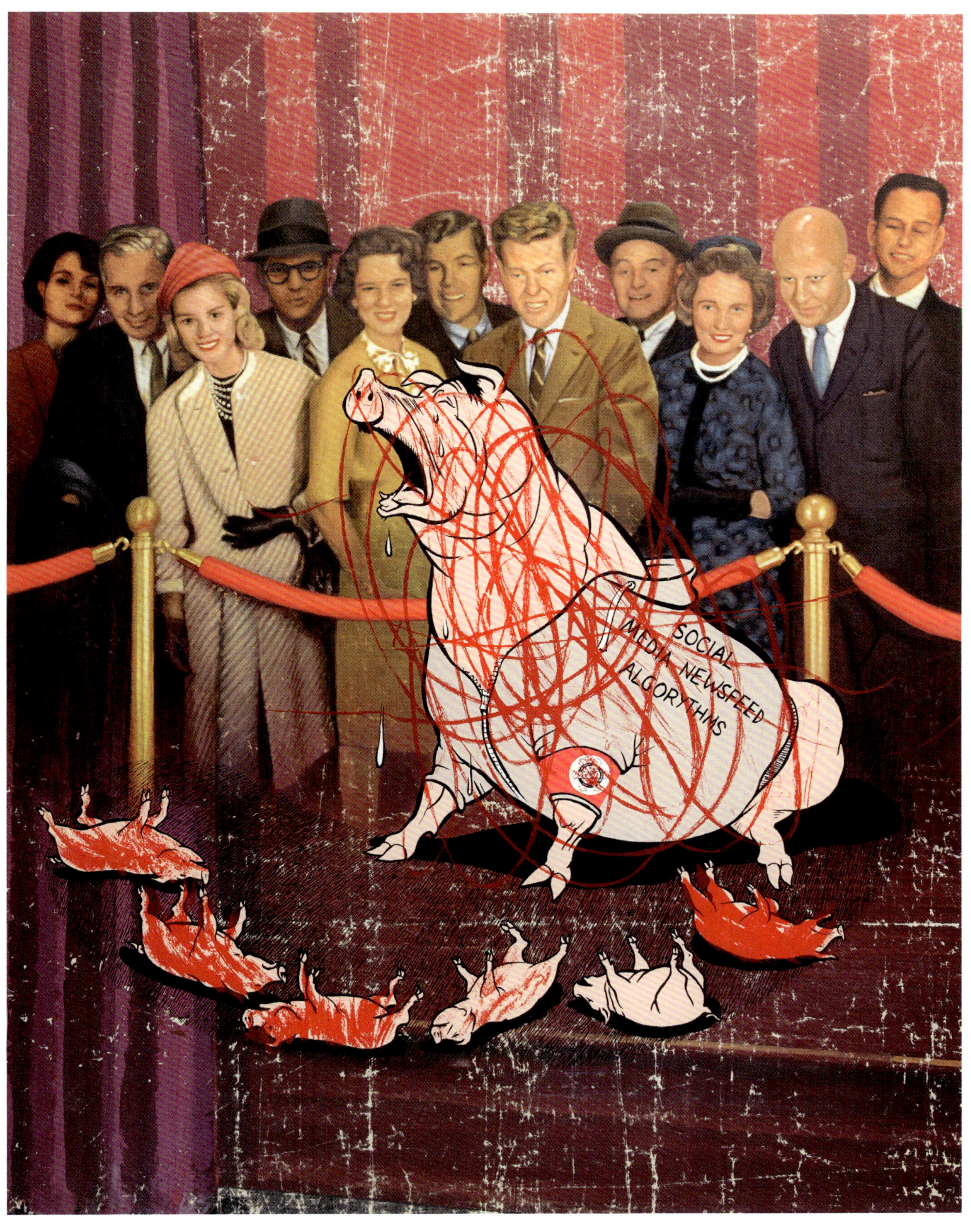

93. Tragedy Display   2018

Acrylic on muslin
153.7 × 121.9 cm (60½ × 48 in)
Private collection

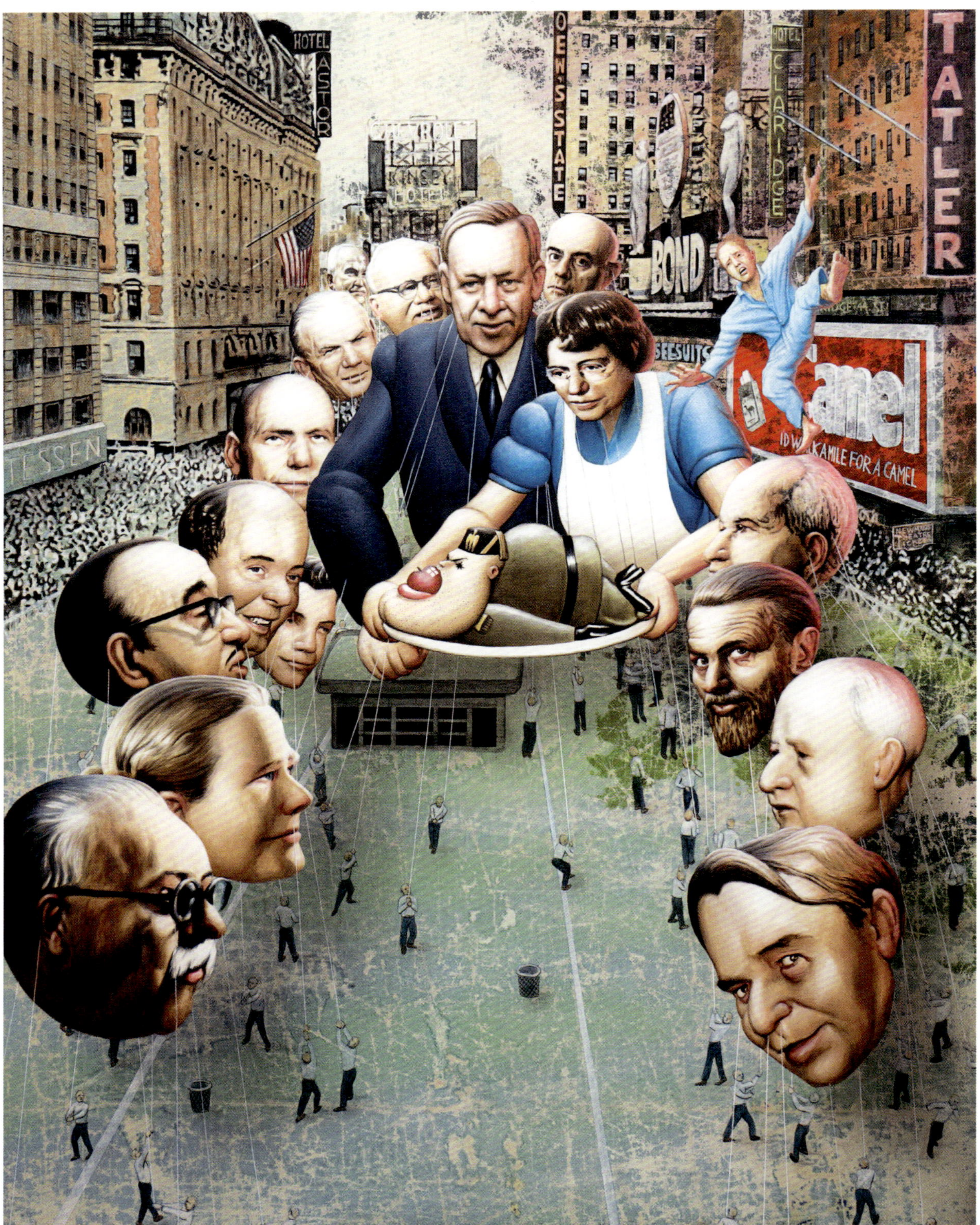

94. Macy's Parade Balloon Floats   2019

Acrylic on muslin
152.4 × 167.6 cm (60 × 48 in)
Courtesy Metro Pictures

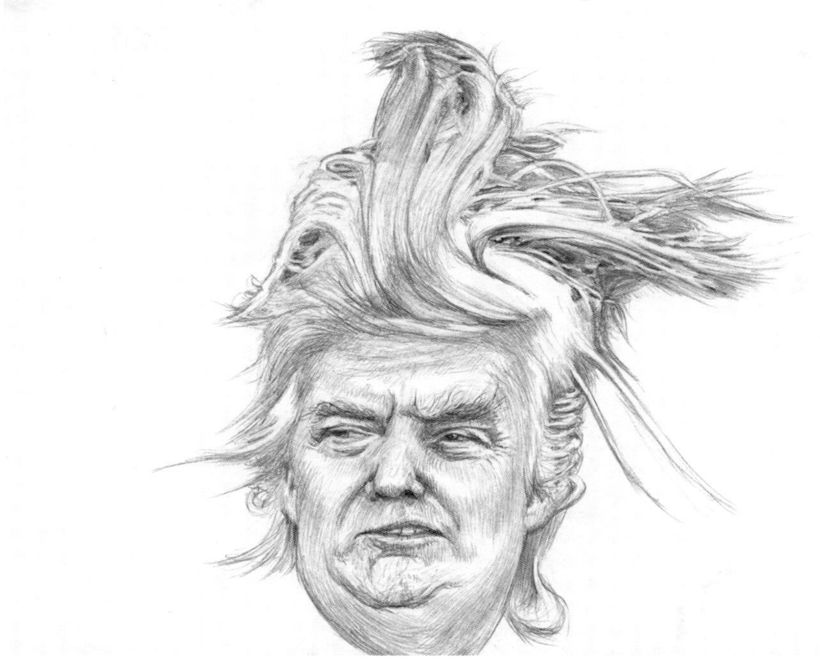

95. Trump Hair Study   2017

Pencil on paper
22.7 × 30.5 cm (9 × 12 in)
Collection of the artist

cartoon of a Nazi sow wailing inconsolably over her six dead piglets, each representing failed Nazi rumors. The fascist sow wears an armband emblazoned with the Facebook symbol. Trump appears in a good number of Shaw's political cartoons, sometimes as a shape-shifting demon (*Small Trump Chaos II*, 2017) (fig.97), sometimes as a Medusa-coiffed menace (*Trump Hair Study*, 2017) (fig.95), and sometimes as a Rorschach inkblot gone bad, despite the silvery shimmer of its decorative patterns (*Trump Wallpaper*, 2018) (fig.96).

Shaw has only made one painting in his *Alt-Right Mythologies* series but it is loaded. *Macy's Parade Balloon Floats* (2019) (fig.94) conflates a series of 1946–53 conferences organized by the Josiah Macy Jr. Foundation with the Thanksgiving Day Parade sponsored, since 1924, by Macy's, a department store chain. The parade is an entertaining spectacle that features balloons portraying cartoon characters and famous personages. The conference featured scholars and scientists brought together to study the likelihood of fascism taking root in America. Shaw's adapted backdrop features both: balloon heads of postwar luminaries, floating as if seated around a table, where the biggest balloons, representing Margaret Mead and Gregory Bateson, serve Benito Mussolini on a platter, laid out as if he were a roasted pig.

Mathematician Norbert Wiener, clinical psychologist Molly Harrower, social scientist Lawrence K. Frank and cybernetic pioneer Arturo Rosenblueth appear on the left. Just behind and slightly beneath their heads bobs the head of Ted Kaczynski, aka The Unabomber, who was sentenced in 1998 to life in prison for killing three people and wounding 23 others with letter bombs. When Kaczynski was

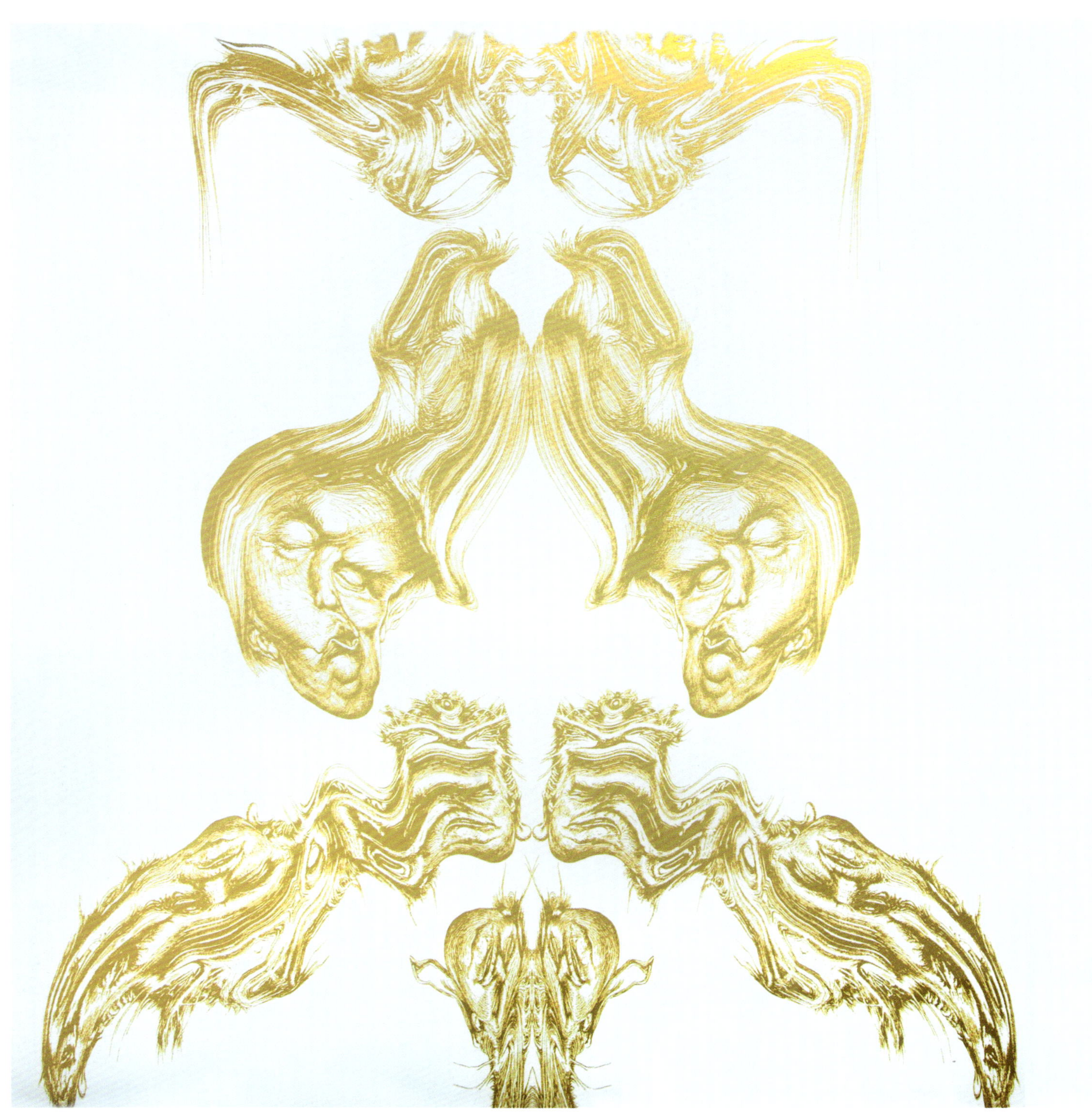

96. Trump Wallpaper   2018

Silver mylar wallpaper
370.3 sq m (1,215 sq ft)
Courtesy Simon Lee Gallery

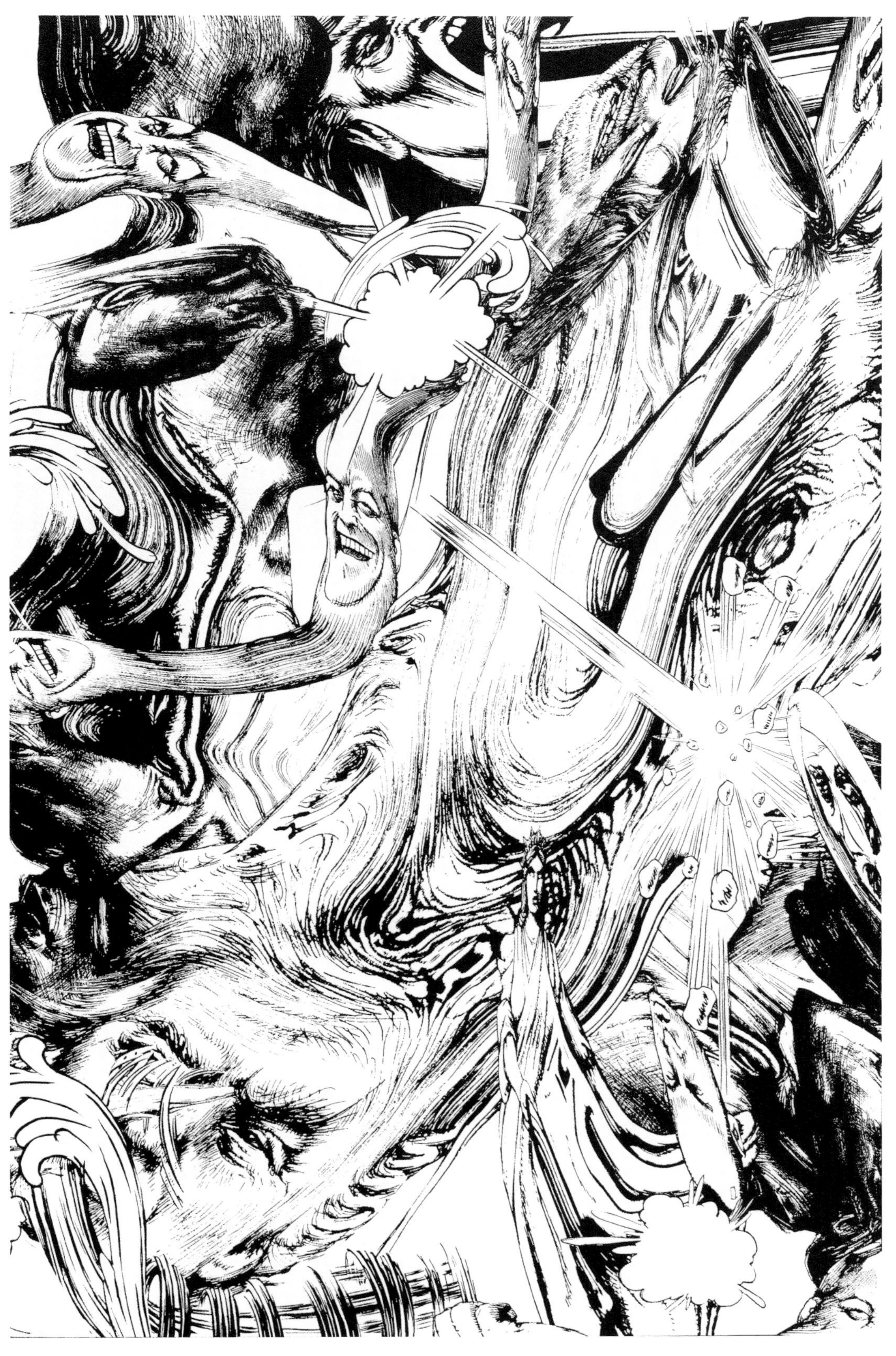

97. Small Trump Chaos II   2017

Acrylic on muslin
151.1 × 100.3 cm (59½ × 39½ in)
Courtesy Metro Pictures

an undergraduate in math at Harvard University, he spent a few hours each week for three years as the subject of a psychology experiment in which he was humiliated and his anger evaluated. Many believe the experiment by psychologist Henry Murray was part of Project MKUltra, the CIA's research into mind-control, which had its origins in the Macy's Cybernetics Conferences.

On the right appear physicist Heinz von Foerster, mathematician and computer programmer John von Neumann, social philosopher Theodor Adorno and neurophysiologist Warren McCulloch. Behind their heads tumbles Frank Olson, biological warfare scientist and CIA employee. No balloon, he is on his way to his death, having mysteriously 'fallen' from his hotel's tenth-story window, nine days after being covertly dosed with LSD by his CIA supervisor and a few weeks after revealing his discomfort with the United States government's use of germ warfare in Korea. In Shaw's seemingly celebratory painting, the best intentions go sideways – and then every which way. Like religion, scholarly research gets turned inside out and upside down when power-mongers get involved.

Shaw's most recent stretched muslin paintings navigate a collision course between absurdity and actuality. In the world given form by his painted political cartoons, freakish unbelievability and everyday ordinariness go hand in hand; fact and fiction intermingle like nobody's business; and dreams and nightmares often seem to be one and the same. Throughout it all, an individual's capacity to distinguish between knowledge and belief is, at best, diminished – not because our visual and intellectual acuity have been dulled, but because objective reality has gotten weirder and wackier and less rational over the four decades that have passed since Shaw was in grad school.

His art invites us to look at reality as if it were not only not what it appears to be, but something far more fascinating, improbable and mind-blowing: an impossible con job perpetuated by powers and players whose purposes ordinary folks will never know fully, much less understand or be able to explain to anyone else, without being taken for a lunatic, or worse. But the alternative is worse. So the only option is to go along with Shaw, trying to glimpse the big picture without being overwhelmed by the insanity of it all.

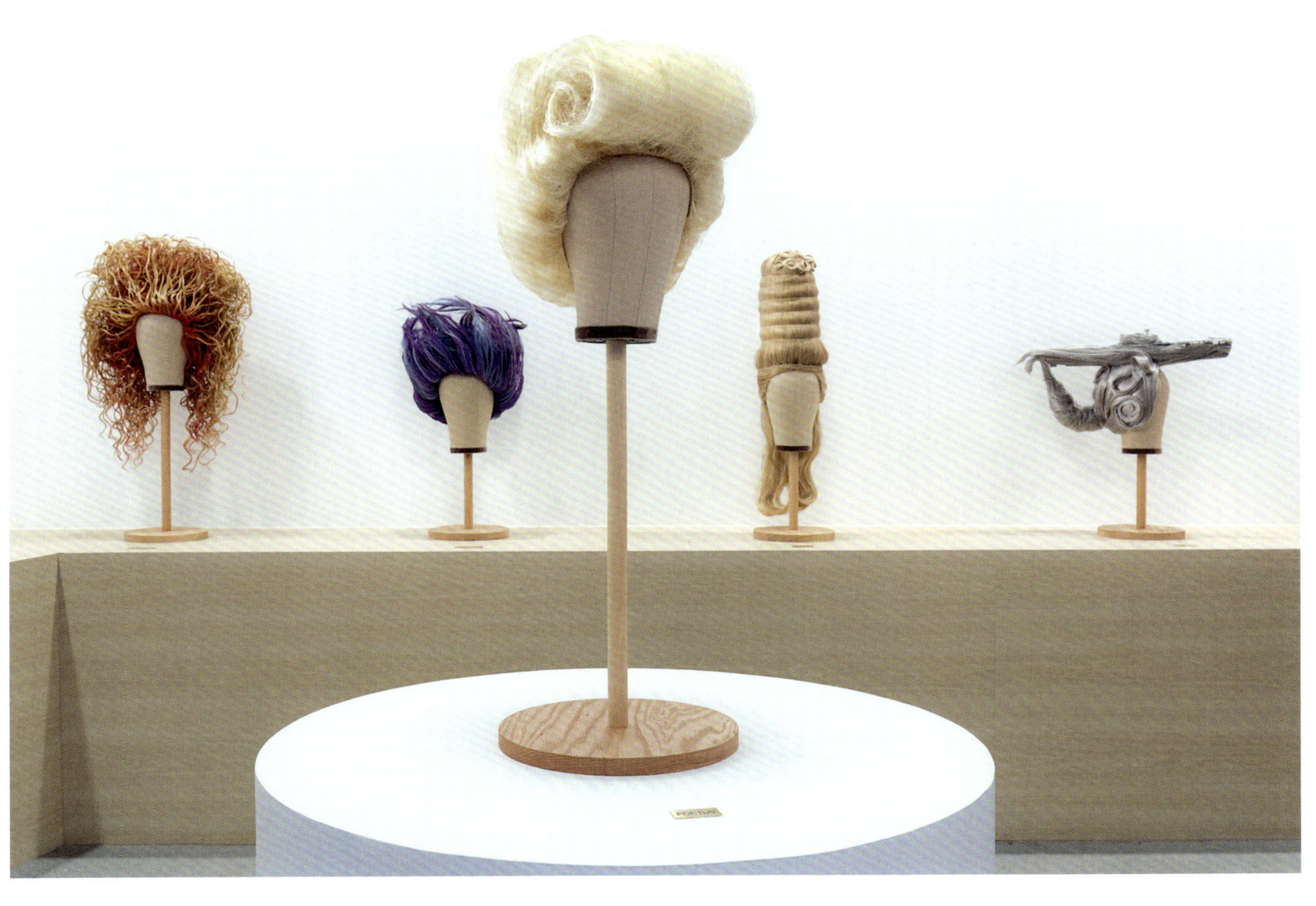

98. The Wig Museum (detail)   2018

Mixed media
Dimensions variable
Marciano Art Foundation

Notes

1. *Jim Shaw, Everything Must Go*, p.56, Casino
   Luxembourg – Forum d'Art Contemporain,
   Luxembourg; Musée d'Art Moderne et
   Contemporain (MAMCO), Geneve,
   Switzerland; Smart Art Press, Santa Monica,
   1999
2. Email from Jim Shaw to David Pagel, 22
   February 2019
3. *Jim Shaw: Left Behind, Essays*, p.10, CAPC
   Musée d'Art Contemporain de Bordeaux,
   2010
4. *Jim Shaw: Left Behind, Essays*, p.28, CAPC
   Musée d'Art Contemporain de Bordeaux,
   2010
5. Conversation with David Pagel, 12 December
   2018
6. *Jim Shaw: The Rinse Cycle*, p.152, BALTIC
   Center for Contemporary Art in association
   with Koenig Books, Ltd, 2012

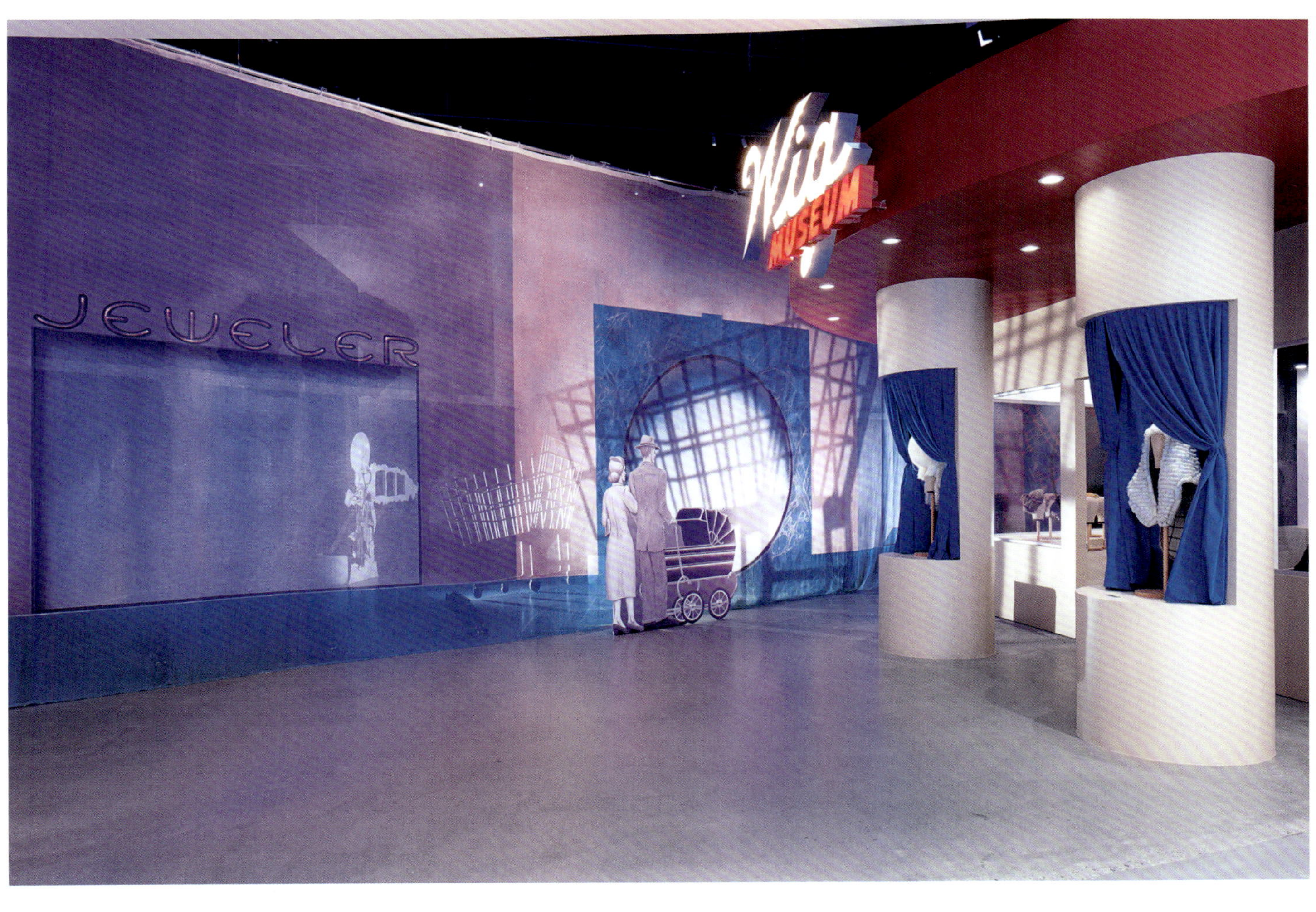

99. The Wig Museum (installation view)   2018

Mixed media
Dimensions variable
Marciano Art Foundation

Bibliography

Alteveer, Ian and Douglas Eklund, *Everything is Connected: Art and Conspiracy*, New York: The Metropolitan Museum of Art, 2018

Bovier, Lionel and Stroun, Fabrice, *Jim Shaw: O*, Le Magasin, Grenoble and Kunsthaus Glarus, 2003 *Une Collection Pour Une Région, 1982 – 2002*, Haute-Normandie, France

Carrion-Murayari, Gary, and Massimiliano Gioni, *Jim Shaw: The End Is Here*, New York: New Museum/Skira Rizzoli, 2015

Colburn, Bolton; Linton, Meg; Williams, Robert, *In the Land of Retinal Delights: The Juxtapose Factor*, Laguna Beach, California: Laguna Art Museum; Corte Madera, California: Gingko Press, 2008

Fréchuret, Maurice; Leeman, Richard; Nancy, Jean-Luc; Poisay, François; Sans, Jérome; Shusterman, Ronald, *Dormir, rêver...et autres nuits (To sleep, to dream...and other nights)*, CAPC, Musée d'Art Contemporain de Bordeaux, Bordeaux et Fage éditions, Lyon, 2006

Goldstein, Ann; Morse, Rebecca; Schimmel, Paul, *This Is Not to Be Looked at: Highlights from the Permanent Collection of The Museum of Contemporary Art, Los Angeles*, Los Angeles, California: Museum of Contemporary Art, 2008

Gudis, Catherine, ed., *Helter Skelter: LA Art in the 1990s*, The Museum of Contemporary Art, Los Angeles, 1992

Hoek, Els, Sjarel Ex, and Hans Smits, *XXXL Painting: Jim Shaw, Klaas Kloosterboer, Chris Martin*, Rotterdam: Museum Boijmans Van Beuningen, 2013

Laubard, Charlotte, ed. *Jim Shaw: Left Behind*. Bordeaux: CAPC Musée d'Art Contemporain, 2012

Nusser, Uta, *Thrift Store Paintings: Jim Shaw*, Kunsthalle Wien, Vienna, Austria; Deichtorhallen Hamburg, Germany, 1993

Payne, Ursula, ed., *Jim Shaw: Realisms*, Saint Petersburg: The State Hermitage Museum, London: Halcyon Gallery, 2016

Roberts, John and Ralfph Rugoff, *Amateurs*, San Francisco, California: CCA Wattis Institute for Contemporary Art, 2008

Saltz, Jerry, 'American Art of the 80's', Museo d'Arte Moderna e Contemporanea di Trento, Italy, 1991

Shaw, Jim, *The Hidden World: Jim Shaw, Didactic Art Collection*, London: Koenig Books, 2014

Shaw, Jim, *My Mirage*, Zurich: JRP Ringier, 2011

Shaw, Jim, *Rather Fear God: Dream Drawings, Dream Objects*. Additional texts by Doug Harvey and Marc Strauss, Brussels: Praz-Delavallade, 2016

Shaw, Jim, *True Stories*, ICA, The Mall, London, England, 1994

Sillars, Laurence, *Jim Shaw: The Rinse Cycle*, Baltic Centre for Contemporary Art, with Koenig Books, London, 2012

Catalogues

1991 Biennial Exhibition, Whitney Museum of American Art, New York

Everything Must Go: Jim Shaw 1974-1999, essays by Doug Harvey, Noelle Roussel, Fabrice Stroun, Amy Gerstler; interview with Mike Kelly, Casino Luxembourg, Luxembourg

Faces and Figures (Revisited), New York: Marc Jancou Contemporary, 2008

Jim Shaw: The Wig Museum, text by Doug Harvey; interview with Philip Kaiser, Los Angeles: Maurice and Paul Marciano Art Foundation, 2017

In Geneva No One Can Hear You Scream, Geneva: Blondeau Fine Art Services; Zurich, Switzerland: JRP/Ringier, 2008

Jim Shaw: Distorted Faces & Portraits, 1978-2006, Blondeau Fine Art Services, JRP/Ringier, Zurich, Switzerland

Jim Shaw: Selected Dream Drawings, Patrick Painter Inc., Santa Monica, California, 2006

Jim Shaw Traume, Frnkfurter Kunsteverein, 1998.

Sunshine & Noir, Louisiana Museum of Modern Art, Humlebaek, Denmark; Kunstmuseum Wolfsburg, Germany; Castello di Rivoli, Museo d'Arte Contempotnae, Italy; UCLA at the Armand Hammer Museum of Art and Cultural Center, Los Angeles, 1997

Dreams, Santa Monica, California: Smart Art Press, 1995

Biography

1952
Born 8 August in Midland, Michigan

1970
Enrolled at The Cooper Union for the
Advancement of Science and Art, New York, but
left before the first week of school ended

1970–2
Earned a certificate in art at Delta College,
Midland, Michigan

1974
Founded art band, Destroy All Monsters, with
Mike Kelley, Cary Loren and Niagra

1974
Received Bachelor of Fine Arts degree from
University of Michigan, Ann Arbor

1977–8
Worked at Don Post mask factory, airbrushing
Halloween masks

1978
Received Masters of Fine Arts degree, California
Institute of the Arts, Valencia, California

1987
Included in *CalArts: Skeptical Belief(s)* exhibition,
organized by the Renaissance Society at the
University of Chicago; Newport Harbor Art
Museum, Newport Beach

1990
Exhibited *My Mirage* in Los Angeles, Berkeley,
Saint Louis and New York
Exhibited *Thrift Store Paintings* in Los Angeles,
Glendale and New York

1991
Included in *Biennial Exhibition*, Whitney Museum
of American Art, New York

1992
Included in *Helter Skelter: L.A. Art in the 1990s*,
Museum of Contemporary Art, Los Angeles

1993
Married Marnie Weber

1994–8
Taught at the University of Nevada, Las Vegas;
California Institute of the Arts; University of
California, Los Angeles; and Art Center College
of Design

1996
Moved into Craftsman home on two lots in Eagle
Rock, California

1999
Daughter, Colette, born

2014
Moved studio into Spanish-style house in
Altadena, California

2015
Jim Shaw: The End is Here exhibition, New
Museum, New York

2017
Inaugural Project Series exhibition at the
Marciano Art Foundation, *The Wig Museum*

Exhibitions

Selected Solo Exhibitions

2019
The Family Romance, Metro Pictures, New York, NY
Praz-Delavallade, Paris, France

2018
Drawings, Simon Lee Gallery, London, UK
Simon Lee Gallery, Hong Kong

2017
Blum & Poe, Los Angeles, CA
Massimo De Carlo, Milan, Italy
Metro Pictures, New York, NY
The Wig Museum, curated by Philipp Kaiser,
  Marciano Art Foundation, Los Angeles, CA

2016
Rather Fear God, Praz-Delavallade, Paris and
  Vedovi Gallery, Brussels, Belgium

2015
Entertaining Doubts, Massachusetts Museum of
  Contemporary Art, North Adams, MA
Jim Shaw, Simon Lee Gallery, London, UK
The End is Here, New Museum, New York, NY

2014
Oeuvres choisies: dessins, peintures, sculptures, vidéo,
  Galerie Guy Bärtschi, Carouge, Switzerland
I Only Wanted You to Love Me, Metro Pictures,
  New York, NY

2013
Jim Shaw, Simon Lee Gallery, Hong Kong
Blum & Poe, Los Angeles, CA
*The Hidden World: Jim Shaw Didactic Art
  Collection,* Chalet Society, Paris, France; traveled
  to Centre Dürrenmatt, Neuchâtel, Switzerland

2012
Dream Drawings, Los Angeles County Museum of
  Art, Los Angeles, CA
The Rinse Cycle, Baltic Centre for Contemporary
  Art, Gateshead, UK

2011
Thrilling Stories from the Book of 'O', Praz-
  Delavallade, Paris, France

*Cakes, Men in Pain, White Rectangles, Devil in the
  Details,* Patrick Painter Inc., Santa Monica, CA

2010
New Works, Bernier/Eliades, Athens, Greece
Left Behind, CAPC Musée d'Art Contemporain
  de Bordeaux, Bordeaux, France

2009
Wet Dreams, Erotic Dream Drawings by Jim Shaw,
  Praz-Delavallade, Paris, France
The Whole: A Study in Oist Integrated Movement,
  Simon Lee Gallery, London, UK

2007
Dr. Goldfoot and His Bikini Bombs, Metro Pictures,
  New York, NY
2012 – Montezuma's Revenge, Galerie Praz-
  Delavallade, Berlin, Germany
The Donner Party, P.S.1 Contemporary Art
  Center, Long Island City, NY
Distorted Faces & Portraits, 1978–2006, Blondeau
  Fine Art Services, Geneva, Switzerland

2006
My Mirage 1986–91, Skarstedt Fine Art, New
  York, NY
Bernier/Eliades, Athens, Greece

2005
The Inky Depths/The Woman in the Wilderness,
  Metro Pictures, New York, NY
The Dream That Was No More A Dream, Patrick
  Painter Inc., Santa Monica, CA

2004
Emily Tsingou Gallery, London, UK

2003
Kill Your Darlings, Patrick Painter Inc., Santa
  Monica, CA
O, Magasin, Centre National d'Art
  Contemporain, Grenoble, France; Kunsthaus
  Glarus, Switzerland

2002
The Goodman Image File and Study, Swiss Institute,
  New York, NY

The Rite of the 360°, Praz-Delavallade, Paris, France
Massimo de Carlo, Milan, Italy
O-ist Thrift Store Paintings, Metro Pictures, New
  York, NY

2001
Dreamt of Drawings, Emily Tsingou Gallery,
  London, UK
Jim Shaw, Metro Pictures, New York, NY
Praz-Delavallade, Paris, France

2000
Thrift Store Paintings, Institute of Contemporary
  Arts, London, UK
Johnen + Schöttle, Cologne, Germany

1999
Praz-Delavallade, Paris, France
Everything Must Go, Casino-Luxembourg,
  France; traveled to Musée d'Art Moderne et
  Contemporain, Geneva, Switzerland; The
  Contemporary Arts Center, Cincinnati, OH
  (exh. cat.)

1998
Frankfurter Kunstverein, Frankfurt, Germany
Rupertinum – Museum of Modern Art, Salzburg,
  Austria

1997
The Deep, Tokyo, Japan
Bookbeat, Detroit, MI
Rosamund Felsen Gallery, Santa Monica, CA

1996
The Sleep of Reason, Metro Pictures, New York, NY
Dreams, Cabinet Gallery, London, UK

1995
*What Exactly is a Dream and What Exactly is
  a Joke...,* Donna Beam Fine Art Gallery,
  University of Nevada, Las Vegas, NV
*I Dreamed I was performing in an Alternative Space
  w/ my Maidenform Bra,* Rosamund Felsen
  Gallery, Santa Monica, CA

1994
Dreams That Money Can Buy, Rena Bransten
  Gallery, San Francisco, CA

1992
Horror A Vacui, (with Benjamin Weissman),
    Linda Cathcart Gallery, Santa Monica, CA
Texas Gallery, Houston, TX
Galleria Massimo de Carlo, Milan, Italy

1991
Jim Shaw: My Mirage, Saint Louis Museum of
    Art, Saint Louis, MO
Feature Inc., New York, NY
Thrift Store Paintings, Metro Pictures, New York,
    NY

1990
Linda Cathcart Gallery, Santa Monica, CA
Jim Shaw: My Mirage, Matrix Gallery, University
    Art Museum, University of California,
    Berkeley, CA
Feature Inc., New York, NY

1989
Dennis Anderson Gallery, Los Angeles, CA

1986
The Nuclear Family, EZTV, Los Angeles, CA

1981
Jim Shaw: Life and Death, Zero Zero Club, Los
    Angeles, CA

Selected Group Exhibitions

2019
Men of Steel, Women of Wonder, Crystal Bridges
    Museum of American Art, Bentonville, AR
Hate Speech. Aggression and Intimacy,
    Künstlerhaus, Halle für Kunst & Medien,
    Graz, Austria
Psyche and Politics, Staatliche Kunsthalle Baden-
    Baden, Germany

2018
Mad World, Marciano Art Foundation, Los
    Angeles, CA
I Dream My Painting and Then I Paint My Dream,
    Praz-Delavallade Los Angeles, CA

Everything is Connected: Art and Conspiracy, Met
    Breuer, New York, NY

2017
Michigan Stories: Mike Kelley and Jim Shaw, Eli
    and Edythe Broad Art Museum at Michigan
    State University, East Lansing, MI

2016
*Realisms: Mitch Griffiths, Tony Matelli and Jim
    Shaw,* The State Hermitage Museum, Saint
    Petersburg, Russia
Physical: Sex and the Body in the 1980s, Los Angeles
    County Museum of Art, Los Angeles, CA

2015
Magnificent Obsessions: The Artist as Collector,
    Barbican Art Gallery, London, UK

2012
*Faking It: Manipulated Photography Before
    Photoshop,* Metropolitan Museum of Art, New
    York, NY

2011
*Return of the Repressed: Destroy All Monsters
    1973–1977,* Prism Gallery, Los Angeles, CA
Secret Societies, Schirn Kunsthalle, Frankfurt,
    Germany; CAPC Musée d'Art Contemporain
    de Bordeaux, Bordeaux, France
The Spectacular of Vernacular, Walker Art Center,
    Minneapolis, MN; Montclair Art Museum,
    Montclair, NJ

2009
*I DREAMED I WAS TALLER THAN
    JONATHAN BOROFSKY, Le Printemps de
    Septembre,* les Abattoirs, Toulouse, France

2007
Eden's Edge: Fifteen LA Artists, The Armand
    Hammer Museum of Art and Cultural Center,
    Los Angeles, CA

2006
*Magritte and Contemporary Art: The Treachery of
    Images,* Los Angeles County Museum of Art,
    Los Angeles, CA

2005
Drunk vs. Stoned 2, Gavin Brown Enterprises,
    New York, NY

2004
100 Artists See Satan, Grand Central Art Center,
    Santa Ana, CA (exh. cat.)
100 Artists See God, organized by Independent
    Curators International; Naples Museum of Art,
    Naples, FL; Jewish Museum, San Francisco,
    CA; Laguna Art Museum, Laguna Beach, CA;
    Memorial Art Gallery, University of Rochester,
    NY; Institute of Contemporary Arts, London,
    UK; Contemporary Art Center of Virginia,
    Virginia Beach, VA; Albright College Freedman
    Art Gallery, Reading, PA; Cheekwood
    Museum of Art, Nashville, TN

2002
L.A. Post-Cool, San Jose Museum of Art, San Jose,
    CA
2002 Biennial Exhibition, Whitney Museum of
    American Art, New York, NY

2000
Made in California, Los Angeles County Museum
    of Art, Los Angeles, CA

1999
*In Sickness and in Health: Jim Shaw and Marnie
    Weber, Recent Works,* Project Gallery, Wichita,
    KS

1998
Pop Surrealism, Aldrich Museum of Contemporary
    Art, Ridgefield, CT

1997
Sunshine & Noir, Louisiana Museum of Modern
    Art, Humlebæk, Denmark; Kunstmuseum
    Wolfsburg, Germany; Castello di Rivoli,
    Museo d'Arte Contemporanea, Italy; Hammer
    Museum of Art, Los Angeles, CA

1994
Facts and Figures, Lannan Foundation, Los
    Angeles, CA

Public Collections

1993

Prospect '93, Frankfurter Kunstverein/Schirn Kunsthalle, Frankfurt, Germany

Four Centuries of Drawing: 1593–1993, Kohn Abrams Gallery, Los Angeles, CA

1992

Helter Skelter: L.A. Art in the 1990s, Museum of Contemporary Art, Los Angeles, CA

Just Pathetic, American Fine Arts Co., New York, NY

LAX, Galerie Ursula Krinzinger, Vienna, Austria

1991

1991 Biennial Exhibition, Whitney Museum of American Art, New York, NY

Presenting Rearwards, Rosamund Felsen, Los Angeles, CA

Ovarian Warriors vs. Knights of Crissum, Sue Spaid Fine Art, Los Angeles, CA

The Store Show, Richard/Bennett Gallery, Los Angeles, CA

1990

Thrift Store Paintings, Brand Library Art Galleries, Glendale, CA; traveled to Contemporary Arts Forum, Santa Barbara, CA

1987

L.A. Hot and Cool: The Eighties, MIT List Visual Arts Center, Cambridge, MA

Cal Arts; Skeptical Belief(s), The Renaissance Society at the University of Chicago, Illinois; Newport Harbor Art Museum, Newport Beach, CA

1986

Social Distortions, Los Angeles Contemporary Exhibitions, Los Angeles, CA

Hang 12, Piezo Electric Gallery, Venice, CA

1985

B & W, Los Angeles Institute of Contemporary Art, Los Angeles, CA

TV Generations, Los Angeles Contemporary Exhibitions, Los Angeles, CA

1984

The Floor Show, Los Angeles Contemporary Exhibitions, Los Angeles, CA

Albright-Knox Art Gallery, Buffalo, NY

CAPC Musée d'Art Contemporain de Bordeaux, Bordeaux, France

Centre d'Art Contemporain, Geneva, Switzerland

Centre Georges Pompidou, Paris, France

Colección Jumex, Mexico City, Mexico

Des Moines Art Center, Des Moines, IA

Eli and Edythe Broad Art Museum, MI State University, East Lansing, MI

Fri Art Museum, Fribourg, Switzerland

Fond National d'Art Contemporain, Paris, France

FRAC, Normandy, France

Galleria d'Arte Moderna e Contemporanea, Palazzo Forti, Verona, Italy

The Hammer Museum, Los Angeles, CA

Los Angeles County Museum of Art, Los Angeles, CA

Marciano Art Foundation, Los Angeles, CA

The Metropolitan Museum of Art, New York, NY

Musée Cantonal des Beaux-Arts, Lausanne, Switzerland

Musée d'Art Moderne et Contemporain, Geneva, Switzerland

Musée National d'Art Moderne, Centre Georges Pompidou, Paris, France

Museum Boijmans Van Beuningen, Rotterdam, Netherlands

Museum of Contemporary Art, Los Angeles, CA

Museum of Contemporary Art, San Diego, CA

National Gallery of Victoria, Melbourne, Australia

New Museum, New York, NY

San Francisco Museum of Modern Art, San Francisco, CA

Solomon R. Guggenheim Museum, New York, NY

Walker Art Center, Minneapolis, MN

Whitney Museum of American Art, New York, NY

Acknowledgments

First and biggest thanks to Jim Shaw, for doing what he has been doing all his life and for putting up with my endless questions. Next, to Daniel Hawkins and Daniel Hope, for tracking down pictures near and far, always with great enthusiasm and speed. Also big thanks to Barry Schwabsky, for inviting me to be a part of this series and for giving me my first break in New York in 1989. Finally, to my folks, Don and Marita, my wife, Alisa Tager, and kids, Leila and Marcus, who all make it all possible.

Image Credits

Bernier/Eliades Gallery, Athens: 30

Blum & Poe, Los Angeles/Tokyo/New York: 37, 52, 53, 54, 59 (Photo © F. Deval, Mairie de Bordeaux); 68, 69, 85, 86 (Joshua White)

Feature Inc., New York: 10

Jim Shaw Studio: 2, 14, 17, 18, 21, 25, 26, 79, 94, 96; (and Blondeau & Cie, Geneva: 19, 20); (and Ilmari Kalkkinen: 44, 45, 87); (and LeeAnn Nickel: 1, 22, 29, 31, 32, 33, 34, 35, 41, 42, 43, 46, 47, 48, 49, 50, 55, 57, 63, 64, 65, 70, 71, 72, 73, 74, 75, 76, 77, 78, 80, 81, 82, 83, 84, 88, 89, 90, 91, 92, 93, 95, 97, 98, 99); (and Frederik Nilsen: 6, 7, 9); (and Praz Delavallade: 15, 16, 29); (and Joshua White: 40, 56)

Les Abbatoirs: 58

Linda Cathcart Gallery, Santa Monica: 8, 11, 12, 13

Massachusetts Museum of Contemporary Art, North Adams, MA/Gregory Cherin: 24

Metro Pictures, New York and Blondeau & Cie, Geneva: 5, 51, 66, 67

Molly Tierney: frontispiece

Patrick Painter Inc., Santa Monica: 38, 61, 62

Phillips, London/New York: 27, 28

Praz Delavallade, Paris/Los Angeles 3, 4, 15, 16, 29, 39, 58

Simon Lee Gallery, London, Hong Kong, New York: 60

First published in 2019 by Lund Humphries

Lund Humphries
Office 3, Book House
261a City Road
London
EC1V 1JX
www.lundhumphries.com

ISBN: 978–1–84822–328–8

A Cataloguing-in-Publication record for this book is available
from the British Library.

Copy-edited by Anna Norman
Designed by Mark Thomson
Set in Custodia (Fred Smeijers)
Printed in Germany

Frontispiece: Jim Shaw in his studio, photograph by Molly Tierney

Cover: *All the President's Men*, 2018, Acrylic on muslin,
121.9 × 177.8 cm (48 × 70 in), Private collection